"To significantly increase the success of a digital transformation, it is crucial to build a strong organizational foundation. Such a foundation should be rooted in the organization's ability to manage change, form partnerships and innovate, coupled with a well-integrated and managed IT infrastructure and applications. Susan Snedaker's book, *Renovating Healthcare IT: Building the Foundation for Digital Transformation*, offers a comprehensive guide to defining, assessing, and establishing a high-performance IT foundation. From IT strategy, governance, operations, architecture to staffing and leadership, the book covers all aspects essential for the digital transformation of healthcare. With the need to digitally transform healthcare, following the guidance in this book is paramount, as it offers a masterful guide to achieving success."

**John Glaser, PhD**
Executive in Residence, Harvard Medical School
Former CIO, Partners HealthCare

"Healthcare is in desperate need of a digital transformation. In this instructive book, Snedaker skillfully leads readers from the principles of digital transformation to IT building blocks to a final map of designing a digital future. This informative, eye-opening book is essential reading for those looking to lead or deepen their understanding of the digital healthcare revolution."

**Katherine Gergen Barnett, MD**
Department of Family Medicine, Vice Chair of Primary Care Innovation
and Transformation, Boston Medical Center
Clinical Associate Professor, Boston University Medical School
Affiliate, Harvard Center for Primary Care
Health Innovators Fellow, Aspen Institute

"As the demands of our industry continue to increase and our technology rapidly evolves, it can be difficult to keep up. Due to limited resources and time constraints, our IT architectures often remain unchanged for decades. In order to break free from this cycle of stagnation, industry leaders should look to Susan Snedaker's latest book, *Renovating Healthcare IT: Building the Foundation for Digital Transformation*. Snedaker's in-depth meta-analysis and clear-eyed grasp of the situation show us how to interrupt this cycle, transforming the traditional cycle of evolution into a path of renovation."

**Anthony Fonze**
Former hospital CEO, healthcare network CIO,
and HIE Chief Innovation Officer

"Susan Snedaker's book *Renovating Healthcare IT: Building the Foundation for Digital Transformation*, provides a comprehensive guide to navigating a fluid post-pandemic landscape and offers a clear roadmap for success as organizations adapt to the future of patient care. Expertly dissecting the challenges faced by the industry, from budget cuts to cybersecurity threats, Snedaker offers actionable solutions for optimizing IT infrastructure, fostering innovation, and driving digital transformation. This is an essential read for hospital and healthcare decision-makers, both inside and outside of IT, who aspire to make a meaningful impact in the constantly evolving future of digitally driven patient care."

**Roshni Mark**
Public Funding Advisor, Cisco Systems, Inc.

"In our rapidly changing digital economy, the challenges and priorities for healthcare IT leaders have never been more significant. Susan Snedaker's *Renovating Healthcare IT* covers the crucial building blocks for organizational IT readiness – strategy, governance, finance, data management, analytics, cybersecurity, hiring, and more – offering practical organizational insights to navigate the complexities of this transforming digital landscape."

**Rachel Linonis, MS**
Director, Digital Solutions, UCLA Population Behavioral Health

# Renovating Healthcare IT

Healthcare IT is under tremendous pressure in today's environment: Budgets are shrinking; staff are in short supply; cloud, mobile, and data are driving expansion and innovation. Consumer expectations are high while agility and speed to market for many HIT organizations is low. The exponential growth of data sources and the need to empower healthcare with data-driven intelligence is pushing capabilities. The words "digital transformation" are infused in just about every discussion and serve to amplify organizational expectations of IT. In this environment, IT departments have to retool, rethink, and revise their way of operating. Few have the option of starting from scratch; the vast majority of organizations have built IT functions over decades. Now, it's time to remodel and renovate for the future. This book walks the reader through the process of determining what type of IT function they have today and what they'll need tomorrow. It discusses how to assess and analyze IT capabilities and then develop and implement a plan to renovate in place. By retooling now, the IT function can successfully meet the growing demands of the organization in the future. When approached in a planful manner, this process of renovating can energize the entire organization and help foster innovation and transformation along the way.

# Renovating Healthcare IT
## Building the Foundation for Digital Transformation

Susan T. Snedaker

Routledge
Taylor & Francis Group

A PRODUCTIVITY PRESS BOOK

First published 2024
by Routledge
605 Third Avenue, New York, NY 10158

and by Routledge
4 Park Square, Milton Park, Abingdon, Oxon, OX14 4RN

*Routledge is an imprint of the Taylor & Francis Group, an informa business*

ISBN: 978-1-032-45442-9 (hbk)
ISBN: 978-1-032-45441-2 (pbk)
ISBN: 978-1-003-37702-3 (ebk)

DOI: 10.4324/9781003377023


Typeset in ITC Garamond
by KnowledgeWorks Global Ltd.

# Contents

## SECTION II  IT BUILDING BLOCKS

# Foreword

What an honor to write the foreword to Susan Snedaker's new book, *Renovating Healthcare IT.* As an accomplished healthcare IT expert with over 15 years of experience in the field, Snedaker has a wealth of knowledge to share with readers looking to improve their overall organization through the strategic application of Digital Transformational Strategies.

There has never been a time in human history where renovation, transformation and even revolution is needed for the United States healthcare system, and in fact, across the globe.

Healthcare has always been an essential aspect of human life. Throughout history, people have sought to improve their health and wellbeing, often turning to traditional medicine, herbal remedies, and other non-conventional treatments. However, with the advancement of technology, healthcare has evolved rapidly, and digital transformation has revolutionized the industry.

The digital transformation of healthcare has impacted virtually every aspect of the healthcare ecosystem, from patient care to clinical research and development. Healthcare providers can now leverage digital technologies to improve the quality and efficiency of their services, reduce costs, and ultimately, save more lives. The power of digital technology has enabled healthcare providers to connect with patients in new and innovative ways, making healthcare more accessible and convenient than ever before.

The healthcare industry has embraced digital transformation, recognizing its potential to transform the way healthcare is delivered and consumed. Healthcare providers are increasingly turning to digital technologies to enhance their services, improve the patient experience, and optimize outcomes. In doing so, they are unlocking new opportunities to innovate, collaborate, and deliver more effective healthcare solutions.

However, digital transformation in healthcare is not without its challenges. Healthcare is a highly regulated industry and ensuring compliance with regulatory frameworks can be complex and time-consuming. Moreover, healthcare providers must grapple with issues such as data privacy and security, which are critical to ensuring that patient data is protected at all times.

Despite these challenges, digital transformation is rapidly reshaping the healthcare industry. The power of technology is driving new levels of efficiency and collaboration, enabling healthcare providers to achieve better outcomes for patients while reducing costs and improving the overall quality of care.

This book explores the various aspects of digital transformation in healthcare, examining the ways in which technology is transforming the healthcare industry and the challenges and opportunities that this presents. This book delves into topics such as telemedicine, electronic health records, artificial intelligence, and machine learning, exploring the ways in which these technologies are being leveraged to enhance patient care and drive innovation in the healthcare industry.

Throughout the book, real-world examples are examined on how healthcare providers are implementing digital transformation strategies to improve the quality of care, reduce costs, and enhance the overall patient experience. The book also explores the challenges and potential pitfalls in healthcare IT, providing insights and guidance to help healthcare IT leaders transform their IT function to enable digital transformation.

As the healthcare industry continues to evolve, digital transformation will undoubtedly play an increasingly critical role in shaping its future. This book is intended to provide healthcare IT leaders with the insights and guidance they need to navigate this dynamic and rapidly evolving landscape.

In *Renovating Healthcare IT*, Susan provides a comprehensive guide to navigating the complex world of healthcare IT. From understanding the current state of healthcare IT to implementing new technologies and managing IT projects, Susan offers practical advice and insights that are relevant to healthcare IT professionals at all levels. Her book is an invaluable resource for those looking to improve the efficiency, effectiveness, and security of healthcare IT systems.

**Russell Branzell, CHCIO, FCHIME, FACHE, FHIMSS**
*President & CEO, CHIME*

# Acknowledgements

Writing a book is as hard as it sounds and it requires a great support system. Heartfelt thanks to my partner and wife, Lisa Mainz. Your unwavering support is the foundation of my success. Thank you, Lisa.

I've had the privilege to work with my Senior Editor at Routledge, Kristine Rynne Mednansky, on several book projects. Your immediate enthusiasm for this book's concept inspired me to spend the next 12 months writing it. Thank you, Kris.

Many thanks and deep gratitude to Tony Fonze for being a trusted colleague, friend, and sounding board on so many topics in healthcare. I continue to learn and grow from every conversation we have. Thank you, Tony.

Sincere thanks to Lisa Avellino, Chief Information and Technology Officer at Moses Weitzman Health System, an incredibly talented colleague and friend, for her feedback and input on many topics in this book. Our discussions on the challenges in healthcare IT over the past couple of years have helped me gain insight into many of the topics in this book. Thank you, Lisa.

And finally, very special thanks to the entire El Rio Health IT team and in particular, the IT leadership team – Asha, Chris, Andrea, Lydia, Bryan, Scott, Daniel, Crystal, and Rebecca as well as my outstanding assistant, Isabelle. We have done amazing work together over the past couple of years and achieved so many important milestones, including successfully renovating critical aspects of our own IT function. The passion, expertise, and commitment you bring to the job inspires me every day. I am very excited to see what the future holds. Thank you, team.

# About the Author

 **Susan Snedaker**, MBA, is a renowned healthcare IT executive, consultant, and author with more than 15 years of experience in the industry. Susan is a leading voice in the world of healthcare IT and has helped numerous organizations improve patient outcomes through innovative IT solutions. As Chief Information Officer (CIO) for a large Federally Qualified Health Center (FQHC) system, and previously, as Information Security Officer (ISO) for a major community hospital system, Susan has a wealth of experience leading healthcare IT departments and implementing cutting-edge technologies.

Her expertise has been recognized by her peers, earning her prestigious certifications as a Certified Healthcare CIO (CHCIO), Certified Healthcare Information Security Leader (CHISL), and Certified Digital Healthcare Executive (CDH-E). Susan is also an accomplished author, having written several books on healthcare IT and leadership, as well as numerous articles and white papers. Her thought leadership has been featured in leading industry publications and she is a sought-after speaker at conferences and events. Susan's passion for healthcare IT and her commitment to sharing her expertise are reflected in her latest book, *Renovating Healthcare IT: Building the Foundation for Digital Transformation*.

# Introduction

As I reflect on the past three years since the COVID-19 pandemic began, I see how much our world has changed. We have come to rely on new ways of interacting. We now routinely shop online and have our orders dropped off on our doorsteps. Meetings are regularly held online, regardless of whether staff are on-site or not. Our work-from-anywhere world has persisted, though many companies are trying to re-establish the pre-pandemic rhythms of working together in a physical location.

Only time will tell if these changes will remain, but one thing is abundantly clear: technology has enabled many of these changes in our daily lives and will continue to do so at an accelerated pace.

Over the past few years, I've frequently read about the need for digital transformation in healthcare. The pandemic showed us glimpses of some of those changes, such as the almost overnight acceptance of telehealth for health care. But as I looked around at healthcare IT and read about all the demands being placed on healthcare organizations to transform, I was struck by the clear disconnect.

Many healthcare IT solutions have been cobbled together over the past decade or two. We have a mashup of technologies that add complexity and risk to our organizations. We have more demand than capacity. Our staff support new technologies and faces new problems every day, but our training often doesn't keep pace. These problems are the roadblocks to digital transformation. Without reworking our IT functions, we will be unable to fully realize the potential of these transformational efforts.

In order to digitally transform our organizations, we must first fix what's broken in IT. Using the renovation analogy, we should not put a new roof on a building that is about to collapse. And, things that were acceptable fifty years ago are no longer (asbestos and lead paint come to mind). We can't just level the building and start over, either. So, we must fix what's in disrepair and bring the building up to code through our renovation project. This gives us a unique opportunity to examine our IT functions, assess how we're doing and where we have opportunities, and renovate these before jumping fully into digital transformation. In fact, it's the only sustainable approach. Before we can digitally transform healthcare, we must first renovate healthcare IT.

This book is divided into actionable sections.

**Section One** provides an overview of the environment in which we're working, akin to the neighborhood in which your renovation project will take place.

**Section Two** examines each of the building blocks of a strong healthcare IT function. These are the building materials for your renovation.

**Section Three** includes assessments for each of the capabilities covered by the building block chapters. These chapters provide the site survey, to assess the strengths and weaknesses throughout the structure.

**Section Four** steps you through creating a successful renovation project plan and implementing those changes. This is where you rebuild and restructure your IT function so it's strong and reliable for whatever comes next in healthcare IT.

This modular approach will help you successfully renovate your entire healthcare IT function and lay the foundation for a successful digital transformation.

# INTRODUCTION TO HEALTHCARE IT RENOVATION

# Chapter 1

# Overview of Healthcare in the U.S.

We begin by exploring the overall environment of healthcare, the equivalent of the neighborhood in which you'll be doing your renovation project. It's impossible to create a plan to meet the future needs of the organization without understanding the drivers in the industry. As information technology (IT) continues to move to the center of many strategic initiatives, healthcare IT (HIT) leaders must fully understand all elements of the business and be prepared to bring effective ideas and innovative solutions to the table. We cover these aspects in this chapter to set the stage for the rest of our work.

## U.S. Healthcare Overview

Healthcare is a vast and complex topic. The players are many and varied, and the segments of healthcare are also numerous. Here's a *partial* list of players/segments in the healthcare space:

| | |
|---|---|
| • Inpatient | • HC service providers (remote monitoring, etc.) |
| • Outpatient | • Skilled nursing facilities |
| • Urgent care | • Long-term care |
| • Emergency care | • Home healthcare |
| • Primary care | • Infusion clinics |

DOI: 10.4324/9781003377023-2

| | |
|---|---|
| • Specialty care | • Home infusion |
| • Dental care | • Employer health |
| • Behavioral healthcare | • Providers (MD, NP) |
| • Social needs care | • Clinical staff (RN, LPN, MA) |
| • Pharmacy | • Ops staff (HIM, revenue cycle, patient access, etc.) |
| • Specialty pharmacy | • Medical device vendors |
| • Imaging | • Healthcare technology vendors |
| • Specialty diagnostics | • Payors/insurance companies |
| • Retail clinics | • Pharmaceutical companies |

That's a long list, and it's not comprehensive. We know healthcare is complicated; anyone who works in healthcare deals with this complexity on a daily basis. Healthcare information technology (HIT) is at the center of all of this, addressing the rapidly evolving needs of the industry. It's no wonder that HIT is such a challenge and that the IT environment is one that's often a patchwork of solutions.

Many have said U.S. healthcare is broken. Some would say that we don't spend enough time or money on primary care and prevention; others would say American lifestyles are primary contributors to chronic conditions and acute care demand, which accounts for about 80% of the cost of healthcare in the U.S. There are numerous and complex reasons the U.S. healthcare system is the way it is today, and that discussion is outside the scope of this chapter and this book. That said, it is important to understand the basic operating environment in U.S. healthcare today in order to understand what's driving change. The concepts around healthcare delivery complexity, IT renovation, and digital transformation will apply to almost any HIT organization in the world, but the U.S. context will be covered in this chapter.

As we explore the current healthcare environment, keep in mind that the changes on the horizon will impact everyone – payors, providers, health plans, acute care, sub-acute care, long-term care, primary care, home care, dental and behavioral care, pharmacies, medical device companies, and more.

In 2022, many U.S. healthcare organizations began reporting significant operating losses. Most of these were hospitals and hospital systems. Many have seen much higher costs along with staffing shortages, causing nursing units to close or scale back, surgeries to be postponed, and non-clinical teams being reduced through layoffs or mandatory time off. Financial pressures in the post-COVID-19 environment are pushing many organizations to drastic measures, and a record number of organizations are closing. [1.1]

Where healthcare delivery goes from here is a subject of much discussion. The path is not yet clear. We do know that the overarching trends of consumerization of healthcare, using more technology, and finding ways to deliver better care at a lower cost will continue to be common themes.

## Healthcare and Technology

Most healthcare organizations in the U.S. have implemented an electronic health record (EHR) system sometime in the past 20 years. Many were implemented in the 2005–2010 timeframe. In 2022–2023, we saw more healthcare systems switching EHR vendors. Of course, many are going to one of the two top vendors in this space: Epic™ and Oracle Cerner ™. That said, not everyone is headed to the big EHR vendors; some organizations are opting to use smaller vendors or those that are custom-built for their healthcare segment.

We also know that the interconnectedness of systems is increasingly important for providing continuity of care. It is no longer acceptable to discharge a patient from a hospital without also electronically notifying the patient's primary care provider or providing the patient with an electronic copy of their discharge instructions. Many healthcare systems have 50–100 (or more) different interfaces to EHR. This includes health information exchanges (HIEs), national disease registries, lab, imaging, real-time insurance eligibility checking, and payment gateways.

The data inside an EHR are becoming increasingly critical to continuity of care as well. We're seeing primary care providers look to data for population health management, including chronic condition management, care plans, addressing social determinants of health (SDOH), and preventive care, to name a few. We are also seeing primary, specialty, and acute care providers looking at data to find ways to improve outcomes, reduce costs, improve the patient experience, or streamline operations. The use of reporting, predictive analytics, and machine learning (ML) are beginning to make a positive impact on care decisions.

We are seeing pressure on healthcare supply chain leaders to improve inventory management (cost, availability, and supply). As we saw during the pandemic, organizations that were able to proactively manage supplies of personal protective equipment (PPE), for example, were in better shape than those who were unable to plan ahead. Using technology, including artificial intelligence (AI) and ML to monitor and analyze supply chain factors such as vendors, availability, lead time, par levels, bulk discounts, and more, leading healthcare organizations are able to reduce costs and improve service levels to clinical operations.

On the IT infrastructure side, we're seeing dramatic changes in IT architecture. Not only is the move to cloud-based platforms accelerating but also we are seeing demand for edge computing driven by the proliferation of the Internet of Things (IoT) and 5G cellular network deployments. The demand to move computing power closer to the place data is being generated is fueling this shift. According to Gold and Shaw in an article on edge computing,

> The early goal of edge computing was to reduce the bandwidth costs associated with moving raw data from where it was created to either an enterprise data center or the cloud. More recently, the rise of real-time applications that require minimal latency, such as autonomous vehicles and multi-camera video analytics, are driving the concept forward. [1.2]

In healthcare, the growing data demand is for intelligent clinical automation (e.g. hybrid operating rooms using AI applications), remote patient monitoring (RPM) devices, population health analytics, and revenue cycle management, among others. Of course, edge computing comes with potentially higher cybersecurity risks, so with the promise of faster IT comes the risk of higher vulnerability to attack.

The use of cloud-based technologies has accelerated despite the move from capital to operational spending. As healthcare systems now face serious financial losses in the post-pandemic economy, we may see shifts again in how these solutions are leveraged. Cloud solutions clearly reduce the need for capital expenditures, enable faster deployment of solutions, and remove the need (in some cases) for specialized IT staff to manage a variety of platforms. However, this all comes with a cost. Many healthcare organizations have seen significant increases in utilization, which is often difficult to manage. This, in turn, increases operating expenses at a time when there's strong downward pressure on expenses. Each organization will approach this differently and assess the pros and cons of cloud solutions. As we'll see, HIT departments must develop a strategy, architecture, and roadmap for cloud adoption that are specific to the needs of their organizations.

Finally, we know that cybersecurity remains a top concern and a top focus for healthcare executives. Even with strong downward pressure on costs, investment in cybersecurity solutions is a requirement. Implementing real-time monitoring, alerting, and remediation solutions is imperative. Paying attention to the basics is equally important. Healthcare has been notoriously slow in implementing some of the fundamentals of cybersecurity, such as ensuring all systems are patched to current levels in a timely manner, hardening systems and servers through automation, encrypting sensitive data at rest and in transit, and utilizing multifactor authentication wherever possible. These rapidly evolving areas will require HIT leaders to remain up-to-date with emerging threats, vulnerabilities, and solutions. It will also require leaders to manage the ever-growing complexity of HIT. Part of the IT renovation process is removing, deselecting, and simplifying the environment, so HIT cybersecurity leaders should be at the table for the entire renovation project.

# Current Trends

The almost overnight shift from reluctance to acceptance of certain digital technologies in healthcare because of the COVID-19 pandemic has been well-documented. Most notably, the immediate acceptance of telehealth solutions during the pandemic has left an indelible mark on how healthcare is delivered today. Many other types of changes that are underway were initially begun (or at least contemplated) prior to the pandemic. Some were accelerated due to the pandemic; others were delayed. In this section, we'll look briefly at some of the trends shaping healthcare delivery today. These trends will certainly impact HIT strategies, so starting with these environmental factors will inform your renovation plan.

## *Growth in Medicare Population*

We know the population of the U.S. is aging. According to the U.S. Census Bureau, the over-65 age group grew over 34% over the past decade.

The 65-and-older population has grown rapidly since 2010, driven by the aging of Baby Boomers born between 1946 and 1964. The 65-and-older population grew by over a third (34.2% or 13,787,044) during the past decade, and by 3.2% (1,688,924) from 2018 to 2019. The growth of this population contributed to an increase in the national median age from 37.2 years in 2010 to 38.4 in 2019, according to the Census Bureau's 2019 Population Estimates. [1.3]

We can expect to see U.S. Medicare spending increase as more of the population reaches the age of eligibility. Both traditional Medicare (government) and Medicare Advantage (private health insurers) plans will see enrollment climb in the coming decade. "The aging of the population, growth in Medicare enrollment due to the baby boom generation reaching the age of eligibility, and increases in per capita health care costs are leading to growth in overall Medicare spending." [1.4]

With the aging of the population (a worldwide phenomenon, not just in the U.S.) come a number of key changes. First, there will be fewer people in the workforce. This will exacerbate the situation healthcare is facing today with staffing shortages and people opting out of work, opting for part-time work, or only being willing to work from home.

Second, it will increase our healthcare costs as older populations tend to have multiple chronic conditions that are more expensive to treat and manage. As healthcare providers look to improve the quality of life for patients and reduce the cost of healthcare, we will see trends like care at home and RPM increase in use.

Third, the aging population will strain our healthcare system if we don't change the way care is delivered. The pandemic demanded instantaneous change to some methods of care, which seemed to have broken the dam of resistance to change as many of the modifications resulted in a positive experience both for providers and for patients. As a result, we're seeing an acceleration in these changes, including RPM, hospital at home, telehealth, provider-patient communication via SMS, and more.

Of course, reimbursement models need to keep pace with these changes in care delivery. For example, there is a strong use case for leveraging nurses in certain aspect of patient care, but their services are often not included in reimbursement models. This can preclude organizations from better leveraging the right provider type for the right care at the right time. The next several years will determine whether reimbursement will continue to evolve along with changing care models or remain largely based on traditional provider fee-for-service models.

All of these changes require HIT to be at its very best, to lead, facilitate, and support groundbreaking changes in the way care is delivered. And, in order to do that, we must renovate the IT function. It's an incredibly exciting opportunity, and the timing is perfect to undertake this journey.

## *Increase in Chronic Condition Management*

According to the U.S. Centers for Medicaid and Medicare Services (CMS), an estimated 117 million adults have one or more chronic health conditions, and one in four adults have two or more chronic health conditions. [1.5]

Managing and treating chronic conditions account for 90% of U.S. healthcare costs. Heart disease and stroke account for about $216 billion in annual healthcare costs. Obesity costs the U.S. healthcare system nearly $173 billion annually. Alzheimer's disease, a form of dementia, impacts about 5.7 million Americans. "In 2020, the estimated cost of caring for and treating people with Alzheimer's disease was $305 billion. By 2050, these costs are projected to be more than $1.1 trillion." [1.6] While these estimates are alarming, the increasing use (and usefulness) of AI and ML in researching the treatment and cure for some of these debilitating diseases is also showing strong potential. For example, in April 2023, the U.S. National Institute on Aging (NIA) announced a six-year, $300 million database project to accelerate Alzheimer's research. [1.7] The clinically proven use of AI is expanding exponentially and will continue to do so at an accelerated rate as AI continues to mature.

Lifestyle choices impact wellness and chronic conditions as well. "Cigarette smoking is the leading cause of preventable death and disease in the United States. More than 16 million Americans have at least one disease caused by smoking. This amounts to more than $240 billion in direct medical spending that could be reduced every year." [1.8] Even physical inactivity takes its toll in contributing to chronic conditions and costs the U.S. about $117 billion a year for related healthcare costs.

Many chronic conditions can be prevented through early diagnosis, lifestyle modifications, and treatment. Obesity is one of the key underlying conditions of several chronic conditions, including diabetes, heart disease, and congestive heart failure. Working to prevent chronic conditions requires the use of population health management and primary care tactics such as enrollment in care plans, providing group education and activities, and monitoring more continuously at home (vs. just office visits). The methods of effectively managing these conditions will require healthcare systems to better leverage current and emerging technologies.

## Population Health

As EHR systems enable a broader view of patient populations, healthcare providers can better manage populations of patients. According to the American Hospital Association, "Population health management refers to the process of improving clinical health outcomes of a defined group of individuals through improved care coordination and patient engagement supported by appropriate financial and care models." [1.9] This includes coordinating care across the healthcare delivery system and addressing chronic and complex conditions. Managing patients with multiple chronic conditions, including substance use (opioids) and mental health needs, is a focus of population health management. The objectives are to improve the quality of life of patients while simultaneously reducing the overall cost of healthcare. Value-based care models that reward quality outcomes through shared financial incentives are increasingly being used to drive the population-based outcomes, but more work is needed to continue to align reimbursement for preventive care (including monitoring and care navigation) vs. episodic fee-for-service models.

## Patient-Centric Model of Care

Consumers have begun to demand a more consumer-friendly healthcare system. Consumers today are using personal fitness trackers, fitness apps, sleep apps, calming apps, and more to find ways to reduce stress, increase fitness, eat better, and maintain healthier lifestyles. Consumers are spending between $300 billion to $400 billion on their own health and wellness beyond qualified medical spending, according to a McKinsey report. [1.10] Consumers are also demanding a more friendly and seamless experience. They want to be able to schedule, change, and cancel appointments online; use virtual visits for some types of care; pay online; receive electronic copies of required documents; use electronic signatures to sign consents, disclosures, etc.; and use text or a patient portal to communicate with their care team about prescription refills, medication use, lab results, medical questions, appointment follow-up, and more.

Virtual care got a boost during the pandemic, but the trend toward using telehealth for a variety of different care models is enduring. Telehealth (whether audio/video or audio only) for prevention and wellness appointments, follow-up appointments, and, in some cases, even urgent care has become an accepted solution. Use of telehealth technologies for behavioral health appointments is very popular and, in many cases, preferred over an office visit for many patients. The ability to have a behavioral health appointment in the privacy of one's own home, without waiting rooms or travel time, is something many patients find comforting and an improvement in the provision of care. Not all providers are enthusiastic about these changes; some prefer to see patients in clinics. Of course, not all medical visits can be successfully conducted using virtual means, and in-clinic visits will still be needed. However, the mix between in-clinic (or in-hospital) and virtual visits will continue to change. Going forward, we're likely to see the mix of delivery methods evolve as providers and patients find the most effective and efficient way forward. Of course, reimbursement models have a significant influence on these care decisions.

The use of RPM rose dramatically during the pandemic from 2020 to 2022. Providers were able to collect vital health data from patients, and patients were able to provide this data from the comfort of their homes. The use of both telehealth and RPM is expected to remain high. Medicare, Medicaid, and private insurance companies provide inconsistent coverage and reimbursements for these services in 2023, but as the cost-benefit analysis continues to show strong results, it's possible reimbursement will improve. Many EHR patient portals can be interfaced with consumer-facing apps on smartphones, which connect to Bluetooth-enabled home medical devices such as pulse oximeters, blood pressure monitors, blood glucose monitors, and body weight scales, to name a few. This meets the current CMS requirement for continuous data to be available to the practitioner for analysis and treatment. [1.11] Additionally, as consumers continue to drive changes to healthcare delivery options, these types of consumer-friendly healthcare solutions are expected to grow.

While virtual models have the potential to transform how care is delivered, it is important to recognize that the technology used in delivering this care is not universally available. As HIT leaders, we must always look at the continuum from high tech to low tech to no tech to find solutions that will address the healthcare needs of our populations. Without due consideration of these factors, HIT has the potential to exacerbate disparities in care rather than ameliorate them. RPM and care at home are great concepts, given the patient has a safe, permanent residence with access to cellular or Internet connectivity. That is not universally true.

## Patient-Centered Care and the Patient Experience

We're seeing the shift toward patient-centered care, where patients as consumers of healthcare services have more influence in the delivery of care. There will be increased demand from patients to improve the patient experience. In today's environment, patients have multiple patient portals, information is still fragmented, and experiences are often a mash up of processes – call for this, text for that, log on to your portal for the other. The need to streamline and improve the patient experience as the patient moves to the center of the circle will be crucial for providing timely, effective care.

While patients want and use more technology to access care, healthcare organizations must be diligent. The phrase "digital front door" has been in popular use in healthcare for about a decade. Yet, using our renovation example, the digital front door might be shiny, fancy, and new, but the house is falling down around it or the entry way has a huge hole in the floor. This kind of hype and hyperbole can serve to place disconnected demands on IT organizations. To extend the metaphor, of course, we can deploy a 'digital front door' solution, but we need to make sure our patients don't twist an ankle in a hole in the floor the moment they cross the threshold.

### Patient Engagement

Patient engagement is often discussed in the context of using technology to engage and manage the patient through the care journey, though it's not always a digital solution. For example, engaging a patient and their family at discharge from an acute care facility may involve providing printed instructions, care demonstrations (how to change a dressing, how to take a medication, etc.), and ensuring the patient understands how, where, and when to get follow up care. The use of technology to facilitate and streamline these processes is certainly part of patient engagement, but these efforts are not well-integrated across most healthcare systems today.

Often technology can be useful, such as emailing or texting a patient-specific follow-up instructions or even setting up the follow-up appointment automatically so there are no gaps in care. Studies have shown that care gaps after discharge are most often related to patients not understanding what to do next, which frequently results in re-admission. Studies show that up to 30% of re-admissions are avoidable. In a survey of 861 respondents,

> Roughly half reported having high-cost follow-up care after their acute event (and as high as 73 percent of respondents who receive Medicaid) …. Thirty-three percent of all respondents with unplanned, high-cost follow-up care reported reasons that they considered avoidable, such as not getting clear post-discharge instructions or receiving inadequate post-acute care. [1.12]

When technology is used effectively to provide post-discharge instructions, re-admissions from these types of situations can be reduced, which ultimately provides better patient outcomes, a better patient experience, and reductions in healthcare costs. Post-discharge instructions provided on paper, via email or text, and in the patient's portal in the patient's preferred language; video instruction delivered via the patient portal; automated follow up calls or texts to ensure the patient knows what to do next and understands how to take those next steps are all examples of how technology can be used to improve patient outcomes.

## Continued Disparities in Care

At the same time we're shifting toward more consumer-driven care, we're also seeing increasing disparities in access to healthcare and in quality outcomes. SDOH factors continue to impede access to high-quality care. This was evident during the COVID pandemic, when access to vaccines was lower in low-income, non-white neighborhoods; mortality was higher, and access and use of telehealth was hindered by various factors, including poverty, digital illiteracy, and limited access. As a nation, we still see higher rates of mortality across a spectrum of conditions for non-white compared to white patients, despite decades of work by community health centers (Federally Qualified Health Centers, FQHC) and other healthcare organizations across the country.

The 2022–2023 acquisition of One Medical by Amazon is a trend hailed by some as innovative and by others as dangerous. Fans see the opportunity to innovate in healthcare; critics see the culling of the healthiest, privately insured patients by a for-profit big tech company. Regardless of the outcome of that venture, the trend toward boutique medicine, concierge services, and the like may create an even larger divide between those with government insurance (Medicare and Medicaid) and those with private insurance. Those with private insurance often have the means to pay for upscale medical options. Technology can help address some of these disparities, and the use of analytics in population health initiatives may help remove some of the barriers to care for those sometimes left behind in for-profit healthcare settings. That said, the use of technology to improve how, when, and where care is provided may ultimately provide additional tools for caring for our most vulnerable populations more effectively and compassionately.

## Change in Site of Care

Earlier in this chapter, we mentioned that the site of care for patients is shifting away from acute care and offices and into ambulatory care, community care, and home care. How this evolves in the coming years is still undetermined, but as healthcare continues to be pushed to be more patient-centric, we will likely continue to see a move away from provider-centric locations. This is already underway and takes many forms. We're seeing primary care providers at local retail grocery stores or pharmacies, primary and urgent care centers on corners in neighborhoods, care at home technologies that allow patients to receive care at home or at assisted living facilities, and the proliferation of healthcare services at home such as dialysis, lab work, and more. The use of telehealth and RPM, discussed in the previous section, also continues to shift care away from the clinic and into the patient's home.

The change in the site of care will fundamentally alter the provider-patient relationship by putting the patient, their location, and their care preferences in center court. As healthcare shifts and, in some sense, becomes less centralized, HIT departments will need to deliver necessary IT services and connectivity securely, reliably, and quickly in a whole new environment. This, too, demands a renovation of HIT to prepare for the new future that is on our doorstep.

One of the potential challenges we'll contend with is the cobbling together of various locations, services, and technologies. While the shift in sites can be beneficial, it also carries the risk of injecting complexity (interfaces, locations, providers, and staff) into the equation. The potential for creating another patchwork of solutions is high. For example, the use of a hybrid computing environment, while perhaps cost-effective, adds a layer of complexity that some HIT departments are ill-equipped to support. Additionally, as we look at providing connectivity and IT solutions in locations other than our primary sites (hospitals, clinics, and sites we own or control), it gets even more complicated. How do we deliver an IT solution for patients at home? For mobile caregivers? The answers are there, but trying to do that within our current (and often outdated) environments may not be feasible.

## Shift from Acute Care to Outpatient Care

The shift in care from acute to outpatient settings began prior to 2020 but non-urgent care was often deferred during the pandemic. Patients were reluctant to go to urgent care and emergency rooms or become patients in hospitals. As COVID spread, hospital capacity was reserved for the most acute cases. Though this resulted in millions of Americans delaying care or not receiving timely care for important health issues, it also forced the healthcare system to rapidly innovate. From using video apps to help hospitalized patients talk to loved ones at home to using video apps to enable providers to assess patients remotely, thereby reducing the use of PPE when it was in short supply, the healthcare system quickly adopted mobile technologies. Patients wanted more flexible options, and this was one of the pivot points.

Looking forward, we see a growing shift from high-cost hospitals and post-acute care facilities to lower cost outpatient centers and home care. With technology for remote and home-based monitoring increasingly accessible and affordable, many consumers are choosing more convenient and less expensive care options, when available. The growing use of high-deductible plans is also driving a more value-based mindset for many consumers who are asking about prices and shopping around for high-quality, lower cost care.

These trends will continue to push less acute care out of hospitals and into community settings. For the HIT leader, this is important to understand and evaluate as part of your organization's long-term positioning in the marketplace. If you work in an acute care setting, this will impact many facets of your organization, including potentially creating downward pressure on budgets, increasing competition for medical specialties, and increasing the acuity of the patient populations you serve in an in-patient setting, for example.

If you work outside of acute care, the landscape is shifting even faster. Outpatient ERs are popping up in shopping centers; outpatient surgery centers seem to be on every corner. The push for these outpatient options is strong, driven by the numerous factors we have discussed.

The one area that has seen steady demand, except during the height of the pandemic, is primary care. The number of primary care providers in most areas is lower than the demand. That means many patients do not have a primary care provider and receive healthcare in an episodic manner. That is the least beneficial for the patient and has the highest cost to the system. That slowly may be changing as we see an increasing focus on value-based payment models. This model is intended to improve health and reduce cost, but it does not address the overall shortage of primary care providers in our communities.

## *Mental Health Needs*

Another factor in healthcare that gained attention during the pandemic was the mental health needs not only of the general population but also that of the caregivers. Mental health needs were openly discussed, and much of the stigma around seeking help dissolved. However, the demand for mental and behavioral healthcare far surpasses the capacity in most communities, with rural communities being the hardest hit. The upside is that the acceptance of telehealth and virtual visits in general healthcare became a favored solution for behavioral health visits. According to a 2022 report by the Kaiser Family Foundation and Epic Research, prior to the pandemic, telehealth visits for both medical and behavioral health issues were less than 1% of visits. At the height of the pandemic, telehealth visits for regular medical visits were about 11%, while 40% of behavioral health visits were via telehealth. In 2022, after the height of the pandemic had passed, medical telehealth visits had drifted down to about 8% of visits, while behavioral health telehealth visits were still 36% of all behavioral health visits. This trend toward telehealth for providing behavioral health will continue because of strong demand, the convenience of visits for both providers and patients, the ability to provide faster, on-demand emergency services, and hopefully improved reimbursement as payors see value in this care delivery model. [1.13]

## Provider Burnout and Nursing Shortages

Provider burnout was a serious factor in healthcare in the pre-pandemic era but became even more prominent during and after the wave of hospitalizations and deaths that came in the first two years of the pandemic. Burnout and staff shortages among nurses and other care providers also spiked.

Numerous studies indicate that better EHR experiences can help reduce provider burnout. By making the system easier to use, reducing clicks, improving automation, and ensuring an encounter can be quickly and easily documented are all elements that reduce burnout. Providers who don't have to complete documentation at home after hours ("pajama time") are more satisfied and less burned out. Preventing burn out is just one way of retaining providers in the face of growing demand. Many hospitals were forced to scale back services due to staffing shortages. These staffing shortages are beginning to ease slightly as many who resigned during the pandemic are starting to return to work. The aging of the workforce, however, means that this staffing shortage will continue far into the future. Provider burnout can be reduced by well-implemented technology, including the use of AI, but technology is only one factor in a complex mix. Addressing provider satisfaction and burnout must be an organizational initiative driven by executives and provider leaders.

## Increase Use of Analytics

As EHR systems capture more data and systems become better integrated, the available data sets are becoming more complete and more useful. We are seeing significant advances in the use of analytics in population health management, including chronic condition management, patient engagement, and revenue cycle improvement, to name just a few. We will continue to see this trend grow as cloud-based solutions enable ever larger data sets to be managed and utilized. The use of AI and ML technologies to improve both individual and population health will grow exponentially in the coming years. This means IT departments must be capable of storing, securing, managing, and leveraging these massive data sets. That requires new IT skills that not all HIT departments currently have.

## Revenue Cycle Enhancements

With strong financial challenges facing many healthcare organizations today, the efficiency of the revenue cycle function is vital to long-term financial health. In recent years, there has been a shift toward patients bearing more of the cost of care, including utilizing high-deductible insurance plans with Health Savings Accounts (HSA) and Flexible Savings Accounts (FSA). With more self-pay comes more bad debt for healthcare providers.

> Between 2010 and 2016, for example, the deductibles for families of four with employer-sponsored health insurance rose 15–70%, depending on the plan type. During that time, average American incomes largely remained flat, leaving patients with less disposable income to pay their growing healthcare bills. [1.14]

At the same time, there has been a shift from traditional government health insurance (Medicare) to managed portfolios (Medicare Advantage Plans). This may be significant because early studies have shown these managed care plans perform claims reviews differently than traditional government plans and may also pay in a different timeline (e.g. slower reimbursements). Coupling this with changes in requirements around claim management such as the more granular International Statistical Classification of Diseases and Related Health Problems (ICD-10) coding system, stricter documentation requirements, or more substantive scrutiny of claims and healthcare organizations could see the reduction or delay in payments over time. The impact of receiving payment after 30 days or after 90 days can be significant if this payor class is one heavily represented in an organization's revenue mix.

All of this increases the complexity of the revenue cycle process in a healthcare system. This also tends to increase the costs of the revenue cycle process, including training providers on proper, detailed clinical documentation, training coders to effectively utilize the proper codes to capture all eligible reimbursement, and ensuring documentation adequately reflects the patient's condition. Denials are on the rise for these reasons, which becomes another source of cost (working denials) and possibly a source of revenue loss. Using technology, including AI for coding and automation of claims processing with advanced analytics, can help relieve some of the burden and improve revenue cycle performance.

## Artificial Intelligence/Machine Learning in Healthcare

There has been much talk about using AI and ML in healthcare for diagnostics, disease management, and more. Much of the successfully implemented AI clinical use cases in 2023 still revolve around utilizing AI in imaging, which has proven to be very effective at finding issues the human eye misses. Outside of imaging use cases, though, much of the work is still in proof-of-concept stages. AI and ML are increasingly used in research on massive data sets. Some of the larger healthcare systems, including those associated with academic healthcare centers, have developed strong use cases in disease management, and these will continue to accelerate as technology, AI, and methodologies advance.

There has also been discussion about the potential of bias in AI, which could exacerbate some of the disparities in healthcare delivery we see today. In this current AI environment, there's been evidence of inadvertent bias built into some systems. For example, AI that is better at pinpointing disease in white vs. non-white patients or assesses male vs. female data differently. These are areas that are emerging as potential concerns. So, while the AI field looks very promising, it also poses risks that must be addressed going forward. AI is not a magic bullet, but it certainly holds immense potential. [1.15]

## Increase Use of Healthcare Technology

From personal fitness trackers to mobile apps that measure and track personal health data to software platforms that manage these data, the use of technology in healthcare will continue to grow in all directions. According to a McKinsey report, there was a 2.8x increase in HIT venture and private equity funding between 2014 and 2021, much of the acceleration happening in 2021. [1.16] We have seen large, well-funded tech giants enter the healthcare market, so we can expect to see further changes as these companies pursue profit via technology and automation. While that has the risk of leaving vulnerable populations behind, it also holds the potential to innovate and drive positive change in the healthcare space.

We know that personal health devices, like fitness trackers and Bluetooth-enabled health monitoring devices, can assist with personal wellness at home. Studies are mixed as to the actual efficacy of these devices in driving better health outcomes when used outside of a clinical care program (e.g.

an individual chooses to use these devices but not because their provider has put them on a care program). Results from studies of patients in clinical care programs using personal health devices are still in early stages, but preliminary results show there often is an improvement in patient metrics through more frequent monitoring and clinical contact. In other words, it may not be about the technology as much as the patient's awareness and the provider's engagement with the patient that are driving better outcomes. As technology helps providers more easily touch base more frequently with their patients with complex conditions, we should see continued improvement in health metrics for these populations.

Medical devices, such as blood pressure cuffs, glucose monitors, pulse oximeters, and body weight scales, can be used at home and monitored by the care team. Using Bluetooth-enabled devices connected to mobile apps, which interface to an EHR, patients can upload their personal data to the EHR and interact with their care team when vital metrics change. As the shift to care at home continues, as patients have become more comfortable with remote care, and with the increasing use of smartphones and mobile apps, this trend will accelerate in the coming years.

On the provider side, we will continue to see a focus on streamlining and improving the EHR systems in use today. Reducing provider burnout has been a key focus for several years now, and there is a direct correlation between the ease of EHR use and provider burnout. [1.17] While most of the research has focused on physician provider burnout, the same holds true for anyone in healthcare who works within an EHR system, including nurses, medical assistants, patient care technicians, lab, pharmacy, imaging, medical records, and business office staff to name a few. Everyone in healthcare uses technology in some aspects of their jobs. As AI and ML continue to grow in function and use, as technology itself evolves, it increasingly will be used in every aspect of healthcare.

This is important for many reasons, but one very important aspect stands out. Not everyone in every healthcare organization is savvy or competent in the use of common technologies, including websites (patient portals), smartphones, smartphone apps, and texting. We have people at one end of the spectrum who can barely navigate a web browser and people on the other end who grew up with social media instant messaging platforms as their common means of communicating, and everything in between. We have patients who are on that same spectrum. As HIT professionals, we must understand how technology and people intersect and interact. We must understand how to *meet people where they are* and we must provide the easiest IT experience possible. That's a tall order even in the best of times, but as we move forward, it will be one aspect that separates successful organizations from those that struggle or fail. This is absolutely the perfect time to plan your HIT renovation. It will set the stage for future success, no matter what type of healthcare organization you work for and no matter what state your current HIT is in.

# The Healthcare IT Imperative

In 2016, McKinsey published a report titled "Partnering to shape the future – IT's new imperative" in which they indicate IT must become a strategic business partner rather than just a service provider. The pressure to perform at higher levels will require IT to rebuild their operating model. The report states that organizations where business and IT work collaboratively as partners perform better in several dimensions. While the survey results in this report are now more than seven years old, the data at the time suggested something somewhat surprising. When IT and non-IT executives were asked about what IT's priorities should be, non-IT executives overwhelmingly ranked things like improving efficiency of IT and improving cost efficiency of the business higher than reducing IT costs. This is important because when IT and business leaders align, the conversation shifts from IT as a *cost center* to IT as a collaborative partner helping to improve the business and achieve organizational goals and objectives. [1.18]

The data also show the shift in job skills required within the IT department. As we'll see in upcoming chapters, the need for skilled workers in IT is increasing, and at the same time, the skills and competencies required in IT are changing. As the McKinsey data show, the two most pressing needs in 2016 for IT leaders were IT talent in analytics and business/IT skills. [1.19] As we have seen in the intervening years since the report was published, the demand for data analytics skills has grown exponentially. Equally important, but far less touted, is the need for strong business skills in IT. This means not only standard business skills like finance, accounting, contracting, and customer service (or in healthcare, patient experience) but also that IT people need to deeply understand the business of the organization. In HIT, that means the leaders, and the Chief Information Officer (CIO) in particular, need to be very well-versed in IT and in the business itself.

Clearly, it's impossible to collaborate with business counterparts if you have little understanding of their domains. In the evolving world of HIT, new leaders will need to understand the business and become more than just the department that provisions and maintains technology. The new IT leaders will be those who understand the business and can develop a vision that drives value to the business through the intelligent use of technology. That is the challenge facing us in the coming years. It's an exciting challenge because most IT professionals have long advocated for a seat at the strategic table. Now, we're not only being invited but we're also expected to arrive fully prepared to help lead our organizations to an optimized, digitized future state. This book will help you develop exactly those perspectives and plans to enable you and your IT team to become the valued, trusted, and relied upon business partners your healthcare organizations need.

In a sentence, the HIT imperative now is to renovate, grow, and transform. To be sure, this is going to be a messy process. HIT has been cobbled together over decades. Most organizations are working with a multitude of platforms, technologies, applications, interfaces, and capabilities. To compound the complexity, we have users with a wide range of technology skills and processes that are an jumble from years of initiatives. If you've worked in healthcare for more than a decade or so, you can probably count four or five major organizational initiatives intended to clean up some of this. Total Quality Management (TQM), Six Sigma, Lean, and Agile are four that pop immediately to mind for most. All of these are legitimate systems to drive standardization and process improvement. Almost all of them were implemented with great fanfare and enthusiasm. Almost none of them survive in healthcare in tact today. Remnants of many of these systems remain – a smattering here, a dab there. Why? Because healthcare is very resistant to change, and generally for good reason. We don't want our providers hopping around from theory to theory when treating congestive heart failure or diabetic retinopathy. We want tried-and-true, safe, reliable, and effective care. So, when it comes to making change, the stakes are very high in healthcare. It's a legitimate reason for the reluctance to change, but it sometimes is a rationale we hide behind to avoid really making substantive change that will improve care across the board.

## Summary

We know that healthcare is evolving rapidly now that the pandemic has served as a jackhammer to the status quo. The challenge now is how we rebuild, re-envision, and re-align healthcare to truly improve the care we provide to everyone at the lowest possible cost and with the highest quality outcomes. Now that consumer demands are shifting, payors and providers are looking at new ways to deliver care. All of that will involve HIT leading and enabling change. But we can't drive change from a place of chaos. The chapters that follow provide a straight-forward method for clearing the rubble and renovating HIT while still running the business.

# References

[1.1] Condon, Alan, "19 Hospital closures and bankruptcies in 2022," November 11, 2022, https://www.beckershospitalreview.com/finance/19-hospital-closures-bankruptcies-in-2022.html, accessed January 9, 2023.

[1.2] Gold, Jon, and Keith Shaw, "What is edge computing and why does it matter?" May 31, 2022, https://www.networkworld.com/article/3224893/what-is-edge-computing-and-how-it-s-changing-the-network.html, accessed August 23, 2022.

[1.3] U.S Census Bureau, "65 and older population grows rapidly as baby boomers age," Release Number CB20-99, June 25, 2020, https://www.census.gov/newsroom/press-releases/2020/65-older-population-grows.html, accessed August 20, 2022.

[1.4] Cubanski, Juliette, Tricia Neuman, and Meredith Freed, "The facts on Medicare spending and financing," August 20, 2019, https://www.kff.org/medicare/issue-brief/the-facts-on-medicare-spending-and-financing/, accessed August 20, 2022.

[1.5] U.S. Centers for Medicare & Medicaid Services, Chronic Care Management, August 1, 2022, https://www.cms.gov/About-CMS/Agency-Information/OMH/equity-initiatives/chronic-care-management, accessed August 23, 2022.

[1.6] Centers for Disease Control and Prevention, Health and Economic Costs of Chronic Diseases, March 23, 2023, https://www.cdc.gov/chronicdisease/about/costs/index.htm, accessed August 23, 2022.

[1.7] Steenhuysen, Julie, "Exclusive: US to build $300 mln database to fuel Alzheimer's research," April 3, 2023, https://www.reuters.com/business/healthcare-pharmaceuticals/us-build-300-mln-database-fuel-alzheimers-research-2023-04-03/, accessed April 9, 2023.

[1.8] Centers for Disease Control and Prevention, Health and Economic Cost of Chronic Diseases, op. cit.

[1.9] American Hospital Association, https://www.aha.org/center/population-health-management, accessed August 20, 2022.

[1.10] Singhal, Shubham, Nithya Vinjamoori, and Mathangi Radha, "The next frontier of healthcare delivery," March 24, 2022, https://www.mckinsey.com/industries/healthcare-systems-and-services/our-insights/the-next-frontier-of-care-delivery-in-healthcare, accessed August 23, 2022.

[1.11] CMS Telehealth Guidelines, last updated May 11, 2023, https://telehealth. hhs.gov/providers/preparing-patients-for-telehealth/telehealth-and-remote-patient-monitoring/, accessed January 4, 2023.

[1.12] Bestsennyy, Oleg, and Jenny Cordina, "The role of personalization in the care journey: An example of patient engagement to reduce readmissions," August 5, 2021, https://www.mckinsey.com/industries/healthcare-systems-and-services/our-insights/the-role-of-personalization-in-the-care-journey-an-example-of-patient-engagement-to-reduce-readmissions, accessed August 20, 2022.

[1.13] Lo, Justin, Matthew Rae, Krutika Amin, Cynthia Cox, Nirmita Panchal, and Benjamin F. Miller, "Telehealth has played an outsized role meeting mental health needs during the COVID-19 pandemic," March 15, 2022, https://www. kff.org/coronavirus-covid-19/issue-brief/telehealth-has-played-an-outsized-role-meeting-mental-health-needs-during-the-covid-19-pandemic/, accessed August 6, 2022.

[1.14] Holloway, Sarah Calkins, Michael Peterson, Andrew MacDonald, and Bridget Scherbring Pollak, "From revenue cycle management to revenue excellence," June 5, 2018, https://www.mckinsey.com/industries/healthcare-systems-and-services/our-insights/from-revenue-cycle-management-to-revenue-excellence, accessed August 20, 2022.

[1.15] Sjoding, Michael W., Robert P. Dickson, Theodore J. Iwashyna, Steven E. Gay, and Thomas S. Valley, "Racial Bias in Pulse Oximetry Measurement," New England Journal of Medicine, December 17, 2020, Updated February 23, 2021, https://www.nejm.org/doi/full/10.1056/NEJMc2029240, N Engl J Med 2020; 383:2477–2478, DOI: 10.1056/NEJMc2029240, accessed January 4, 2023.

[1.16] Singhal, Shubham, and Neha Patel, "The future of U.S. healthcare: What's next for the Industry Post-COVID-19," July 10, 2022, https://www.mckinsey. com/industries/healthcare-systems-and-services/our-insights/the-future-of-us-healthcare-whats-next-for-the-industry-post-covid-19, accessed August 20, 2022.

[1.17] O'Reilly, Kevin B., "New research links hard-to-use EHRs and physician burnout," November 14, 2019, https://www.ama-assn.org/practice-management/digital/new-research-links-hard-use-ehrs-and-physician-burnout, accessed August 26, 2022.

[1.18] Khan, Naufal, Jason Reynolds, and Christoph Schrey, "Partnering to shape the future – IT's new imperative," May 11, 2016, https://www.mckinsey.com/capabilities/mckinsey-digital/our-insights/partnering-to-shape-the-future-its-new-imperative, accessed August 29, 2022.

[1.19] Ibid. P. 7.

# Chapter 2

# Digital Transformation

The phrase *digital transformation* is everywhere these days. It's the topic of conferences and seminars, articles, and blog posts. You can't read anything about information technology (IT) without seeing a reference to digital transformation. That's especially true in healthcare, where the promise of transforming health care with technology is an ever-present theme. Of course, technology vendors are adding to the hype because they believe their solution will trigger or enable this transformation. In this chapter, we're going to look at some of the hype and some of the reality around digital transformation in healthcare. This will lay the foundation for the subsequent chapters because the bottom line is this: you cannot engage in a digital transformation without first fixing what's broken.

In his 2023 book titled "Digital Transformation: Strategy, Execution, and Technology," author Siu Loon Hoe aptly described the situation in this way:

> Many organizations rush into digital transformation initiatives without first addressing the fundamental business issues and IT problems. Prior to embarking on a full-scale digital transformation exercise, it is important to first close the existing business gaps and resolve any underlying process inefficiencies. [2.1]

Of course, if you work in healthcare, your very next thought might be, "*If that's true, we may never be able to begin a digital transformation journey.*" Healthcare processes are often inefficient for many reasons – some good, some not so good. We can't wait until the business has sorted itself out before undertaking digital transformation. We also can't digitally transform

DOI: 10.4324/9781003377023-3

our business without first fixing some of the things that are broken, both in the business but especially in IT.

This is not a linear processor nor a single-pass process. It is iterative and sometimes circuitous. You can develop a plan to address IT issues either in advance of, or in parallel with, your digital transformation initiatives. If you try to renovate your IT function while also trying to transform it, you are likely to end up with a bit of a muddled mess. It will be hard to tell if you're working on renovation, innovation, or some odd combination of the two. Thus, the focus of this book is on the renovation needed to build the IT foundation for your digital transformation. This chapter provides a very focused look at digital transformation in healthcare, so you understand the big picture and the long view of where healthcare is headed. It will give context to your IT renovation project and help inform you as you decide where to put your efforts first.

## What Is Digital Transformation

Let's start out with a basic definition or two. Numerous experts, including Hoe, have made a distinction between *digitization*, *digitalization*, and *digital transformation*. While there are various views on this, the basic distinctions really have to do with where they fall on the technology spectrum and the overall impact on the business. Let's start with Figure 2.1, Overview of Digital Transformation.

As you can see, *digitization* is usually the first step for any organization. One could argue that the first major healthcare digitization project was the move from paper to EHRs. Paper records were scanned, or, in some cases, transcribed, into an EHR. The primary objective of digitization is to create or convert information into an electronic format. Information assets are the primary targets of this first phase.

The second phase is *digitalization*. In this phase, the business focuses on converting business processes in a way that leverages technology. Many of the EHR optimization projects would fall into this category. Automating claim submissions or using scheduling templates to optimize turnaround times in operating rooms (ORs) are examples of digitalization. The target in this case is business operations or the overall business operating model. The objective is to streamline and improve existing operations using technology.

The third phase is *digital transformation*. Most experts agree that digital transformation entails completely reimagining the business to create entirely

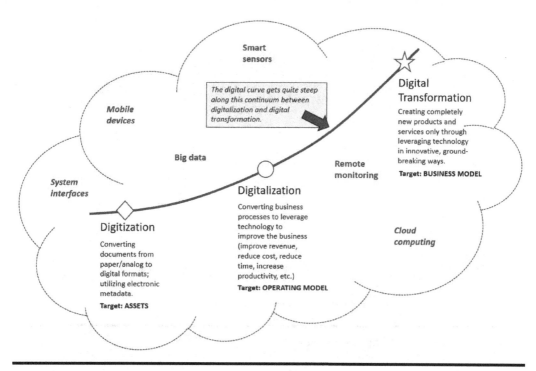

**Figure 2.1    Overview of digital transformation.**

new products and services that could only exist through the innovative use of technology. We have seen examples of digital transformation in other industries that make this concept easier to understand. For example, online retailing (now a relatively "old" example), music streaming sites, or ridesharing companies and apps all demonstrate how business can be completely reimagined using technology. Netflix ™ is an oft-cited example. They started out by disrupting the video rental market by mailing CDs to people, getting people to sign up for monthly subscriptions, then morphed into an online streaming service and, most recently, a production company creating award-winning original content. All of this was enabled by evolving technology and digitally transforming the company. In this case, the target was the business model itself.

Digitally transforming any business, including a healthcare organization, is an enterprise project that entails reimagining how businesses can create new operating models using digital technologies. Digital transformation must be preceded, at least to some degree, by digitization and digitalization. It would be difficult to go from paper records to telehealth without a few interim steps. Figure 2.2 depicts the conceptual journey that most organizations go through when moving from digitization to digital transformation. The dashed line boxes indicate the progression of technology over time, which

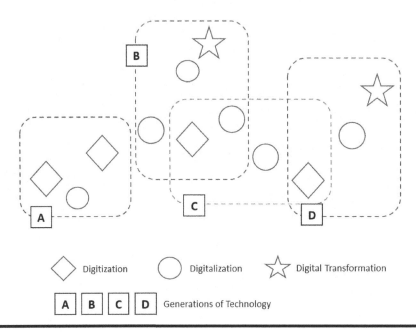

**Figure 2.2   Conceptual digital journey.**

never ends. Technology implementations often contend with ever-newer generations of technology solutions appearing on the horizon, threatening to render obsolete that which is still being implemented.

Digital transformation clearly leverages new and emerging technologies to create new business models, new ways of operating. Later in this chapter we'll discuss three current examples of digital transformation underway in healthcare today.

In Chapter 1, we talked about the future of healthcare and what digital transformation efforts are likely to bring in the coming years. However, we know healthcare organizations are notoriously difficult to change, primarily because it's a complex, high-risk environment with many stakeholders, from governmental regulators to patient populations, payors to providers, and everyone in between. Your organization's digital transformation efforts will be heavily influenced by all of these factors as well as by the accelerating rate of change in technology.

The failure rate of digital transformation projects is enormous – most data suggest the failure rate is around 70%. [2.2] Part of that failure is due to moving into uncharted territory, part is due to organizational change management (or lack thereof), and part of it is due to trying to build a new structure on top of one that is in decay. You can improve your odds of success through this renovation effort by performing the assessments and remediations we'll discuss.

## *The Digital Landscape*

Digital transformation has been underway in one form or another for more than a decade. According to most sources, the phrase *digital transformation* was first used by Deloitte research in 2015 to describe the efforts of the best digital transformation projects. Since then, the term has been used, overused, and misused in every imaginable way.

However, there is a long-term change underway, and transformation really does best describe what's happening. Businesses not only have to digitize manual processes in order to remain competitive, they also have to re-invent their business processes to be more customer-centric. In today's environment, that means streamlining processes and allowing the customer to engage with the business in a fully digital manner. [2.3]

Many in healthcare IT are a bit leery of the phrase digital transformation because it seems to denote something the IT department has to do, and that's completely inaccurate. Technology can be applied to various aspects of healthcare in order to transform that part of the business. IT is uniquely qualified to implement these transformative solutions. Yet these efforts must be led by operational experts who fundamentally want to change how healthcare is delivered. In many cases, IT provides innovative ideas about what's possible using technology, but it is the organization as a whole, and senior leaders specifically, who must have the desire and vision to transform care delivery.

Digital transformation is not a straight-line journey, nor does it ever really end. In healthcare, there is often limited tolerance for the time, cost, resources, and disruption that come with digital transformation. Yet, every C-suite executive is impatient to see results and to leverage new digital capabilities to improve the business.

In a January 2022, Harvard Business Review article entitled "The 4 Pillars of Successful Digital Transformations" authors Furr, Shipilov, Rouillard, and Hemon-Laurens outline both the current challenges with digital transformation and a path forward.

> Despite years of discussion, understanding what digital transformation means for established companies remains a daunting challenge. Leaders put in charge of a digital transformation feel pulled in many different directions, with competing demands from IT, marketing, sales, and operations…. The key to cutting through the confusion is to see that digital transformation is not a single thing, but a multi-faceted journey …. [2.4]

The authors indicate that without a clear understanding of what digital transformation is or should be, organizations put the wrong people in charge, assign the wrong resources, and put the wrong performance measures in placc.

Clearly, the data indicate that digital transformation is neither fast nor easy. Transformation in healthcare requires a focus on quality of care and improved outcomes. These don't happen simply because of technology, nor do they happen quickly. As we look at digital transformation in healthcare, we have to look both at the organization's appetite for change and its ability to manage that change. We also have to look at the IT function in healthcare. As we've discussed, demand typically far exceeds capacity, and there's usually constant downward pressure on budgets. These factors often keep IT stuck fighting for resources and reacting to changes rather than leading transformative efforts.

These demands to accelerate change, to digitize, and to automate are almost constant, but there's no space for this to occur inside the cramped and battered IT structure we find in most healthcare organizations. Built over decades, sometimes (figuratively) cobbled together with baling wire and duct tape, our IT house is a bit of a hazard. Digital transformation efforts have about a 30% chance of success, as noted earlier. Part of the reason for that low success rate is that IT departments are not positioned to enable transformation. Renovating your IT function is the key to creating an environment in which digital transformation has a better chance to be successful.

## Operational Transformation

Increasingly, efforts to digitize and digitalize are being referred to as *operational transformation*. Just as digital transformation became a buzz phrase a few years ago, operational transformation now is increasingly being discussed. Maybe that's because operational transformation is a good precursor to digital transformation. As shown in Figure 2.1 earlier, these efforts to digitize and digitalize lead to capabilities that ultimately support digital transformation.

As you review your environment throughout this renovation process, be aware that operational transformation also requires the basic IT house to be in order. Certainly, there are numerous opportunities to improve operations in parallel with your renovation work, but be on the lookout for potential pitfalls.

One of the most common operational transformation initiatives is automation. This may be work IT initiates or work requested by operational leaders, but it must be preceded by process improvement. You should not automate a convoluted or illogical process. If you don't improve workflows *before* you automate, you'll simply speed up a poor process. The current state may not contain the right actions in the right order, or it might involve the wrong people (or miss the right people), or it simply may not be needed anymore. If you're being pressed for organizational transformation, you still need to sort out some of your IT functions. Digitization or digitalization efforts require an initiative to document the workflow, improve the workflow, then design the transformed process. In Lean terms, it would involve a *kaizen* or an improvement event, before change is made. So, include opportunities to improve IT and organizational processes in your overall renovation plans and resist creating a few one-off projects that may create unneeded distractions and diversions along the way. Buzz phrases aside, your mission is to improve fundamental IT functions so you can transform both your IT function and your organization.

## Enterprise Architecture and Digital Transformation

In this section, we will briefly discuss how enterprise architecture (EA) and digital transformation are linked. EA as a body of knowledge has been around since the 1960's, but it more recently has gained traction as technology has become more central to business operations. There are many models used to envision, manage, and transform EA. Resources at the end of this chapter point you to additional references if you're interested.

Let's begin with a brief definition of EA.

> Enterprise architecture (EA) is the practice of analyzing, designing, planning, and implementing enterprise analysis to successfully execute on business strategies. EA helps businesses structure IT projects and policies to achieve desired business results and to stay on top of industry trends and disruptions using architecture principles and practices, a process also known as enterprise architectural planning (EAP). [2.5]

EA is the link between business strategy and technical implementation. It defines how the business is (or wants to) operate and how technology will enable and amplify those business objectives. Done effectively, EA can coalesce business and IT objectives to deliver value. EA helps IT understand what the business is trying to achieve and which technical solutions will drive those outcomes. EA helps the business clarify its objectives and outcomes by partnering with IT leaders to develop plans to implement the next generation of technologies. As such, it's easy to see how EA supports and drives digital transformation efforts.

Another benefit of EA is that it can help align various business segments to IT so that common IT components can be effectively used across the organization, including infrastructure, applications, and data systems. Thus, EA can help an organization decide among multiple opportunities or multiple technical paths to find a common thread that will best create value in the organization.

Having a basic understanding of EA can help you develop your IT renovation project even if you do not have a formal EA function in place.

## Artificial Intelligence and IT Operations

Generative AI is a broad category of AI that can generate something new – new text, images, and sounds, for example. In the past couple of years, user interfaces to these AI engines have emerged, providing broad access to AI capabilities. The release of ChatGPT by OpenAI in November 2022 was one of the pivotal events around access to AI.

With the broad access of AI, we will certainly see it influence IT operations in a significant way going forward. Having AI generate code, test scripts, reports, or perform complex tasks is all within the reach of IT staff. AI is augmenting the technical skills of our teams, expanding their ability to generate reliable code or test that code faster and more accurately. AI can create test cases and then run tests against a complex set of criteria. This can enhance our ability to test our security, for example. The flip side is also true. Malicious actors will have broader access to tools that will perform a variety of attacks, even if AI engines refuse to write malicious code, there are simple workarounds that currently outsmart AI.

Thus, we will see the acceleration of technical capabilities, for good and for bad. As healthcare professionals, we should determine how AI can help augment our staff and accelerate our knowledge uptake or capabilities. We also need to be prepared for much more sophisticated attacks on our networks and electronic assets.

According to a March 2023 article on the use of this capability in IT operations,

> Generative AI can be used to produce original content in response to queries, but it can also be used to code or operate as a virtual assistant. Other generative AI examples include GitHub's Copilot, based on OpenAI's Codex, which can create software application code based on natural language prompts, Salesforce's CodeT5; and Tabnine's code completion tool. This week, generative AI also surfaced in new AI assistants for Microsoft Azure and Office 365, as well as updates to Google Cloud and Google Workspace. [2.6]

As AI continues to make inroads in IT operations as well as healthcare, we will see it being used for more tasks, but it won't replace humans in the near term. Some roles will change or become obsolete, but new roles will be needed to manage AI operations and the challenges that come with that change.

## Digital Transformation in Healthcare

Digital transformation in many industries is tied to increasing revenue or increasing consumer loyalty (in order to increase revenue). It can be argued that in some cases, it's about generating (or capturing) digital data, but that in turn is used in some manner to generate revenue.

In healthcare, digital transformation typically is not solely about increasing revenue, though that certainly can be one element. Other aspects include improving time to diagnosis, improving quality of care, or providing new modes of treatment. As discussed, some examples of digital transformation in healthcare are the use of AI, telehealth, and personal health devices, which fall under the category of the IoT.

### *Artificial Intelligence*

According to IBM,

> At its simplest form, artificial intelligence is a field, which combines computer science and robust datasets to enable problem-solving. It also encompasses the subfields of machine learning and

deep learning, which are frequently mentioned in conjunction with artificial intelligence. These disciplines are comprised of AI algorithms which seek to create expert systems which make predictions or classifications based on input data. [2.7]

While AI might enable the problem-solving capabilities of humans, it can also greatly augment those capabilities. A machine can be programmed to ingest massive volumes of data and spot trends a human would miss. It can be programmed to read digital images with higher accuracy than the human eye. In healthcare, one of the primary goals currently is to use AI to improve diagnosis and treatment across populations.

Disease prevention and treatment will evolve faster as larger data sets and larger populations can be evaluated through ML and AI. Looking at which interventions are most effective for specific populations can dramatically improve health outcomes. For example, data might show that a particular treatment protocol is more effective in one population than another. This allows providers to fine-tune treatment plans to achieve more optimal outcomes.

## Telehealth

The use of the Internet and mobile devices has certainly transformed how care is delivered. It wasn't long ago that healthcare was only provided in person at a clinic or hospital. Care was provider-centric; patients went to the provider's location. Since the pandemic, statistics show that telehealth (and telepsychiatry) have been well-received by providers and patients. Acceptance by seniors, rural patients, and behavioral health patients is high because, in a sense, the provider virtually goes to the patient. Coupled with IoT devices, discussed next, many aspects of clinical care can be effectively delivered in this manner. While there is no substitute for an in-person provider/patient encounter, in some cases, these virtual methods expand the options for patients to receive care in the manner most suitable for them. This is a fundamental shift in the approach to provider-centric healthcare. We are moving toward a more balanced model where both provider and patient needs are met.

## Internet of Things

Wearables such as smartwatches, Bluetooth-enabled (BT) blood pressure cuffs, or fitness trackers are all part of the IoT category. These electronic devices connect to apps and portals, delivering data that can be recorded and analyzed. Perhaps more importantly, the ability of people to see their own personal metrics often facilitates better prevention or management of chronic conditions.

These electronic devices also enable RPM in both passive and active modes. Passive monitoring might include providing a body weight scale to a patient and having them begin tracking their weight over time. Being significantly overweight, for example, is often the precursor to numerous other chronic health conditions. Using a BT-enabled scale connected to an app on a smartphone connected to a patient portal in an EHR enables a care team to monitor data and intervene as needed.

Active or real-time monitoring, such as cardiac monitoring, is also being conducted from the patient's home, allowing the patient to remain in a more comfortable (and lower cost) environment while still having the safety net of medical monitoring available.

Modern EHRs can take patient-provided data, analyze it, and automate alerts to the care team. For example, if a patient is monitoring blood pressure and it's slowly climbing or it jumps suddenly, AI can analyze the trend data and alert the care team or the patient via text. RPM services can monitor and alert, causing a healthcare team member to contact the patient to investigate abnormal or dangerous results.

Additionally, these technologies allow a range of medical devices to be used at home by the patient in conjunction with their provider. These so-called "doc in a box" solutions can provide an electronic stethoscope, blood-pressure monitor, thermometer, glucose monitor, and pulse oximeter all in an easy-to-use setup for the patient. This enables a well-child visit, annual physical exam, or a monthly senior check-in to be conducted virtually. These will not replace in-person provider care, but they can certainly augment care.

These are the most common uses of technology in healthcare that would fall under the term digital transformation. There are many other changes underway that utilize technology, but following Hoe's definitions, many would be more closely aligned with digitization and digitalization than digital transformation.

In the future, we'll continue to see innovation and digital transformation in the healthcare industry. Numerous big tech companies are investing in healthcare and will likely drive changes both in how care is delivered and in how technology is utilized. This has both benefits and risks. Clearly, the benefit is that big tech has the money to invest in these innovative experiments, and some of them will no doubt be successful. However, big tech is typically profit-driven. The risk is that big tech companies will focus solely on profit and take care of the wealthiest of patients while leaving those less profitable (or unprofitable) patients to be cared for by others. They may potentially move into spaces not to provide the best quality care but to control or acquire the most consumer data and leverage that data for profit. These are some of the potential pitfalls of big tech in healthcare. However, big tech innovation in healthcare delivery could ultimately improve access to quality care and reduce the cost of care for everyone. Only time will tell how this will play out.

## Summary

We've touched on the topic of digital transformation in a cursory manner because this book is not about digital transformation, per se – it's about preparing your IT function for digital transformation. Digital transformation is about fundamentally changing the way business is conducted. In this case, it's about radically changing the way healthcare is delivered. Those changes can't be successfully navigated if you're working with hardware that's ten years old or operating systems that never get patched or a mash-up of software applications that have gaps and overlaps and no clear function. There are additional aspects that influence your renovation and ultimately, your digital transformation that we'll cover in upcoming chapters.

Digital transformation will create massive organizational improvements if done well, but it cannot be done well with an outdated and underskilled IT function. You will need to navigate your IT renovation project with speed and diligence.

## References

[2.1] Hoe, Siu Loon, Digital Transformation: Strategy, Execution, and Technology, CRC Press, Boca Raton, FL, 2023. P. 18.
[2.2] Argenti, Paul A, Berman, Jenifer, Calsbeek, Ryan, and Whitehouse, Andrew, "The secret behind successful corporate transformation," September 14, 2021, https://hbr.org/2021/09/the-secret-behind-successful-corporate-transformations, accessed January 28, 2023.
[2.3] Xperience, "Short.history of digital transformation: The world's longest revolution," September 21, 2020, https://www.xperience-group.com/news-item/short-history-of-digital-transformation-the-worlds-longest-revolution/, accessed August 15, 2022.

[2.4] Furr, Nathan, Andrew Shipilov, Didier Rouillard, and Antoine Hemon-Laurens, "The 4 pillars of successful digital transformations," January 28, 2022, https://hbr.org/2022/01/the-4-pillars-of-successful-digital-transformations, accessed September 23, 2022,

[2.5] White, Sarah K., "What is enterprise architecture? A framework for transformation," October 16, 2018, https://www.cio.com/article/222421/what-is-enterprise-architecture-a-framework-for-transformation.html, accessed August 27, 2022.

[2.6] Pariseau, Beth, "How ChatGPT and generative AI will affect IT operations," March 17, 2023, https://www.techtarget.com/searchitoperations/news/365532540/How-ChatGPT-and-generative-AI-will-affect-IT-operations, accessed March 19, 2023.

[2.7] IBM, "What is artificial intelligence?" https://www.ibm.com/topics/artificial-intelligence, accessed January 8, 2023.

## Resources

Enterprise Architecture Body of Knowledge, https://eabok.org/ (defunct as of 2020 but data remains available online), accessed August 28, 2022.

Ross, Jeanne W., Peter Weill, and David C. Robertson, Enterprise Architecture as Strategy: Creating a Foundation for Business Execution, Harvard Business Press, Boston, MA, 2006.

The Art of Service, Enterprise Architecture Body of Knowledge: A Complete Guide - 2021 Edition, November 2020. ISBN-13: 978-1867429548.

The Open Group, "TOGAF Standard Version 9.2", no date, https://pubs.opengroup.org/architecture/togaf9-doc/arch/index.html, ISBN: 1-947754-11-9, accessed August 28, 2022.

Wager, Karen A., Francis W. Lee, John P. Glaser, Health Care Information Systems: A Practical Approach to Health Care Management, 5th Edition, Boston, MA, Wiley & Sons, Inc., 2022.

# Chapter 3

# Assess the Environment

In the first two chapters, we looked at where healthcare, technology, and digital transformations are headed. In this chapter, we look at the overall environment in which we are operating. We will look at the environment of healthcare, your organization, and your IT department. There's a blueprint at the end of the chapter, so you can develop your own action plan for assessing your environment.

## Healthcare Environment

In Chapter 1, we looked at the megatrends in the healthcare environment. Let's take a quick look at what's happening in healthcare right now that will impact your IT renovation project.

At the annual HIMSS Conference in 2021, Tom Kiesau, senior partner with the Chartis Group, discussed the findings from a survey of 220 healthcare executives on such issues as digital health, machine learning, and AI. Kiesau warned that new technology plus an old organization equals a costly old organization. [3.1] Indeed, when we layer on new technology without going through the renovation stage, we have an unwieldy and expensive array of solutions that create significant risk. As organizations are facing financial pressure in the post-pandemic environment, the need to renovate HIT is even more critical.

The HIMSS "2022 Future of Healthcare Report" indicates healthcare organizations worldwide understand the need to move toward more digital solutions. However, looking five years down the road, 54% of organizations expect to be in "planning" stages and just 46% in "implementation" phases. [3.2] Contrast this with data from the same report showing that 70% of

DOI: 10.4324/9781003377023-4

clinicians support the use of digital tools and believe those tools could potentially enable better disease management, prevention, and coordination of care. Granted, digital transformation is an evolution with layers of iterations over time. Still, the expectations around this progress five years out seem to lag a bit behind consumer and clinician expectations.

As a backdrop for your assessment, we will take a moment to walk through some methods for doing this research on your own every year or two. As an IT leader, it's important to not only see where healthcare as an industry is headed, but also to discern points-of-view in the data. Table 3.1 shows a sampling of data sources and their potential relevance to your research. While this is not an exhaustive list, it provides ideas for where you might source

**Table 3.1   Data Sources for Healthcare Environment Research**

| Data Points of View | Who/What | Relevance |
|---|---|---|
| Thought leaders in HC | Well-known leaders in healthcare | Highly relevant for healthcare trends |
| Thought leaders in IT | Well-known leaders in IT | Highly relevant for IT trends that may or may not impact HIT |
| Industry leaders in HC | Respected, innovative organizations and their leaders | Highly relevant for healthcare trends and best practices |
| Industry leaders in IT | Respected, innovative organizations and their leaders | Highly relevant for IT, may not clearly connect to HIT |
| HC organizations | Organizations in the middle of the pack indicate current state | Reflects typical adoption and innovation rates, may be a good reality check |
| IT vendor organizations | Often includes IT organizations in or breaking into healthcare | Reflects current capabilities and is sometimes biased by their own offerings |
| Scientific research | Governmental and think-tank publications | Can reflect a possible future state, but sometimes is too academic to apply |
| General media | Millions of outlets for general information | Can often be inaccurate, but shows popular trends that are often accurate |
| Social media | Possible subject matter experts as well as uninformed opinions | Social media collectively can indicate trends; experts may share unique perspectives on social media sites; can also be the source of misinformation |

your data. Once you've validated a data source and understood its perspective and potential bias, you can include the data in your future research.

By understanding how various sources present data and what their perspectives (or biases) are, you can more clearly see how the data can assist you in understanding what future trends are likely to come to fruition and impact your organization. For example, about 8% of healthcare executives saw artificial intelligence and machine learning as an important future priorities and about the same percentage said AI and ML were "distractions." [3.3] Compare that to data in the same article indicating 80% of providers surveyed are interested in the use of AI for clinical use cases. What does that tell you? Providers will be pushing for AI while executives may be tapping the breaks, due to costs, capabilities, or other priorities. As a HIT leader, what does this conflicting data tell you? How does your organization view AI and ML today, and how is that influenced by your executive team, your provider team, and your IT team?

Vendor perspectives are also influential, though often biased toward their own solutions. Cloud vendors see cloud technologies as the next big thing. AI vendors see AI and ML as the next must-have capabilities. Regardless of your view about these vendors' capabilities and technologies, large vendors do drive perception; perception drives reality, which in turn drives IT spending. For example, a decade ago, it was not uncommon to find a healthcare organization that had no cloud presence. Today, every healthcare organization has implemented some version of a hybrid strategy (though "strategy" might be too strong a word; some perhaps have stumbled their way to the cloud) to meet the evolving needs of the organization and the changing technical requirements for delivering healthcare. As we're all aware, cloud technologies do offer viable solutions, but they are not a cure-all by any means.

In healthcare, there are organizations known to be well-oiled machines that can implement leading-edge technologies and solutions to light the way for those that follow. However, most healthcare organizations fall somewhere in the middle of the pack. They may agree with trends and priorities but lack the resources or capabilities to implement leading-edge solutions. Often, the organization simply lacks the vision, will, or budget to explore these solutions. So, they allow the market leaders to experiment and refine, then consider implementing later once a technology or solution has moved from trend to norm. Business intelligence and analytics followed this trajectory in healthcare. AI and ML are following a similar path now.

As a HIT leader, you are aware of what's trending, what's hyped, and what's helpful. By looking at trends, market leaders, industry experts, and other sources of data, you compile a view of the future that is most relevant for you and your organization. You are probably also keenly aware of the capabilities and constraints of your own organization, its appetite for growth, change, and risk; and its position in the marketplace. We will cover that in more detail later in this chapter. First, let's look at three mega-trends in the healthcare space today: financial challenges, staffing challenges, and the shift to value-based payments.

## Financial Challenges

Many healthcare organizations are struggling financially for several reasons. The payments made during the pandemic to keep organizations financially afloat have largely ceased. These payments did help, but in some cases, they also masked some of the underlying problems that have now started to show up. For acute care providers, the lack of inpatients, lack of surgeries, and lack of emergency room visits all hit the bottom line. For ambulatory surgery centers and some specialty providers, demand dried up as everyone tried to avoid these services unless they became critical.

At the same time, there have been strong upward cost pressures in the supply chain. Everything from wages to personal protective equipment, medicines to fuel prices – costs have gone up across the board. This has led to significant challenges for some organizations. Headlines are full of announcements of large healthcare providers with significant operating losses. [3.4]

These factors are impacting most healthcare organizations, including yours. How organizations respond will vary. Some will cut operating budgets, close certain lines of business, or temporarily close portions of the business (such as reducing the number of inpatient units to better staff ICUs and EDs). Some will scale back or close. Others will look to stabilize finances or hold steady until they see how the multi-year financial picture looks.

## Staffing Challenges

We have discussed the aging of the workforce and the impact that is having on all industries. Healthcare is particularly impacted as healthcare is delivered by humans and much of the work cannot be automated. While technology can reduce the need for some types of staff, it cannot replace patient care techs, medical assistants, nurses, or physicians. If well-implemented, technology can take on some of the mundane, repetitive tasks, freeing humans up to do more meaningful and value-added work.

In addition to the aging workforce, we are seeing people move out of the workforce or into other kinds of roles. The pandemic made hard work even harder for healthcare professionals, and some are leaving the healthcare field.

When they leave, they not only create a staffing gap but also a knowledge gap, as many of these individuals are highly skilled and experienced professionals. Even if the role can be filled, it is often with someone with less experience and who will require time to reach the same level of expertise.

## *Shift to Value-Based Payments*

Some financial models are beginning to shift, gravitating toward value-based care instead of fee-for-service. This changes the equation in terms of how care is provided. However, these models are not consistently in place across the healthcare environment. The fee-for-service model is still the predominant reimbursement method, so organizations are stuck in the middle. Many want to move to value-based care models because it reimburses them for providing comprehensive care to the patient, but reimbursements and guidelines are inconsistent in some areas. Payors have to be onboard with this shift and it's a long, slow process. Compensation must make sense for all parties, and incentives must drive the proper outcomes. This is a slowly evolving area, but one that impacts how organizations generate revenue and how providers provide care.

These three high-level trends are impacting all healthcare organizations and will continue to evolve in the coming months and years. As a HIT leader, it is important to understand the trends in healthcare so you can see how they influence your specific organization. This provides the context for your organization and, ultimately, for your IT organization.

## *IT Marketplace*

Finally, it's important to understand what's happening in the broader IT marketplace. Though not all innovations and implementations will be suitable for healthcare, they are important to factor into the overall picture. We have seen the rise of virtualization, machine learning, big data, IoT, and automation in recent years. Figure 3.1 shows the flow of influence to consider as you assess your environment.

IT in an organization is influenced by the organization, by the healthcare industry and by the IT market. Similarly, the organization is influenced by the industry, the available IT solutions (IT market), and the IT solutions in place in the organization. The continuum across these dimensions is unique for each organization, but the influence of each segment should be acknowledged as renovation plans are created. How is your IT function influenced by these segments, and how are these segments influenced by your IT function?

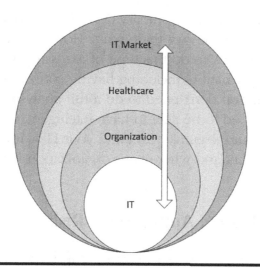

**Figure 3.1    The flow of influence in healthcare IT.**

## Your Organization's Environment

We have discussed the healthcare environment in several different ways. Now, let's turn our attention to your organization. When you look at your organization, begin by assessing your overall organization. What segment of healthcare is it operating in? What are the specific characteristics of that segment? Where is your organization positioned in that space? For example, are you with a large, well-funded organization or a smaller, budget-conscious company? Are you a local PCP group or a regional hospital system? Are you a market leader or a follower? Does your organization actively pursue innovation today, or is it barely getting along as is?

In the context of healthcare and renovating your IT function, understanding your organization's relative position in the market is an important starting point. It tells you about the overall 'personality' of your organization and what you can expect in terms of how you will need to approach your renovation project.

One area of inquiry should be the competitive environment in which your organization is operating. Who are the primary competitors and what are they doing? What is your organization's competitive advantage? Is another organization making inroads in that area, or are you still a singular leader in that regard? What is happening in your city/region/state that might impact your competitors and you? How are you doing compared to your competitors in terms of patient acquisition, patient engagement, and patient experience? How are these three aspects viewed within your organization (prioritized, mentioned, or forgotten)? What have been the primary demands on your IT department from the organization over the past three years? How do you see that shifting?

You don't need an MBA to do this type of assessment. It takes reviewing various sources of information, including having conversations with leaders in your organization. You don't need to do a full analysis of any of these aspects, but you do need to be able to have intelligent, well-informed conversations with your executive team and your IT team about the competitive environment and where your organization is headed.

## Tolerance for Change, Appetite for Risk

Among the most important elements to assess after the overall nature of your organization is its tolerance or appetite for change.

### Tolerance for Change

As we've discussed, healthcare is notoriously hard to change for many reasons. As you look around your organization, look at various change initiatives in the past to see how they have fared. Also look to see what artifacts from prior change projects are still hanging around. This is not to judge, but to see how the organization responds to change. If prior projects such as Six Sigma or Lean are still pretty much intact, you know you have an organization that can maintain processes. In this case, you may choose to leverage the framework to manage your IT renovation project. In other cases, you will see a smattering of numerous different improvement projects. You will know that change is hard won in your organization. That should cause you to really look at what it will take to drive change in the organization and in your department. For example, your organization may be very resistant to change, but you may have real change champions in the IT department who can envision and implement change (including process change) in the department. How might that influence the success of your IT renovation? How might that influence the C-suite?

Conversely, you might have an IT department that is very resistant to change and is clinging to old, manual ways of doing things while the organization seems to have begun to embrace its digital future. How might that impact your IT renovation plan?

Understanding the tolerance for change in your organization as well as in your IT department is crucial to developing a realistic and sustainable IT renovation plan. There are very few right or wrong answers, but a mismatch of organizational culture and your expectations around change will result in either failure or muted success. We discuss organizational change management in depth in Chapter 29, so be sure to refer to that chapter as you develop thoughts about change in your organization.

## Appetite for Risk

All organizations strive to be successful, but what are they willing to risk to achieve that success? We've all read news headlines about companies that fight hard to achieve innovation or risk a lot to achieve a new milestone. We have also seen or worked for organizations for whom the status quo was quite acceptable, where risk was avoided to the extent possible. There is no right or wrong answer here; it's really about understanding the fundamental nature of the organization you're in. If you try an aggressive approach with a status quo organization, you will likely run into strong headwinds. Conversely, if you take a slow-and-steady approach to change in a very innovative organization, you are likely to be criticized for not moving fast enough.

Some of these traits are driven by the type of healthcare organization, such as whether it is for-profit, publicly held (often driven by quarterly results), not-for-profit, or governmental. The nature of the organization is also formed by the Board of Directors and the executive team. Their desire for change, for aggressively pursuing growth, or top-line revenue will create one type of organization. If the CEO or the Board want to maintain and perfect what is already in place, if it is not beholden to outside stakeholders (like publicly held companies, e.g.), it will become a different type of organization.

Understand your organization's tolerance for change and appetite for success and what (and who) drives it so you can develop your renovation plan and timelines accordingly.

## Strategic Leadership and IT

We have looked at the healthcare environment and at your organization. Now it's time to turn our attention toward the leadership in your organization and its views about IT. Clearly, some healthcare executives are very tech-savvy, and some are the opposite. Some embrace technical innovation; some run from it. Some enable digital transformation by championing change, others actively or passively obstruct the path. Their reasons are almost always anchored in what they believe is best for the organization and the services they are delivering. However, their backgrounds and biases, coupled with their own personal comfort levels with technology, often define an organization's digital personality. This will also inform how you, as the IT executive, approach your renovation project.

Let's look at a few hypothetical examples. First, the CEO, who came up through the ranks on the financial side of healthcare. She is likely very focused on revenue, productivity, quality, expense control, and returns on investment. She is also likely to appreciate the role technology plays in the organization but may be focused primarily on cost vs. capability. When working with your CEO and executive peers to define the opportunity, you are likely to emphasize waste in terms of dollars lost or upside revenue opportunities rather than the technical capabilities themselves.

Next, the CEO who came up through the clinical ranks. He is likely someone who appreciates technology's promises but is leery of it actually delivering on those promises. He may press very hard for data that shows how technology has been successfully used in organizations just like yours. It's also possible he finds technology a 'necessary evil' or feels it gets in the way of great patient care, or he might feel that technology has been a great enabler for the care team. Your approach with this type of leader is to highlight successful clinical implementations of technology in the past and how they have improved patient care or the provider experience. Showing data from other organizations, industry leaders, or thought leaders in the technology space can help cement support.

Finally, you may have a CEO who came up through the operations side of things. She may fully understand the promise and complexity of technology in healthcare. She may also know how often projects fail and at what cost. She may require broad operational buy-in before agreeing to any IT projects. She may ask for a project plan, rapid deliverables (as in agile methods), and tangible near-term results. Garnering support from other C-suite executives, showing prior project success, and developing a plan that will deliver short-term wins will be the likely keys to approval from this type of CEO.

These are all highly simplified examples to give you insight into how your executive team, including your CEO, may view technology and related projects. In reality, your CEO and executive team likely embody all of these points of view. Knowing their focus and interest can help you hone your messaging as you develop you plans.

# Environmental Assessment Plan

You can develop your own plan for assessing your organization's environment. Table 3.2 provides a starter set of elements to investigate. You can use this to begin your environmental assessment, which is an initial phase of any renovation project.

**Table 3.2   Environmental Assessment Blueprint**

| Focus Area | Focusing Questions |
| --- | --- |
| Healthcare big picture | What's happening in healthcare overall? |
| Healthcare trends | What are the current and emerging trends today? |
| HIT trends | What are the current and emerging HIT trends? |
| HIT trends and your organization | How do these current trends show up in your IT department? How will these trends impact your IT department? |
| Your competitors | Who are your primary and secondary competitors and what are they doing? |
| Your organization's opportunities and threats | Based on the competitive environment, what are the opportunities and threats to your organization? |
| Your organization's strengths and weaknesses | Based on the opportunities and threats, what are your organizations (and your IT) strengths and weaknesses? |
| Your organization's leadership culture | How would you characterize your organization's leadership style and culture? How will that impact IT plans? |
| Your organization's culture | How would you characterize your organization's overall culture? How will that impact IT plans? |
| Your organization's financial status | What is your organization's financial type and status (for-profit, not-for-profit; running profitably, break even, negative)? |
| Your organization's operating environment (city, region, and state) | What's happening in your city/region/state that could impact you and your competitors going forward? |
| Other relevant factors | What other relevant factors should be considered for your specific type of healthcare organization? Regulatory changes, technological innovations, cybersecurity risks, other? |

## Summary

In this chapter, we have reviewed several different dimensions for assessing your organization. This step is important prior to undertaking any renovation work because you need to understand the specific situation your organization is in – both in the industry and with respect to technology. You no doubt know much of this information; the task is to compile and review it in a more organized fashion so you have a clear sense of the environment in which you will be operating.

## References

[3.1] Morse, Susan, "The digital revolution has begun but 52% of executives have not progressed beyond the pilot stage," August 11, 2021, https://www.healthcarefinancenews.com/news/digital-revolution-has-begun-52-executives-have-not-progressed-beyond-pilot-stage, accessed August 7, 2022.

[3.2] HIMSS, "Intelligence and new trends revealed in 2022 future of healthcare report," July 25, 2022, https://www.himss.org/resources/intelligence-and-new-trends-revealed-2022-future-healthcare-report, accessed August 7, 2022. Pp 5-6.

[3.3] Morse, Susan, "The digital revolution," August 11, 2021.

[3.4] Ellison, Ayla, "Financial updates from 14 health systems," August 31, 2022, https://www.beckershospitalreview.com/finance/financial-updates-from-13-health-systems.html, accessed January 7, 2023.

# IT BUILDING BLOCKS

# Chapter 4

# IT Strategy Building Blocks

We begin with IT strategy since it is foundational to all we do in healthcare IT. In this chapter, we will discuss what IT strategy is and how you can develop it. Then, in Section III, we will walk through performing an assessment of your current IT strategy capabilities so you can develop a renovation plan for this important aspect of HIT based on where you are and where you want to go.

## Strategy Defined

Strategies are planned actions you take to achieve defined goals. If you set a goal, the next step is to define objectives to accomplish the goal and define strategies for achieving those objectives. It's important to distinguish strategy, which describes *how* at a high-level from tactics, which describe *how* at a task level. Strategy paints a broad stroke about how you will accomplish your objectives. Tactics are very detailed tasks or steps to achieve those strategies. We will walk through some examples later in this chapter to illustrate this distinction.

Strategy is developed by examining goals and determining the best approach to achieving those goals. Goals are typically set by the organization at a high level and then by each division. The division goals (such as IT) should align with, or support, the organization's goals. Sometimes those goals are financial, sometimes operational, and sometimes they are aspirational. In healthcare, organizational goals almost always include maintaining and improving the quality of care as well as financial goals. Therefore, IT goals can be developed to support these two key drivers – quality of care and financial outcomes.

DOI: 10.4324/9781003377023-6

# IT Strategic Planning

Developing a strategy involves prioritizing options and selecting the steps and actions needed to realize those priorities. To determine those priorities, an organization would begin with its vision and mission. These usually don't change much from year to year. From there, the organization will set goals and define specific strategies to achieve those goals. IT strategies should align with organizational goals.

Some healthcare IT departments lack a strategic plan because they find the organization changing direction so frequently, they feel they cannot execute on anything strategic. While this may be true, there are also opportunities to develop a more flexible strategic plan for IT that both keeps the IT function on track with important strategic objectives and allows IT to respond quickly to the changing demands of the organization.

IT strategy in any organization starts with understanding where the organization is positioned in the market and what its current state is. In Section One, we looked at the overall healthcare environment as well as what digital transformation will look like going forward. This gives you a solid starting point for beginning your conversations with your organizational peers and your IT leadership team. You know that IT strategy must fully support and enable the business to accomplish the company's objectives. You can also see what's on the horizon from a technological standpoint. Together, these serve to inform your planning and help you develop an effective IT strategy. In short, we need to assess where we are today, where we want to be tomorrow, and what capabilities we will need to create the digital future we envision.

# Healthcare IT Strategic Plan Example

Let's take a look at the strategic plan from the U.S. government's Office of the National Coordinator (ONC) for Health Information Technology shown in Figure 4.1. In the published strategic plan covering 2020 through 2025, they identify four high-level goals along with thirteen related objectives. These are then tied to strategies defining how these objectives will be achieved. Walking through this example helps demonstrate the relationship between goals, objectives, and strategies in a healthcare environment. This should help guide you as you begin to think about your own HIT strategies.

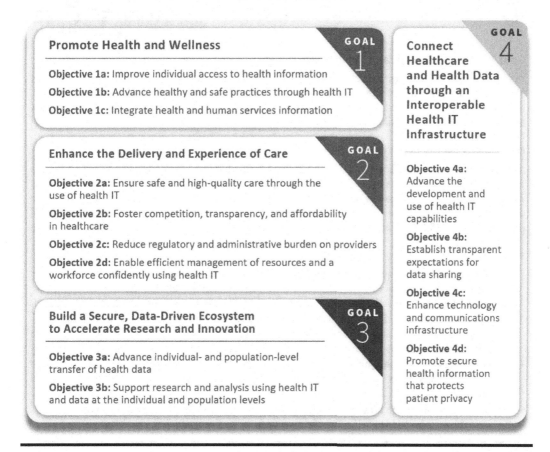

STRATEGIC PLAN
# Framework

**Promote Health and Wellness**                                      GOAL 1

**Objective 1a:** Improve individual access to health information
**Objective 1b:** Advance healthy and safe practices through health IT
**Objective 1c:** Integrate health and human services information

**Enhance the Delivery and Experience of Care**                      GOAL 2

**Objective 2a:** Ensure safe and high-quality care through the use of health IT
**Objective 2b:** Foster competition, transparency, and affordability in healthcare
**Objective 2c:** Reduce regulatory and administrative burden on providers
**Objective 2d:** Enable efficient management of resources and a workforce confidently using health IT

**Build a Secure, Data-Driven Ecosystem to Accelerate Research and Innovation**   GOAL 3

**Objective 3a:** Advance individual- and population-level transfer of health data
**Objective 3b:** Support research and analysis using health IT and data at the individual and population levels

GOAL 4
**Connect Healthcare and Health Data through an Interoperable Health IT Infrastructure**

**Objective 4a:** Advance the development and use of health IT capabilities

**Objective 4b:** Establish transparent expectations for data sharing

**Objective 4c:** Enhance technology and communications infrastructure

**Objective 4d:** Promote secure health information that protects patient privacy

**Figure 4.1   IT strategy from U.S. Office of the National Coordinator (ONC) for Health Information Technology (HealthIT.Gov). (Taken from the draft version as it lays out goals, objectives, and strategies in a more visually effective manner than the final version. [4.1].)**

The first goal is "Promote Health and Wellness." There are three associated objectives as follows:

**Objective 1a:** Improve individual access to health information.
**Objective 1b:** Advance healthy and safe practices through health IT.
**Objective 1c:** Integrate health and human services information.

We'll examine Goal 1 and its associated objectives to better understand how all of this fits together. Figure 4.2 shows Goal 1 and Objective 1a in more detail.

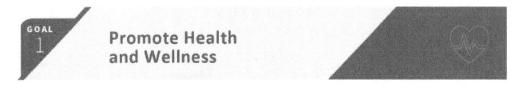

### Goal 1: Promote Health and Wellness

The use of health IT must go beyond the sharing of electronic health information between healthcare providers and the enabling of administrative tasks. Health IT should be used to empower individuals, address patients' full range of health needs, promote healthy behaviors, and facilitate the improvement of health for individuals, families, and communities.

### Objective 1a: Improve individual access to health information

A key aspect of person-centered care is empowering individuals by providing them access to their health information. It allows patients to become more engaged in their care and management of their conditions and alleviates strain on caregivers who manage the care of their loved ones. To expand access to health information, it is necessary to improve access to technology, especially for populations in rural areas, persons with disabilities, racial and ethnic minorities, and those with low socioeconomic status.

**Strategies**

- **Enable individuals to access their health information** by ensuring that they are able to view and interact with their data via secure mobile apps, patient portals, and other tools.
- **Promote greater portability of health information** through APIs and other interoperable health IT that permits individuals to readily send and receive their data across various platforms.
- **Improve access to smartphones and other technologies** needed to attain and use health information, especially for at-risk, minority, rural, disabled, and tribal populations.
- **Build the evidence base on the use of health information,** including on the types of information that will benefit individuals most and the best ways to present information to patients and caregivers.
- **Provide resources on how to access and use health information** so that patients and caregiver understand how to use their data safely, securely, and effectively.

**Figure 4.2    Goal 1, objective 1a from ONC strategic plan.**

Under the goal of Promote Health and Wellness, the objective describes *what* and *why*. Let's look at Objective 1a.

### Objective 1a: Improve individual access to health information

A key aspect of person-centered care is empowering individuals by providing them access to their health information. It allows patients to become more engaged in their care and management of their conditions and alleviates strain on caregivers who manage the care of their loved ones. To expand access to health information, it is necessary to improve access to technology, especially for populations in rural areas, persons with disabilities, racial and ethnic minorities, and those with low socioeconomic status.

[4.1]

The objective is to improve individual access to health information in order to meet the goal to Promote Health and Wellness. The narrative describes *what* that is (person-centered care) and, at a high level, *how* this will happen (access to their own health information through technology). It explains *why* it matters (more engaged patients, involved in their own care), and some of the challenges (improved access to technology, challenges in rural areas, people with disabilities, as well as disparities experienced by racial and ethnic minorities and those of lower socioeconomic status).

The objective describes an element of the goal. Objective 1a identifies one way they are going to try to achieve the goal: through better access to personal health information. It speaks to why this is important and how it supports the goal, but it does not get specific about exactly how it will achieve that, except to note that technology will be an important aspect of the work. Beneath that objective describing the *what* and the *why*, they identify the strategies that describe *how* these objectives will be met. These strategies describe *how* at a high level, not at a task level. Referring to strategies shown in Figure 4.2, we see five bullet points.

- Enable individuals to access their health information.
- Promote greater portability of health information.
- Improve access to smartphones and other technologies.
- Build the evidence base on the use of health information.
- Provide resources on how to access and use health information.

Let's look at each of these in more detail.

## ONC Strategies for Goal 1, Objective 1a

The strategies associated with this objective describe how the objective will be met through strategic activities. [4.2]

> **"Enable individuals to access their health information** by ensuring that they are able to view and interact with their data via secure mobile apps, patient portals, and other tools."

One strategy is to enable people to interact with their health information via various tools and methods. This describes *how* at a high level and does not delve down into exactly how that will happen. For example, it does not describe which tools or what data. This is the right level of detail for how an objective will be achieved through a strategy.

> **"Promote greater portability of hcalth information** through APIs and other interoperable health IT that permits individuals to readily send and receive their data across various platforms."

To improve individual access to health information, a second strategy is to promote the portability of health information through technical interoperability. The level of detail is appropriate. There is no discussion of *which* APIs or *which* platforms will be used. Rather, it describes at a high level how greater portability will be achieved in this strategic plan.

> **"Improve access to smartphones and other technologies** needed to attain and use health information, especially for at-risk, minority, rural, disabled, and tribal populations."

To improve individual access to health information, a third strategy is to improve access to smartphones and other technology, especially for those in at-risk, minority, rural, disabled, and tribal populations. The details of how that access will be provided are not specified at the strategic level of the plan. Those are operational details that will be determined by an assessment of the current state and ideas on how to best improve access.

> **"Build the evidence base on the use of health information,** including on the types of information that will benefit individuals most and the best ways to present information to patients and caregivers."

To improve individual access to health information, a fourth strategy is to build the evidence based on the best way to present information to patients and caregivers. From a strategic perspective, this provides ample guidance as to how to achieve the objective, but it does not specify the types of information or the best ways to present the information. Those are operational details that would not be included in a strategic statement.

> **"Provide resources on how to access and use health information** so that patients and caregivers understand how to use their data safely, securely, and effectively."

The fifth and final strategy associated with this first of three objectives under Goal 1 is to provide resources on how to access and use health information, but it does not specify details such as which resources or how they will be provided. Clearly, this objective could be achieved in many different ways.

It's easy to see that once these strategic directions are defined, a team could be engaged in determining the best ways to approach each of these elements. More importantly, the strategy does not dictate the solution. This allows the IT team to assess the situation, the business context, the constraints, and the risks, and develop a plan that is suitable for the organization. This is how strategic direction can effectively drive IT planning and decision-making.

Hopefully, by walking through this example, you have gotten a better feel for goals, objectives, and strategies and how you might develop them for your IT department. This strategic plan provides a very good example because it shows the what, why, and how at a high level. It does not go into exactly how an objective will be achieved but leaves those decisions to the operational leadership team to determine.

Reading through the whole document may be helpful for two reasons. The obvious one is that it might help solidify your understanding of goals, objectives, and strategies so you can work on your own set of items. The second, less obvious, reason is because it helps you understand where U.S. healthcare is headed from the ONC perspective. This can be a useful input both for your organization's future planning as well as for your IT department's planning.

# IT Strategic Plan

Our focus in this book is on renovating the IT function so you're well-positioned for the future. Your goals might include statements around this fact. A goal could be to have a fully updated and modern IT function. Objectives might be to upgrade infrastructure, better leverage cloud options, and identify opportunities for innovation. Those three objectives would each have strategies that define how you would achieve those objectives. Your objectives might fall along the lines of run-grow-innovate. The key is to define a set of goals, objectives, and strategies that are closely aligned with the organization.

Healthcare organizations typically group goals and objectives around familiar themes such as improving quality metrics, reducing costs, or improving patient outcomes. Sometimes they are referred to as the organization's True North metrics, Key Outcomes, or Core Measures. Group your IT strategies around these organizational themes to signal to both IT and operations how key IT initiatives support these objectives.

It can be helpful to group IT initiatives under the same goals and objectives labels used by the organization to help connect IT to operations. For example, an organizational goal might be "To create a world class patient experience." What would be the associated IT goals and objectives? "To create a world class patient experience" might still be the goal, but the objective might be something like "Create an easy-to-use patient portal." Strategies for an easy-to-use portal might be "Upgrade patient portal, implement online scheduling, enable online bill pay, and streamline the user interface."

By tying these IT objectives to the organizational goal of a world-class patient experience, you ensure alignment and your work remains visible and valuable.

Let's look at another example. Perhaps another organizational goal is to achieve quality measures for hypertension (with defined metrics). How can IT possibly impact hypertension goals? Your objective might be to "Enable system functions and related technology to support hypertension management." Strategies could include working to connect BT devices to the EHR, build and enable Care Plans in the EHR, and implement an integrated text messaging platform for care coordination.

Every time you report on your progress against goals, you are tying back to what the organization is trying to achieve. This repetition and alignment will go a long way in helping company leaders see how IT is contributing to organizational goals and how IT creates value.

Of course, there are many things you need to do in IT that are not directly tied to these organizational goals, such as create a secure, stable, and reliable IT environment. These activities fall under an operational strategic plan.

## Operational Strategies

Since we're undertaking a renovation project, you might also create an operational strategic plan where you set out goals, objectives, and strategies for your IT operations. Your IT strategic plan would contain goals that align closely with business objectives, but your IT operational strategic plan would contain goals that you want to achieve within IT operations. Of course, they should align with your overall plan and with the organization, but they may need to be planned and executed separately or by a different group within IT.

A goal might be to improve the end user experience, to reduce manual and paper processes, or to achieve certain service level metrics. You need to identify what operational capabilities will be required to support the strategic initiatives of IT and the organization. This ties back to the reason you are contemplating an IT renovation project.

Unfortunately, in many organizations, IT is still seen as an operational department, an "order taker" for the business. Transitioning from being operational to strategic can be challenging, especially given the fast-paced nature of demands on IT and the continuing tight budget climate. *Better, faster, cheaper* is a phrase often used to describe what people want from IT, but that sells IT services short. Better, faster, and cheaper are operational improvements at best. Though it may be tempting to look at operational efficiency as strategic, it's really not. For healthcare IT departments, achieving operational efficiency is imperative, but just being better, faster, and cheaper won't suffice in the long-term.

## Innovation and Strategy

Part of the strategy should include assessing business objectives and identifying opportunities to innovate using technology. To use the concepts introduced in Chapter 2, look for ways to *digitize, digitalize*, and *digitally transform* your environment. Some of these initiatives may have to wait until you have completed your IT renovation, but some may be essential elements of your renovation plan. Document ideas that arise through this process to capture fresh thinking on the topic. Innovation doesn't always have to be seismic; sometimes innovation is simply looking at a problem with a fresh perspective and taking a different approach. Keep this in mind as you develop your renovation plan because you'll have plenty of opportunities to fix your IT function through innovative thinking. That's actually one of the exciting parts of the renovation project – identifying areas that need to be improved and taking an innovative approach to solving them.

## Summary

We've discussed goals, objectives, and strategies for IT that map directly to organizational goals and how that maintains alignment and drives visibility. By reviewing the ONC goals, objectives, and strategies, you saw how these are linked and what an appropriate level of detail is for each item. It's important to give thought to both IT strategy and IT operational strategy because they are two sides of IT that have to remain in balance. You have a unique opportunity to look at all of this with fresh eyes and come up with some very innovative solutions along the way.

## References

[4.1] The Office of the National Coordinator for Health Information Technology, Office of the Secretary, United States Department of Health and Human Services, "Federal Health IT Strategic Plan, 2020-2025," https://www. healthit.gov/sites/default/files/page/2020-01/2020-2025FederalHealthIT%20 StrategicPlan_0.pdf, accessed January 13, 2023. Page 21.
[4.2] Ibid. Pages 21–22.

# Chapter 5

# IT Governance Building Blocks

IT governance is the organizational function that ensures IT demand and capacity are well managed. The demand for IT resources in every organization is almost infinite. Every day, an end-user, a departmental manager, or a division leader thinks, "wow, wouldn't it be great if IT could ..." Or they read a blog post about a new application, a new device, or a new capability and think it would be great to implement. They might see an opportunity to improve their operations through deploying technology in a different way or deploying a new technology altogether.

We cannot control organizational demand; it will always be near infinite and budgets will never be. However, we can manage IT capacity so it best aligns with the priorities and strategies of the organization. That is most successfully done through effective IT governance.

IT demand will continue to grow, yet no organization can afford to simply keep increasing IT budgets and staff. In fact, that would be detrimental to the organization. There is an optimal size for an IT function in almost every business. While that optimal size can be a challenge to identify, it can be defined through the IT governance process. As we'll discuss, balancing capacity and demand through governance allows the organization to decide how much it wants to invest in IT. The caveat here is a significant one: IT must be efficient and effective. If the department is ineffective, all investments in IT will seem like a waste. The assessment and renovation process is intended to improve efficiency and reduce waste. Once you've tuned up your IT function and are prepared for digital transformation, you'll also be better armed with data about how much actual

DOI: 10.4324/9781003377023-7

IT capacity you have. Then you can guide the organization in determining how best to utilize that capacity to further the goals and objectives of the organization.

This ties in nicely with our conversation on IT value creation in Chapter 15. Value in IT is derived from investing in the right technologies and the right projects at the right time and at the right cost for the organization. Value is also created by ensuring that IT objectives are closely aligned to strategic objectives as we discussed in Chapter 4.

In healthcare IT, we see continued pressure to reduce staff, reduce cost, and do more with less. While IT leaders can certainly work to optimize IT resources through these renovation plans, there is a limit to operating in deficit mode (do more with less). At some point, the IT function becomes hobbled by sparse resources. This is when organizations struggle to advance or experience significant downtimes or cyber events. The organizational risk of IT cutbacks must be articulated and agreed to by the leadership of the organization. This, too, comes under the IT governance umbrella.

It's important to note that IT governance is not a cure-all. Sometimes, despite a strong business case or a compelling presentation from the CIO, the financial demands are such that IT initiatives are tabled in favor of key clinical expenditures. Investments such as a new hybrid operating room or a new imaging suite, which cost millions of dollars, are sometimes selected because these investments generate a very clear business case. Spend $X, see #Y patients, bill $Z, and the investment pays off in some finite timeframe. And these are involved in direct patient care, so they're visible and are meeting a defined need. IT solutions, on the other hand, are harder to tie directly to those outcomes. Having a stable EHR, for example, is vital to all clinical care, but investing in a storage cluster or a new cloud-based enterprise data warehouse platform in support of that EHR is hard for many non-IT people to fully understand and prioritize.

IT investments are rarely that straightforward, which is why they are sometimes deprioritized. IT cannot always prevail, but having an IT governance process assists in bringing forward key initiatives and needs, and it documents decisions made by the organization. This process can also create a regularly occurring dialog with the organization about IT investments, so the best decisions can be made with complete information. In this chapter, we will discuss IT governance separately from data governance because, while they are both critical IT functions, they have several significant differences. We'll discuss IT governance first.

# About Frameworks

Let's start with a brief note about frameworks in general. In IT, there is a framework for almost every element of the work we do. Like the old expression "there's an app for that," one could easily say "there's a framework for that" when referencing IT. Frameworks can be very valuable in providing a well-vetted approach to managing an aspect of IT.

However, frameworks can have downsides as well. Some organizations try to implement too many frameworks at once (ITIL, EA, Change Management, Agile, etc.) and fail because of fragmented focus. Others find that adherence to the framework becomes the work itself and distracts the team. Still others find that a framework is too detailed, too cumbersome, or too general to fit HIT needs and it's scrapped somewhere along the way. Fragments of failed frameworks can be found throughout HIT.

Many frameworks are discussed in this chapter and throughout this book. They are pointed out as potential topics for consideration. In many cases, understanding what the framework does, what the elements are, and how you might apply portions of the framework can be very helpful. Proponents of these formal frameworks might vehemently disagree with this approach, but HIT is complicated, and trying to implement frameworks can be challenging. These frameworks should work for you, not the other way around.

# IT Governance Definition

Gartner, Inc. provides a very helpful definition of IT governance.

> IT governance (ITG) is defined as the processes that ensure the effective and efficient use of IT in enabling an organization to achieve its goals. IT demand governance (ITDG—what IT should work on) is the process by which organizations ensure the effective evaluation, selection, prioritization, and funding of competing IT investments; oversee their implementation; and extract (measurable) business benefits. ITDG is a business investment decision-making and oversight process, and it is a business management responsibility. IT supply-side governance (ITSG—how IT should do what it does) is concerned with ensuring that the IT organization operates in an effective, efficient and compliant fashion, and it is primarily a CIO responsibility. [5.1]

In essence, IT governance is a business investment decision-making and oversight process. Why does this matter? It ensures the organization understands that the IT function is a series of business requests that have associated costs (hardware, software, project implementation, maintenance, upgrades, break/fix, backup, business continuity, cybersecurity, etc.). While the business may say, "do this project next," it rarely understands all that goes into the IT side of the project or request.

Though it is not important for business leaders to understand *exactly* how some IT functions will be done or what they will cost, it is imperative they understand two things. First, that there *are* constraints regarding how something will be done (timing, method, architecture, regulation, etc.), and second, that there are *organizational* costs in addition to IT costs. These are organizational investments of time, money, resources, process change, change management, end user testing, validation, training, etc., that must be accounted for as part of the cost of doing business.

Aside from IT infrastructure initiatives such as updating firewalls, replacing storage clusters, or moving to cloud-hosted services, IT projects almost always require operational engagement and change. IT governance provides both the language and the process for ensuring businesses understand what they are asking for, what it will take for IT to deliver, and what business operations need to do as well. In other words, it can help clearly define roles and responsibilities for both IT and the organization as a whole. By inference, then, it also holds stakeholders accountable and provides transparency for all required work. If IT fails to do its job, it is visible. If operations fails to do its job, it's also visible. It is much easier to have fact-based discussions when things are clearly defined and articulated.

The objectives of any IT governance program include:

1. Gaining buy-in and building trust with operational leaders.
2. Reducing risk by ensuring IT projects meet regulatory, compliance, and other requirements.
3. Aligning IT operations with business priorities to drive business value.
4. Ensuring organizational and IT roles and responsibilities are clearly documented and understood to drive accountability for results.

As part of the governance function, you may want to include both the projects the organization requests as well as the IT infrastructure projects. Some governance councils only want to focus on the business-facing IT aspects, but this causes the IT infrastructure projects (and associated costs) to be invisible and undervalued. This often leads to infrastructure projects being de-prioritized in favor of organizational projects. However, delaying or canceling critical infrastructure projects ultimately has a negative impact on the entire organization. Thus, bringing them through the governance process can help maintain visibility and priority around these projects.

Including high-level infrastructure initiatives in the governance process can be challenging, as most non-IT leaders do not find infrastructure investments to be particularly interesting or understandable. Still, infrastructure is the foundation for all other IT work, so including it in the governance process will make it more visible and allow it to be prioritized along with business-facing IT initiatives. Typically, these projects are not brought forward for approval as much as for awareness. If you have to upgrade your firewalls due to obsolescence or security vulnerabilities, the organization generally doesn't get to approve or disapprove of this project. (Of course, it should be part of the roadmap and budget, but that is separate from this discussion). Instead, they need visibility as to the need and purpose of the project and awareness of the timing and potential impact on operations. For example, you might need to schedule network downtimes, or you may need to schedule around an application Go Live event. It can also be a good exercise for IT leaders to learn how to communicate IT information using business language instead of IT jargon.

There are many IT initiatives that are not specifically project-related. IT investments such as creating redundant network paths and configuring more Internet bandwidth, replacing network switches with newer ones that have higher throughput, or even a new cybersecurity capability are all requirements to support business efforts. These new projects and initiatives cannot exist in a vacuum. They must be supported by IT infrastructure. Those costs, from new systems to upgrading, patching, and securing existing systems, are all part of this IT environment and should be included to some extent in the IT governance framework. When discussed in the context of supporting the organization, the investment (IT cost) becomes less of an expense side conversation and more of a strategic investment discussion.

## Implementing IT Governance

There are numerous frameworks for implementing IT governance including two of the most widely used:  Control Objectives for Information Technology (COBIT) and the Information Technology Infrastructure Library (ITIL).

However, you can choose any framework or process that works for your organization if it meets the objectives of IT governance, is documented, and is applied consistently. There are several best practices you can use to begin implementing IT governance. The key to success, as is true for many types of change initiatives, is to start small and build on success.

These are the five high-level steps. In all cases, these steps along with decisions and outcomes, should be documented. The documents should be stored in a central location so stakeholders can readily access and review them.

1. Develop a template for new initiative/new project requests.
2. Develop a process for organizational leadership review of all project requests.
3. Develop a vetting and prioritization process.
4. Develop a project management process that communicates project status.
5. Develop a process for periodic review of initiatives.

1. **Develop a template for new initiative/new project requests.** The template should include all required fields so the request can be analyzed without several cycles of back-and-forth questions and answers to gather complete information. Many service management solutions can automate much of this. For example, setting required and optional fields and not activating the Submit button until all required data is entered can help reinforce basic processes.
   The information can include:
   a. Project title.
   b. Project description.
   c. Description of what the project is intended to accomplish.
   d. Required project outcome.
   e. Project sponsor (operational owner, not IT) and contact information.
   f. Executive sponsor (senior leader/C-suite executive sponsoring this initiative).
   g. Strategic alignment and organizational benefit.
   h. Organizational change leader and anticipated changes.
   i. Assessment of resources needed (high level: staff, IT systems, location, supplies, etc.).
   j. Additional information – regulatory, timeline, dependencies, and constraints.

This is a short and simple way to get IT governance up and running. As the organization becomes more aware of the process and sees how the process facilitates important work being scheduled, people will be more willing to follow the process. In addition, disallowing IT projects to be initiated in any other manner will stop the outliers. If you support this via an organizational policy that says all IT-related projects will be reviewed by the IT Steering Committee (ITSC) except *(specifically name acceptable exceptions),* you can reduce the number of outliers. This way, if you find someone repeatedly doing an end-run to your IT staff, you have two avenues for course correction. One is with the operational person and their leadership chain of command. The other is internally. If IT staff understand there is a policy not to allow end-runs, they can politely push back on those trying to skirt the process. It also gives you a tool to hold IT staff accountable for their role in ignoring policy and procedure, if needed.

One element that might be new for you is *organizational change leader and anticipated changes.* We know change is difficult to implement and maintain. Unless you have clear change leaders and champions taking accountability for assessing and managing organizational change, there is a good chance your project will fail or be less than successful. Organizational change management must be part of the project conversation from the very beginning. Often, failed projects begin with no operational engagement and no organizational change management. You've seen these projects, you've likely led a few of these projects in your career. They are frustrating because IT can create a great project plan and deliver an outstanding solution, but without strong operational engagement, it fails. Part of your renovation plan will be to go through your IT inventory and see what's still there that's not being used – often there are remnants of stalled, cancelled, or failed projects that just never get pulled out of the environment.

If your organization does not yet have an IT governance function or if you're interested in a more formalized methodology, there are plenty of resources available that you can research and utilize. See Resources at the end of this chapter for a few ideas.

2. **Develop a process for organizational leadership review of all project requests.** Once a completed form is submitted, it can be presented at an ITSC meeting by the executive sponsor or someone he/she invites to present. This is not to give a project the green light

to proceed, but to give operational and IT leaders, an opportunity to review and ask questions. These questions should include things like:

1. What problem does this solve for us?
2. What are the risks of this project?
3. Who will do this work after the IT portion is complete?
4. What alternatives did you consider?
5. Are these all the costs, or are there other costs not yet listed or known?
6. What is the operational impact?
7. What sort of change will this inject into the organization? Is that good? Bad? Neutral?
8. What happens if we don't do this project?

There are many more questions you can (and should) ask. Your review process should include a list of questions to discuss. Not all questions will be needed for every project, but you should start out with a standard list of questions and modify as needed.

The objective is to understand enough about the proposed project to ask IT to assess the project and come back with better, more accurate estimates of cost, effort, duration, constraints, risks, and alternatives. Essentially, the executive team says, "Yes, we believe this may have merit. Please spend some time working this up into a more formal and specific project proposal."

Regardless of the outcomes, they should be documented and stored for future reference. The executive and operational sponsors (those asking for the project) should be notified of the decision.

3. **Develop a vetting and prioritization process.** Once IT analysis work is completed, usually through collaboration between the operational owner and IT, the project is brought back to the ITSC with IT recommendations. If the solution would potentially fit into another approved project, it may be folded in. If it is a stand-alone project that meets the standards of the organization (cost, architecture, cybersecurity, interoperability, supportability, timelines, etc.), it can be slotted into the project list based on its relative size, scope, and priority. It might not fit into current project capacity, and the ITSC may decide it's not a good time to undertake such a project. The ITSC may choose to pause or cancel another project in favor of this new one. The project proposal might be put on hold for a defined or open-ended period of time. Finally, it's possible the ITSC might decide the project does not have merit or that the proposed benefits did not pan out as expected.

In that case, the ITSC leaders might decide to decline to proceed with such a project.

4. **Develop a project management process that communicates project status.** If you do not have a formal Project Management Office (PMO) or project management process in place, that should be a top priority. It can be implemented in parallel with IT governance, but be cautious about implementing an IT governance function without a solid project management process.

   A critical element of change management, project management, and IT governance is communication. Ensure that results, decisions, and status are clearly and easily communicated to stakeholders. This could take the form of a simple project status email, or, even better, an internal website or location that makes project information easily accessible by all authorized stakeholders.

5. **Develop a process for periodic review of initiatives.** Finally, it's important to recap or summarize accomplishments through this process. The review may be quarterly, semiannually, or annually. It should identify projects that were completed successfully and the value they added to the organization. The value statements should be data-driven and use specific metrics (number of patients, dollars saved, processes improved, etc.) whenever possible. It should also include projects that did not complete successfully (in other words, they did not meet scope, budget, timeline, or quality requirements) or did not complete at all. Results and recommendations from an after-action review should be presented at the time of the project results review.

   In these reviews, take the opportunity to get input and feedback from stakeholders. What's working well? What could be improved? Sometimes the feedback will be project-specific, but often there's an opportunity to hone the process itself so it continues to improve.

   This brief overview is not intended to get you up and running with IT governance (or project management), but to give you a basic checklist to ensure you have some sort of IT governance in place or are working toward that end. IT departments without any governance functions end up being pulled in a thousand directions by the organization. They risk failing to deliver on the highest-priority work. Those with an IT governance function, even one in its early stages, are much more likely to deliver what the organization really needs, delivering true IT value. Almost as important, IT governance will create a less chaotic, more organized environment for IT staff. As we continue to see demand for skilled IT staff increase, we need to create and maintain a positive, productive, and reasonable IT environment to retain top talent. Implementing IT governance can play a part in creating this type of IT environment.

# Data Governance

Data governance differs significantly from IT governance and is typically addressed as a separate function. In smaller organizations, IT and data governance may be combined because the stakeholders are often the same group of leaders. However, in mid-sized to large organizations, these functions should be managed separately so the appropriate stakeholders are engaged and the decisions made in each forum are made by the right people. In essence, data governance is the way organizations make strategic decisions about how it uses its data.

It's important to note that data governance and data management are not the same thing. Governance refers to how the organization governs or manages the use of data. Data management refers to how the data elements themselves are managed, which we'll touch on briefly.

Due to the similarities in function, you can certainly leverage your IT governance process to develop your data governance process. We'll discuss the critical success factors here. In Chapter 17, we'll discuss how to assess your IT and data governance functions so you can build a more robust program.

## *Why Data Governance*

In the past decade, healthcare data has proliferated at exponential rates, in part due to the use of EHRs and in part because of the ability to interconnect electronic systems. The *variety*, *volume*, and *velocity* of data are constantly growing. With all that data come new opportunities and challenges. Data governance is about managing data as a strategic asset to ensure there are controls around the content, structure, quality, use, and security of this valuable organizational asset.

Here's an example, a hospital system admits, treats, and discharges a patient, Diane Garcia. That data is sent electronically to the regional HIE. The PCP for Diane is notified at admission and at discharge. The data from the HIE (or directly from the hospital) is then imported into the PCP's EHR. The PCP refers Ms. Garcia to a specialist, who gets an electronic referral and some data about the patient from the PCP. The specialist's office creates a patient file for Diane Garcia in their practice. Essentially, all that data is duplicated to some extent, but everyone needs that data in their system in order to perform the clinical care, from documentation to coding and billing to diagnosis and referrals. The hospital runs analytics to determine if there are any correlations between the treatments given to Ms. Garcia and the outcomes, length of stay, or cost of care. The PCP may look at data across their population to seek the most effective treatments for patients like Diane using population health analytics that might include clinical data as well as data around SDOH such as income level, race or ethnicity, or zip code location, to name a few. The PCP might also be part of a value-based contract that rewards providers for quality outcomes rather than the typical fee-for-service model. In that case, the PCP will be collecting data about the outcomes and submitting these data to show how quality of care is improving health and reducing the cost of care. This is just one patient's data journey and a relatively common one. You can see not only all the data touch points but also all the data collected by the various systems. In many instances, these systems are connected, and the data points grow.

In healthcare, the availability of data is crucial to all aspects of providing care. The data must be reliable and available to the right people at the right time in the right format. Data needs to be treated as a valuable, strategic asset. Yet, in many organizations, this data is unmanaged or unknown, residing in pockets across organizations without governance or management. This leads to substantially suboptimal use of data in an organization.

Additionally, data governance also helps ensure safeguards against data breaches are in place. As a strategic asset, data stolen by hackers or competitors becomes a valuable asset to someone else. If data is strewn across the organization, there's a high likelihood it's improperly protected (backups, encryption, access controls, and monitoring). There is also a very good chance data is duplicated, (adds to cost and data discrepancies). Finally, there's a very good chance that the data is unreliable. It might be improperly sourced or attributed – the list goes on. Data governance and data management help reduce these risks.

According to a Deloitte study in 2021, only 19% of companies surveyed had strong data governance in place, 48% had ad hoc data governance, and 33% either had no data governance or didn't know if they did (which generally means they don't). [5.2] While this study was not specific to healthcare, it's clear that, though there's a desire to intelligently use data, there is often no actual movement toward formalizing or developing the governance function.

With the explosion of data in healthcare, it is vital to ensure the data are properly managed. Governance supports sound data management. The key reasons for needing strong data management are:

1. Data quality
2. Data protection
3. Information security
4. Regulatory compliance
5. Clinical outcomes
6. Cost savings

Some of the most common challenges organizations face with respect to data are these:

1. No one knows who oversees the data.
2. No one knows who has access to change, edit, add, or delete data.
3. No one knows who is authorized to make changes to data definitions.
4. No one knows how to reconcile information when conflicting data results occur.
5. No one has the skills to manage and govern data.
6. No one sees data as a strategic asset, and therefore no one is willing to invest time, resources, and staff in this effort.

In most organizations, data resides in several places. First, data is generated through some mechanism. In healthcare, and specific to clinical data, it is typically a provider entering data in an EHR, but we know there are many other sources. Next, clinical data are stored in tables in a database inside the EHR. Each table has a label and each data point has a description and some specifications (defining it as text, numeric, date, or zip code for example, etc.). Financial data are typically stored in databases within an electronic financial system, supply chain inventory in yet another. Then, someone in the organization asks a question like, "How many of our patients have a diagnosis of diabetes?" or "How many of our diabetic patients have had a diabetic retinopathy screening in the past twelve months?" or "How many encounters did Dr. Murali have last quarter?" or "What's our cost per visit at each clinic?" Someone pulls data from the EHR into a reporting tool or a spreadsheet. Sometimes that data needs to be correlated with data from other systems, so it's pulled into an enterprise data warehouse. Data is correlated with other non-EHR data and a report is generated.

The report is then presented to several stakeholders. Each has a different question about the data and none agree the data reflect the answers to their questions. This process causes the organization to question the accuracy of the reporting function and to lose confidence in the data in general. This typically leads to departments take reporting into their own hands, which ultimately leads to poor data quality and disagreement across the enterprise around data.

That is exactly why data governance and data management are needed. These activities help ensure data are entered, stored, reported, validated, and presented in a consistent and correct manner and that data requests are properly defined, vetted, validated, and delivered.

Key elements to any data governance program, much like any other program or large project, are these:

1. Define the vision, purpose, and goals of data governance.
2. Identify potential risks and associated mitigation strategies for your data governance program.
3. Define the data governance team. These should be both organizational and IT representatives.
4. Create a RACI chart to clearly assign roles and responsibilities. (Refer to Table 5.1).

**Table 5.1  RACI Matrix**

| | |
|---|---|
| **Responsible** | The person doing the task. |
| **Accountable** | The person who is the decision-maker. |
| **Consulted** | Those people in the organization who need to weigh in on the task or project. |
| **Informed** | Those people who need to be kept informed of progress and overall results. |

5. Create a data governance process document or map that clearly defines how data projects are initiated, defined, staffed, performed, validated, operationalized, and closed out.
6. Identify how reports and ad hoc data are decommissioned and disposed of (i.e. data in the EHR simply stays there, but data pulled out and placed in another container must be managed).
7. Define how data are managed and who the responsible parties are.
8. Develop data governance metrics to track performance over time.

In data governance, it's also important to define roles. You do not necessarily need to define all of these roles, but understanding these elements can help you determine what your data governance functions should cover.

**Data Owner** – accountable for the quality of the data set. This is not an IT role unless the data is IT data.
**Data Steward** – responsible for maintaining the quality of the data.
**Data Producer** – anyone in the organization responsible for creating or capturing data, which in healthcare organizations is almost everyone.
**Data Consumer** – anyone in the organization who is using data for business purposes. They are responsible for defining the minimum necessary quality of the data and for validating data results.
**Data Custodian** – the entity responsible for storing and managing the data. Typically, this is an IT function.
**Data Quality Team** – individuals who are responsible for reviewing and ensuring the quality of the data.

Of course, there are ample data governance resources available for anyone interested. This section is intended to call out the importance of data governance in an environment increasingly flooded with data, especially data that must be protected by law.

In summary, data management focuses on the technical aspects of handling, storing, organizing, and maintaining data. Data governance is broader than that and includes activities to establish policies, procedures, and controls around the data. It also involves defining data ownership as well as roles and responsibilities. The goal of data governance is to help ensure the information captured by the organization is secure and reliable and can be leveraged to create actionable insights to drive business outcomes.

Finally, like IT governance, it can serve the function to prioritize data requests from across the organization to ensure that there are sufficient resources to meet the data needs and that the highest impact data projects are prioritized accordingly.

## Summary

As new technology and the use of AI and big data move to the forefront of healthcare, it is increasingly important to have strong IT and data governance functions. The demand for IT projects will accelerate, and managing demand through IT governance is critical. Demand will always be infinite, and IT resources will always be finite. IT governance is the mechanism by which these two conflicting drivers are resolved.

Data governance and the associated data management functions, used to be seen as optional or nice-to-have in healthcare. However, as new solutions have enabled many organizations to leverage massive data sets and healthcare organizations have developed business intelligence capabilities, the need for strong data governance and management functions is required.

There are many dangers to having weak capabilities in this area, including the organization relying on poor-quality data, making decisions based on erroneous data, or being unable to rely on data because it is not delivered in a timely or accurate manner. Maturing this competency is one of the core elements required for any future state in healthcare. In other words, you don't need to know where HIT is going to know that wherever it goes, strong governance will be needed.

## References

[5.1] Gartner, Inc., IT Governance (Glossary), no date, https://www.cio.com/article/272051/governanceit-governance-definition-and-solutions.html, accessed December 13, 2022.
[5.2] Parakh, Kirti, Dean Paterson, and James Gordon, "Deploying effective data governance to achieve key business priorities," January 19, 2022, https://www2.deloitte.com/us/en/insights/topics/strategy/effective-data-governance.html, accessed January 13, 2023.

# Resources

## IT Governance

Gathright, Travis, "IT governance and organizational effectiveness with IT," April 11, 2013, https://www.hcinnovationgroup.com/policy-value-based-care/staffing-professional-development/blog/13019025/it-governance-and-organizational-effectiveness-with-it, accessed December 13, 2022.

ISACA, "CGEIT, Certified in the Governance of Enterprise IT, Eighth Edition" Schaumburg, IL, ISACA, 2020.

Lindros, Kim, "What is IT governance?" July 31, 2017, https://www.cio.com/article/272051/governanceit-governance-definition-and-solutions.html, accessed December 13, 2022.

## Data Governance

Buttner, Patty, Melanie Meyer, Raymond Mikaelian, Nicole Miller, and Becky Ruhnau-Gee, "Practice brief: Healthcare data governance," December 20, 2021, https://journal.ahima.org/page/practice-brief-healthcare-data-governance-14, accessed December 13, 2022.

Office of the National Coordinator for Health Information Technology, "Patient demographic data quality framework - Data governance," no date, https://www.healthit.gov/playbook/pddq-framework/data-governance/governance-management/, accessed December 13, 2022.

University of Wisconsin, "What is data governance in healthcare?" September 11, 2017, https://uwex.wisconsin.edu/stories-news/data-governance-in-healthcare/, accessed December 13, 2022.

# Chapter 6

# IT Architecture Building Blocks

IT architecture describes three levels of solutions: *technology, solution,* and *enterprise.* Understanding these three elements of IT architecture is important for your renovation plan. The difference among these three disciplines is depicted in Figure 6.1. The key difference is where the focus is on the continuum between technology and strategy. [6.1]

Technical architecture has a strong technology focus and describes how solutions are developed. Technical architects take solutions developed by solution architects and create technological solutions that can be implemented. They have deep technical expertise and an understanding of the overall IT infrastructure and architecture. A technical architect will develop how an enterprise data warehouse solution should be created, provisioned, and managed, for example.

Solution architecture requires a balance between technology and strategy. It describes the technical solutions needed by the enterprise, but it does not get into deep technical detail. A solution architect needs to understand the organization's strategy well enough to develop technical solutions. These are then handed off to the technical architect to develop specific solutions. For example, a solutions architect might develop a solution for an enterprise data warehouse function and hand it off to a technical architect to come up with the specific technical requirements and implement that solution.

Enterprise architecture (EA) is primarily strategy-focused. The enterprise architect understands the business as a whole, its goals and objectives, and develops IT strategies aligned with those objectives. A successful enterprise

DOI: 10.4324/9781003377023-8

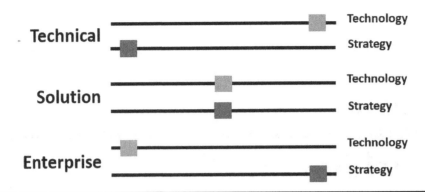

**Figure 6.1 Technology, solution, and enterprise architects. (Adapted from LeanIX "IT Architecture Roles" see Reference 6.1.)**

architect has deep expertise in both technology and business, with a specific ability to translate business objectives into high-level IT objectives. For example, the organization may be contemplating entering a new business line (such as adding ambulatory surgery centers to its hospital system), and the enterprise architect would engage with those business leaders to develop high level IT strategies to support that expansion.

Many healthcare IT organizations do not have technical, solution, or enterprise architect roles defined, though many IT staff perform some of these functions. However, you can imagine the difference between having trained (and potentially certified) staff in these functions vs. general IT staff who have come up through the ranks and are doing the best they can with limited training or knowledge. The results, of course, can be vastly different.

As we are looking at our IT renovation project, we have to consider whether the current state is partly a function of having no one fulfilling these three important roles. As we look at IT architecture in this chapter, you can think through how you might want to go about developing these skills in your IT department over the long-term. These will be important for any digital transformation efforts you may want to undertake later, so incorporating them into your renovation plan will lay the needed groundwork. Without these functions, you are likely to have silos, disconnects, redundancy, and risk.

Since much of the alignment work occurs at the EA level, we will focus on this aspect and assume it also incorporates the solutions and technology architecture layers as well.

We know that a well-managed architecture can optimize IT-business alignment and enhance outcomes. This is especially true when managing large, complex, integrated systems (business systems and technology systems). It also fully supports IT in the capital and operational planning aspects of running an IT function. Instead of implementing Technology X, business and IT leaders can discuss what problem they're trying to solve, what the architecture might indicate as a solution, and how various solutions fit into the architecture. This drives better conversations in your IT Steering Committee meetings. It makes the capital and operational planning processes less difficult and more aligned with business goals, objectives, and strategies.

EA refers to the blueprint or framework for IT across the entire enterprise – all divisions, locations, departments, business lines, etc. It looks at the entire company, the strategic objectives of the whole company, and all the business lines to create a cohesive IT strategy to meet the objectives of the enterprise. This includes all aspects of IT, including applications, interfaces, integration platforms, web/portal/mobile, data and data tools (analytics, enterprise data warehouses, etc.), as well as core IT infrastructure from servers to storage, networks to security appliances.

## Understanding Enterprise Architecture

EA as a body of knowledge has been around since the 1960s, but more recently has gained traction as technology has become more central to business operations. There are many models used to envision, manage, and transform EA. We'll discuss how EA and digital transformation are linked. For more on EA, you can see Resources at the end of this chapter.

Let's begin with a brief definition of EA.

> Enterprise architecture (EA) is the practice of analyzing, designing, planning, and implementing enterprise analysis to successfully execute on business strategies. EA helps businesses structure IT projects and policies to achieve desired business results and to stay on top of industry trends and disruptions using architecture principles and practices, a process also known as enterprise architectural planning (EAP). [6.2]

EA is the link between business strategy and technical implementation. It defines how the business is run and how technology will enable and amplify those business objectives. Done effectively, EA can coalesce business and IT objectives to deliver value. EA helps IT understand what the business is trying to achieve and which technical solutions will drive those outcomes. EA helps the business clarify its objectives and outcomes by partnering with IT leaders to develop plans to implement the next generation of technologies. As such, it's easy to see how EA supports and drives digital transformation efforts.

Why use an EA framework? It has the potential to drive powerful insights into how the business operates. It delineates the technologies in use as well as what will be needed to deliver innovation in the future. Three examples of how EA can enable enterprise and IT success are:

1. **Define business capabilities.** When there's a shared understanding of the business's capabilities today and where it desires to be in the future, business and IT leaders can work from a common set of requirements.
2. **Identify gaps and future opportunities.** Once the environment has been assessed and documented, it is much easier to see where there may be gaps or future opportunities to leverage technology to drive desired business outcomes.
3. **Optimize and support technology assets.** An EA framework allows the organization to see what technologies are in use and to optimize those assets according to business objectives. Additionally, it supports the expenditures (current and planned) on technology, reducing the perception of "IT as a financial black hole."

There are numerous frameworks available for EA, two of the most commonly used are The Open Group Architectural Framework (TOGAF) and The Zachman Framework for Enterprise Architecture.

The TOGAF framework describes four architecture domains: business, application, data, and technology. We'll discuss each briefly here to better understand how EA can impact your organization.

## Business Architecture

Business architecture refers to the business's strategy and the key business lines or initiatives driving that strategy. It also refers to the methods by which the business achieves those objectives – in essence, the *why* and the *how*. The information can be conveyed as a series of value stream diagrams or a matrix of business capabilities, assets, and outcomes per business line. Within this, the IT systems supporting these core processes should be clearly identified. Though not specific to the EA framework, it could be argued that patient-centered objectives, outcomes, and technologies are part of the (healthcare) Business Architecture domain.

## Application Architecture

The application architecture identifies the software used to conduct the business of the organization. In healthcare, that includes EHR software, the myriad of interconnected applications used for patient access, revenue cycle (coding, billing, claims, etc.), and scheduling, to name a few. Additional applications are used for functions such as lab, imaging, pharmacy, infection control, surgery, cardiology, etc., which are all part of an enterprise EHR system or are connected through data interfaces. Other enterprise applications include finance, supply chain, human resources, customer (patient) relationship management, public websites and portals, and enterprise resource planning. All of these come into play in an EA framework. Smaller applications or utility applications, while useful or vital to carrying on the day-to-day work of the organization, might be excluded from a high-level EA view. The objective of the application architecture domain is to identify the interconnectedness of the applications in achieving organizational outcomes and delivering value.

## Data Architecture

Data architecture describes the way data is intended to be used in the organization. It describes definitions and classifications of data as well as data sources. It captures the data collection (sources), storage, and use of data across the enterprise. Most healthcare organizations have implemented some sort of business intelligence or data analytics function to develop, utilize, and deliver value from data. The EA data domain ultimately describes the organization's data management resources and ties them to strategy and organizational objectives.

## Technology Architecture

Technology architecture is likely a domain you are very familiar with in healthcare IT. It describes the hardware and software systems that make up the IT infrastructure and related services. It describes the various platforms in use (on-premises, cloud, and hybrid) as well as network architecture and structure. It should tie back to the organization's strategic initiatives and business drivers to ensure alignment between IT infrastructure architecture and business objectives.

Security architecture is a precursor to application, data, and technology architectures. We've included it as a sub-section of the Technology Architecture section (TOGAF doesn't address Security as a separate domain). It may overlap or intersect with these domains, but should have a distinct architecture that overlays the others. Security architecture crosses business, application, data, and technology domains to provide core information security functions. In healthcare, information security is required by federal law as well as by other rules and regulations to which healthcare organizations are subject. Security should be part of the technology architecture, ensuring all solutions are secure by design.

These four domains encompass all critical elements of a business, including any healthcare organization. Ultimately, organizations need to look at the overall business environment, assess the internal structure of the company, and make strategic decisions about how the company, its technology, and its data align with business objectives. The EA format is what supports and defines this work. Over the past twenty years, the way businesses operate has changed from largely physical, bricks-and-mortar to more virtualized, digitized models. This has been driven by technological changes as well as shifts in consumer expectations and behaviors.

Healthcare has been less driven by the consumerization of business than many other sectors – until recently. As discussed in Chapter 1, there has been a marked shift toward patient-centered care, improving the patient experience, and allowing the patient to have more control over elements of care. Things like on-demand telehealth visits, online scheduling and bill payment have all become more common. These trends will accelerate in the next several years.

All of this points to a need for an overarching plan for the business. While many businesses outside of healthcare may have engaged in EA processes, there are fewer clear examples within healthcare. An EA initiative can reduce cost, reduce risk, reduce complexity, and increase organizational (and IT) agility. It has the potential to create a sustainable competitive advantage when done right. That said, it also requires organizational commitment, including time, resources, and leadership, to deliver those results.

It is clear that EA and digital transformation are closely linked. Using some form of EA methodology can help guide the efforts for companies looking to re-architect their businesses through digital transformation efforts. For example, a healthcare company may decide to look at its business across silos, such as the patient journey. From how the patient first learns of the healthcare organization to how it first interacts to how care is provided, documented, and billed, are all part of the patient's journey. This cuts across standard healthcare silos – from registration to scheduling, provider documentation to labs, imaging, follow-up appointments, and billing. Rather than looking at the business in terms of the scheduling team, the medical records team, and the billing team, healthcare organizations will have to develop organizational structures that span these traditional silos. Technology can't be leveraged in a siloed manner going forward. Integration across these segments requires some form of intentional EA development.

While it is not imperative you use EA for your digital transformation, reviewing some of the highlights and key points from an EA framework will help ensure you have your eyes on the right targets and that your transformation (and renovation) efforts will continue to align closely with the objectives of the organization.

## Summary

IT architecture and EA are closely linked. Most IT departments have some IT architecture capabilities, but many do not employ EA at all. As you renovate your IT function and begin to look at how you will better align with the business and better align with strategic objectives, you'll naturally start looking at elements of EA. Whether you decide to implement an EA framework or simply begin incorporating some of the key concepts is up to you and is largely dependent upon the nature of the organization. As you look to renovate your IT function, keep these capabilities in mind and begin to develop them in-house, or consider getting some outside training or expertise to assist you down the road before beginning your digital transformation work.

## References

[6.1] Image adapted from LeanIX, "The difference between an enterprise architect vs. solution architect vs. technical architect," no date, https://www.leanix.net/en/wiki/ea/enterprise-architect-vs-solution-architect-vs-technical-architect-whats-the-difference, accessed January 16, 2023.
[6.2] White, Sarah K., "What is enterprise architecture: A framework for transformation," November 23, 2022, https://www.cio.com/article/222421/what-is-enterprise-architecture-a-framework-for-transformation.html, accessed January 17, 2023.

## Resources

CMS.gov, "What is enterprise architecture?" December 1, 2021, https://www.cms.gov/Research-Statistics-Data-and-Systems/CMS-Information-Technology/EnterpriseArchitecture, accessed January 14, 2023.

Info-Tech Research Group, "Design an enterprise architecture strategy," no date, https://www.infotech.com/research/ss/design-an-enterprise-architecture-strategy, accessed February 8, 2023.

Quiggle, Jim, "Enterprise architecture for healthcare," 2010, https://healthmanagement.org/c/it/issuearticle/enterprise-architecture-for-healthcare, accessed February 8, 2023.

U.S. Government, Federal Enterprise Architecture, "Federal Enterprise Architecture Framework Version 2," January 29, 2013, https://obamawhitehouse.archives.gov/sites/default/files/omb/assets/egov_docs/fea_v2.pdf, accessed February 8, 2023.

White, Sarah K., "What is TOGAF: An enterprise architecture methodology for business," May 30, 2022, https://www.cio.com/article/228328/what-is-togaf-an-enterprise-architecture-methodology-for-business.html, accessed January 17, 2023.

# Chapter 7

# IT Finance Building Blocks

With the increasing pressure to reduce IT costs in healthcare, IT departments face significant challenges to continue to provide day-to-day support for the organization and deliver secure, reliable, innovative solutions. One of the primary challenges IT departments have in healthcare is communicating the value of IT investments. It can be particularly difficult when IT is competing with clinical leaders for limited funds – such as whether to implement a new software solution vs. upgrade an imaging system in an operating room. It is almost always seen as a simple answer – clinical needs come first. However, without a secure, stable, reliable, and highly available IT infrastructure, no healthcare organization can function effectively. So, how are these trade-offs made, and how do you communicate the value of IT in a way that is useful to organizational leaders? In this chapter, we'll delve into healthcare and HIT finance to better understand how to improve the likelihood of securing appropriate levels of funding to achieve organizational objectives.

## Healthcare IT Finance Overview

Interestingly, though many healthcare systems reported significant operating losses in 2022, it appears they also began to increase their investments in technology. This is significant because it means the value and necessity of leveraging technology to improve quality and cost of care is being recognized, at least in some quarters. A report in Becker's Hospital Review stated, "This year [2023], 95 percent of providers are expected to purchase new technologies; those that can improve productivity or reduce labor

DOI: 10.4324/9781003377023-9

costs are in high demand. Providers cited revenue cycle management, patient intake/flow, clinical systems, and telehealth as the most strategically important investments." [7.1]

A recent article by McKinscy & Company covers a lot of ground in terms of high-level financial drivers in the U.S. healthcare market. If you want to really understand healthcare finance, understanding the factors discussed in the article is important. For example, it covers profit pools for commercial and Medicare Advantage segments, physician offices, and specialty pharmacy. One particularly important note is this: "However, we see solid growth in the sector starting in 2023, especially as technology adoption by providers and payors continues to accelerate. We now estimate a 10 percent CAGR [compound annual growth rate] between 2021 and 2026, to $81 billion by 2026….That would make it the fastest-growing sector in healthcare. We see the greatest acceleration in software and platforms (for example, patient engagement and clinical decision support) as well as data and analytics, with 13 percent and 19 percent CAGRs, respectively." [7.2]

Understanding these financial elements and where your organization fits into the healthcare sector will help you better understand how your organization will be impacted in the future. If these financial elements are somewhat unfamiliar to you, this is a great chance to sit down with one of your finance experts and discuss healthcare finance in your organization. Showing an interest and desire to learn about healthcare finance will help bridge the distance and create a shared understanding. Developing a positive relationship with your CFO and their team is always a good idea.

As we discussed in Chapter 6, building an Enterprise Architecture (EA) function can help span the gap between business and technology to help meld business demand with IT capabilities. When business and IT are aligned because IT understands where the business is headed and business understands how IT can enable success, budget conversations are usually more productive and collaborative. A shared vision of the future helps align these sometimes-disparate interests.

In addition to EA and IT governance functions, IT departments sometimes use chargeback or "show back" methods to make IT expenditures more visible. Both have limitations. While IT costs are known and can be analyzed via financial systems, how these IT systems are used, and by which segments of the organization, are not reflected in financials. When you review your general ledger accounts or your departmental budget file (usually operational expenses against budget), you see IT expenditures.

You don't see things like "new HR software to facilitate more effective on-boarding," or "upgraded network firewalls at Location A to improve security of network segment." Instead, you see a large dollar amount and maybe some subordinate line items under "Software License and Maintenance" or "Hardware Licensing" or a capital line item for "Network Hardware Upgrade." None of these adequately communicate the value IT is generating for the business.

## Chargeback and Show Back Methods

Some organizations implement software solutions to track and manage things like the costs of acquisition, implementation, and support. Then they allocate these costs accordingly, either via an actual charge to the originating department's budget or via a virtual charge, often referred to as a *show back*. This may include the originating or sponsoring department and the number of employees impacted. For example, an HR system is typically used by HR and all employees for managing paid time off, benefits, and schedules, to name a few. So, HR system costs (acquisition, implementation, and on-going support) could be attributed to the HR department, an enterprise software cost, or reflected as a cost-per-employee.

An IT system used just for facilities management, for example, could be charged (or attributed) to facilities, or it could be allocated across each physical location. So, if you have 24 locations, it could be annual cost divided by 24. Alternatively, you could allocate the IT expense on a per-square-foot basis. So, each of the 24 locations is "charged" or "allocated" based on its total square footage. A site that is twice the size of another would account for twice the cost.

There are many methods used across organizations of all sizes in many different industries. In healthcare, there have been iterations of *chargeback* and *show back*, with mixed results. *Chargeback* actually moves IT expenses to other departmental expense accounts so that the acquiring department is charged for the IT expense. *Show back* merely attributes costs without changing budgets. In some organizations, all of IT is expensed across the entire organization as a single administrative expense, sometimes on a percentage of revenue or percent of expense basis. In other words, if inpatient units account for 56% of operational expenses, then 56% of the IT expenses would be attributed to inpatient units.

## Chargeback

Using chargeback has benefits and risks. With chargeback, IT costs are transferred to the initiating or responsible business unit. The upside is that these units must budget for these costs, and therefore the IT budget appears smaller. They also may be required to justify the expense, which can help drive operational accountability for required IT solutions.

The potential downside is that distributed IT costs can make IT spending less transparent, less visible, and less under IT control. It's easy to lose sight of total IT expense when it is in many different departmental accounts. In addition, it often fosters shadow IT, where departments acquire their own IT assets without IT involvement because they have IT funds in their budget.

There's the risk that a vital system requires an upgrade or an expansion and the funds to undertake these efforts will not be budgeted by the operational owners, leaving IT in a bind. Sometimes this process can work well if IT maintains control of these systems, but often what happens is that the operational owner says, in essence, 'If I'm paying for it, then I'm in charge of it.' That may work out until a system upgrade or required enhancement is missed because the operational owner is not well-versed in managing IT systems.

## Show Back

Show back is an alternative in which the costs remain in IT but are attributed to the operational units. This can be an effective method for both maintaining control over the environment (such as adequately budgeting for an upgrade or replacement) and engaging operational units. If these IT costs are shown as line items on their budgets as show back items, it brings visibility. Of course, the downside is if the operational units are not actually held accountable for managing or controlling these costs, it can become a hollow exercise. Still, the opportunity for IT to reflect these costs may outweigh the potential pitfalls.

Think about the cost to implement a new EHR. For most organizations these days, the cost is somewhere in the $10–100M range. If you attribute costs to emergency, inpatient, surgical, and ambulatory care (for example), you can see what the implementation, training, and support costs are per area per year or per patient per area per year. The next time the organization says IT is too expensive, you can refer to the data. For example, suppose your spreadsheet shows all the IT costs associated with the emergency department or a specific ambulatory clinic. The cost of the network infrastructure, the allocated cost of cybersecurity, servers, storage, telephony, end-user devices, printers, as well as all the software used to deliver patient care – from the EHR to document management, dictation solutions, financial management, and supply chain, just to name a few. Then, it becomes clear that these IT investments are made to benefit the organization and enable operations.

There are software systems that help collect, analyze, and visualize this data, but you can do it relatively easily at a high level in a spreadsheet, if desired. For example, if you are an ambulatory healthcare system with twenty clinics, take your total IT cost and divide by twenty. That's the average cost, per clinic, for the IT function. If you want to get more granular, look at patient visits per site or providers per site. You could indicate that the cost of IT is $X per provider or $Y per employee, or $Z per patient. Any metric that ties IT costs to the provision of healthcare services can help connect the dots from cost to value.

For smaller companies, this detailed reporting, tracking, and show back/chargeback is often not feasible for numerous reasons. Still, the effort to attribute costs to organizational units at even its most basic level can be powerful.

## Shifting the Conversation from Cost to Value

Ultimately, you are working to articulate the value of IT for the organization. When the conversation shifts from cost to value, it becomes a more forward-thinking conversation. Rather than asking how IT can cut costs, it might shift to how IT can add more value. Yes, you might still be pressured to reduce costs or add more value at the same cost, but at least that is a more useful conversation than simply being asked to cut your IT costs by 15%. By making IT costs visible, it can also enable useful conversations with the organizational leaders about where they want to invest time and money. Often, operations will indicate they want or need some new technology but sometimes haven't identified all the related costs. Hardware and software acquisition, design, configuration, build, testing, validation, IT training, end-user training, on-going maintenance costs, and upgrades are items often missed in operational conversations. Then, when those costs come to light, the conversation turns to "IT is expensive, there are always surprise costs," or similar.

In Chapter 15, we'll talk more about IT value and a specific framework known as Technology Business Management (TBM), which sets out to help articulate the value of technology investments for the organization. The takeaway for this chapter is that there are methods available to help define and discuss the costs of IT in light of the business value IT drives for the organization.

## Healthcare Finance Overview

Of course, at its most basic level, all business finance is driven by income and expense. At an organizational level, this can be quite complex. In most healthcare delivery settings, income (or revenue) is driven primarily by patient encounters, whether in-patient days in a hospital or patient visits/encounters in primary and specialty care. There are many variations in between, but most income is derived from interacting with patients through what is traditionally referred to as the fee-for-service (FFS) payment model. Healthcare in the U.S. is slowly moving toward some value-based payment models in which revenue is earned through providing services that demonstrate value, such as preventive services or chronic disease management. These ultimately should reduce the total cost of care and produce savings vs. traditional cost of care. These savings are typically shared between the payor and the provider. One of the challenges, of course, is developing contracts with  payors to properly define specific metrics for outcomes and how shared savings would work. What metrics indicate improvements in healthcare delivery? What metrics indicate the total cost of care has been reduced over a period of time? And how are those shared savings distributed? A discussion of FFS vs. value-based payments is beyond the scope of this chapter, but it is important to note the current environment because it impacts both organizational revenues and IT initiatives.

Beyond the payment models, many healthcare organizations receive grants from the government, educational institutions, or private donors for research, capital investments, or special projects. Organizations typically also have retained earnings (profit, net operating income, etc.) that are invested in order to increase the financial strength of the company. These investments are often the source of capital funds for large-scale initiatives such as purchasing a competitor, acquiring a new location, or building a new building. It's often the source of funding for large IT capital initiatives as well as large clinical initiatives like new imaging equipment or new surgical suites, for example.

There are numerous other entities in the mix, including managed care organizations (MCO), accountable care organizations (ACO), Clinically Integrated Networks (CIN), and Independent Physician Associations (IPA) among them. If you are interested in learning more about healthcare finance, you can refer to the resources at the end of the chapter or sit down with your CFO or Director of Finance and discuss how your organization drives revenue and income.

On the expense side, salaries and benefits are typically the largest operational expenses in healthcare, often followed by IT. As IT platforms move from on-premise to cloud-based, these expenses move from capital to operational expenses. For example, purchasing a storage cluster (hardware and software) might cost more than a million dollars in capital and have an associated operational cost of $200,000 per year. The organization must pay the million dollars to purchase the hardware, depreciate the asset over its useful life (IT equipment is typically depreciated over five to seven years), and pay the maintenance or support costs for the duration of the use of the equipment.

If that same capability is purchased from a cloud vendor, there is no capital outlay and no depreciation expense. However, there is typically a higher ongoing monthly fee for using the cloud solution. These expenses often scale with the growth of the organization, which is helpful but can also lead to unfettered increases in operational costs if the organization consumes more cloud-based resources than budgeted or without proper controls in place.

This matters because many healthcare organizations often look at IT costs as a percentage of overall operational expense. As cloud-based solutions are increasingly used, the percentage of operational expense for IT increases rapidly, and may yield the false notion that IT is getting exponentially more expensive. The reduction in capital expense and the associated maintenance and depreciation costs need to be factored in.

Also, many cloud-based solutions are difficult to contain. They are engineered to be easy to provision and easy to expand, which is both good and bad. It's great because it provides very flexible capacity to the organization. It's challenging because it's much easier to grow than to shrink cloud presence, and end users can often consume as much as they want without controls in place. In some cases, this results in the IT operational expense skyrocketing without the ability to manage or control the cost.

As you work through your renovation plan, you'll have to take this into account and work closely with finance and executives to make sure this shift in costs is fully understood.

It is also important to note that in the past decade or so, as companies have migrated to cloud-based solutions, a new industry has emerged to address the burgeoning and often uncontrolled growth of cloud-based spending. For a fee, consultants will analyze your cloud spend and recommend ways to reduce or control that cost. Moving to the cloud also may not have the ROI many firms expected. An article in October 2022 indicates that in a survey of 1,000 KPMG executive clients, two-thirds were re-evaluating cloud spending after failing to achieve a significant ROI. [7.3] This is a notable finding and one worth investigating as you develop your renovation plan.

In addition to capital vs. operational costs, you have to manage annual budgets. Organizations range from extremely rigorous, detailed budgeting processes to very high-level operational planning budgets. Regardless of how your organization approaches budgeting, you should have a list of your operational expenses for staff (salary and benefits), hardware, software, vendors, training, travel (education and conferences), and utilities (such as internet bandwidth, telephony circuits, etc.) for current year and your needs for the subsequent year. If you have a formal budget request process, of course, you can prepare your data, including justifications for the current year (if needed), value provided (or IT accomplishments in the current year), and new needs for the upcoming year. Again, these should be tied to organizational initiatives, expansion of capabilities, new programs, etc. If you are trying to right-size your department based on demand, you might try to find benchmarking data for comparison, so you have facts to substantiate your need.

Analyzing your budget and performance against budget year over year can help you see where costs are changing. You will need to be able to articulate the business value of IT in one way or another and have a solid understanding of the mechanics of budgeting as well as the trends in IT spending year-over-year.

## Managing Cloud Costs

As mentioned earlier, one of the rapidly evolving areas of IT spend is in cloud costs. Consulting companies are increasingly offering services to assess, audit, and help manage cloud-based costs. This is a clear indication that this is a pain point for many companies. Cloud vendors typically make it very easy to provision services, which can make it difficult to manage usage and costs. From a financial perspective, this can be challenging, as IT often pays invoices for cloud services, but end users or operational leaders make decisions around how to use those services. The disconnect between the entity incurring the expense (operations) and the entity paying the invoice (IT) leaves a lot of room for unmanaged growth or contentious discussions.

Most cloud vendors want to enable organizations to move quickly. This often means users self-provisioning cloud resources. However, many IT organizations lack sufficient controls (or even visibility) around this to properly manage these environments. Imagine a user who spins up several servers and large databases for a project. The project concludes, and those resources still sit in some cloud vendor's data center, generating a monthly fee. Without strong controls around provisioning, metering, monitoring, and using cloud-based resources, cloud service costs will spiral out of control. IT is often held accountable even if it lacks control over the spending.

As you evaluate cloud service contracts, your team should analyze these potential cost escalations. Look at how the contract is structured and what controls are in place (or missing). More important, make sure there is clear documentation around how these resources will be provisioned and how costs will be allocated. Additionally, when you evaluate your staffing (see Chapter 13), you will want to ensure you have the skills on your team to effectively manage cloud-hosted solutions, including monitoring and managing user provisioning, use of resources, deprovisioning, and of course, security. Moving from one platform to another may produce immediate cost reductions but contain hidden expenses down the road, so evaluating these proposed solutions thoroughly is crucial.

## Renovating IT Finance

Hopefully, you have a strong ally in your CFO and are working closely to articulate cost and value together. Some healthcare CFOs are very technically savvy and supportive of using IT to transform the business. Others are more narrowly focused on the financial elements of the business, such as payor contracts, productivity, profit and loss, and cash flow. While all CFOs must focus on these elements, CFOs in healthcare who are tech-savvy and supportive can be valuable allies in articulating the value and necessity of IT investments. Strategically leveraging technology can help reduce overall costs, improve cash flow, improve quality, reduce accounts receivable, and more. Being able to speak the language of your Finance department helps forge a shared understanding about the costs and benefits of IT expenditures. Since financial systems are also part of HIT, identifying opportunities to better leverage the capabilities of those systems can be a useful way to both build a solid business partnership with finance. Enabling finance system features that foster better HIT cost conversations with the organization helps the entire organization, not just finance or IT. In other words, renovating your HIT finance systems can be part of your overall IT renovation project plan.

## Summary

Regardless of how you approach your IT costs and the finance function, you need to be able to articulate the value of these IT investments in business terms. Garnering the support of your CFO can certainly help, as can leveraging financial data and frameworks like TBM that help connect the dots between what the business needs and what IT delivers. This process and these relationships need to evolve. Including them in your renovation project will help you mature these capabilities over time. Hopefully, conversations about budgets and IT costs shift from the common narrow focus of cost and expense to a broader discussion about the value of enabling the innovation and transformation of the organization.

## References

[7.1] Condon, Alan, "Health systems boost tech spending to tackle cost, labor pressures," January 18, 2023, https://www.beckershospitalreview.com/finance/health-systems-boost-tech-spending-to-tackle-cost-labor-pressures.html], accessed January 18, 2023.
[7.2] Patel, Neha, Shubham Singhal, "What to expect in US healthcare in 2023 and beyond," US healthcare developments in 2023 and beyond, January 9, 2023, https://www.mckinsey.com/industries/healthcare/our-insights/what-to-expect-in-us-healthcare-in-2023-and-beyond, accessed January 18, 2023. P. 7.
[7.3] Gonsalves, Antone, "Companies search for ROI from cloud spending," October 6, 2022, https://www.techtarget.com/searchcloudcomputing/news/252525820/Companies-search-for-ROI-from-cloud-spending, accessed October 9, 2022.

## Resources

Balakrishnan, Tara, Chandra Gnanasambandam, Leandro Santos, and Bhargs Srivathsan, "Cloud-migration opportunity: Business value grows, but missteps abound," October 12, 2021, https://www.mckinsey.com/industries/technology-media-and-telecommunications/our-insights/cloud-migration-opportunity-business-value-grows-but-missteps-abound, accessed March 4, 2023.

Gapensky, Louis C., George H. Pink, Understanding Healthcare Financial Management, Seventh Edition, Health Administration Press, Chicago, IL, 2015.

Healthcare Weekly Staff, "5 ways technology can reduce healthcare costs," May 30 2018, https://healthcareweekly.com/5-ways-technology-can-reduce-healthcare-costs/, accessed January 17, 2023.

Moriates, Christopher, Vineet Arora, Neel Shah, Understanding Value Based Healthcare, First Edition, McGraw-Hill Education, 2015.

## Chapter 8

# IT Technology Building Blocks

As an IT professional, you are certainly familiar with the building blocks of IT technology. The objective of this chapter is to help you take a 360-degree view of your environment so you don't have any gaps when you perform your assessment and create your renovation plan.

We will discuss what systems, technologies, and data stores are in use, where are they located, who's managing them, who's securing them, and who's patching/updating/upgrading them. Essentially, you will be creating a full inventory of systems and technologies. When you perform your assessment in Chapter 20, you can work from the list(s) you have created here.

## IT Asset Management

Let's start by talking briefly about IT asset management (ITAM), which is an important building block for managing all your IT assets. ITAM has been a topic of increasing interest over the past decade and has matured as a body of knowledge. Many existing IT infrastructure software solutions contain asset management capabilities. Some systems call it the configuration management database (CMDB), some call it ITAM, and some call it inventory management, for example. Many Service Desk software solutions include or have add-ons for ITAM.

The common denominator in all these solutions is the ability to identify, quantify, manage, and store IT asset information. If you have an ITAM or CMDB solution in place, that's your logical starting point. If you don't have

DOI: 10.4324/9781003377023-10

that type of solution in place, your first step might be to see whether an existing solution you have includes this or whether it might be part of an add-on module. You could investigate a stand-alone solution, but you risk going down the project implementation wormhole instead of continuing your assessment and renovation project. If you choose to select a system to assist your efforts, you might consider making it part of your renovation plan instead of a stand-alone project to reduce the likelihood of getting sidetracked.

If you don't have an ITAM solution and don't want to spend time or resources to address that at this point, you can create your own basic database or even use a spreadsheet to capture key data. Regardless of how you approach this, you should develop processes for consistent and repeatable ITAM to accurately track assets across their lifecycle. Continuous auditing and strict change control processes also contribute to successful ITAM.

Of course, the benefits of having this information documented are that you can reduce your total cost of ownership, better manage and secure your assets, reduce the risk of downtime, and make more efficient use of your assets and, by extension, better use of your IT staff's time. Additionally, if you cannot account for every device you've purchased, there's a chance that devices are being 'borrowed,' 'pilfered,' or stolen by anyone who has access to your sites (employees, vendors, contractors, patients, etc.). As a responsible steward of your organization's assets, you should be able to account for these assets throughout their lifecycle.

An often-neglected aspect of ITAM is IT asset disposal, or IT asset disposition. Iron Mountain, a document management vendor, offers seven critical steps for secure IT asset disposition (ITAD) for healthcare [8.1]. These steps include creating a policy, establishing a chain of custody, and requiring a certificate of destruction, among other things. Regardless of whether you destroy decommissioned IT assets in-house (via physical or logical destruction methods) or hire an outside vendor to do so, you need to know what assets you have, where they are, and what protected health information (PHI) or other confidential data might be stored on them. From there, you need to know those assets are securely disposed of to avoid violating security and privacy regulations. This covers all IT assets, regardless of where they are physically located or who is managing them. Using third-party hosted solutions is fine, but who ensures PHI and other confidential data is securely and permanently destroyed when those hosted solutions are no longer needed? How do you verify hosted backups are securely stored and destroyed when no longer needed? These are things to keep in mind when you look at your IT technology environment.

Whatever approach you use, be sure to document everything that matters so you only 'touch' each asset once. For more on ITAM and ITAD, see the information at the end of the chapter.

## Data Centers

Let's begin in the data center. Most organizations still have a data center of some type, even if they've moved a lot of server or storage functions to the cloud. You may have primary and secondary data centers; you may have rented disaster recovery data centers. The list shown in Table 8.1 is a starter list for you.

Your *Data Center – Secondary, Tertiary* may be a cloud-based solution with a major tech provider or with a disaster recovery vendor. If you have hosted solutions, it's helpful to note where that solution is hosted (the vendor, the physical location, or both), as well as who in your IT department is responsible for managing the environment and any relevant renewal dates. If you don't have this data handy now, that's fine, but as you create your spreadsheet to track these data points, you can add detail as you go. By noting the IT owner, you will also be able to quickly delegate the assessment tasks you'll undertake later.

With the increased use of hybrid cloud solutions, it is imperative that you have accurate data about these hosted solutions, including interfaces, backups, configurations, and more. The complexity of some hybrid cloud solutions can create security and operational risks, so it is vital to have a strong grasp on all the details surrounding your cloud presence.

**Table 8.1   Data Center Example**

| Data Center | | Location/Vendor | Point of Contact | Renewal Date |
|---|---|---|---|---|
| 1 | *Data center – primary* | [insert address or location designation along with vendor contract information, if applicable] | [name of responsible person in IT] | [contract terms, costs, and renewal date, if applicable] |
| 2 | *Data center – second, third* | | | |
| 3 | *Disaster recovery – primary* | | | |
| 4 | *Disaster recovery – second* | | | |
| 5 | *Other facilities* | | | |

## Servers, Storage, and Platforms

Next on the technology list is servers. Again, these may be on-premise or cloud-based. They might be public or private clouds, and of course, they may be part of a hyperconverged infrastructure solution running various operating systems, from Microsoft Windows™ to some version of Unix, Linux, or a proprietary operating system. If your servers are virtualized, you should have an inventory of both the virtualization solution and all the virtual machines (VM) in use as well as a process for managing that environment.

Next on our list is storage. Again, you may have on-premise and off-premise storage solutions, from individual solutions to storage clusters. Also include your backup storage solutions in this list, including disk-based, tape-based, or other backup solutions in place.

For both servers and storage, you should include the age of the device as well as the expected end of life (EOL) of the device. If you don't have that information now, you can add that work to your renovation project. Ultimately, you should know the acquisition date, cost, in-service date (if substantially different from the acquisition date), estimated useful life, and announced end of support or EOL for the product. The benefit of digging up all this data about each system is that you can quickly develop a technology roadmap that details when items will be removed from service and what the replacement strategy will be. Ideally, this will be done when you develop your renovation plan. Table 8.2 shows an example of what the basic inventory might look like. You can add elements and, obviously, repeat this for each server or storage solution you have. Some data might be available through prior financial records or capital project archives. If you cannot locate the data, use estimates.

If you have orchestration, virtualization, or presentation platforms, you should include them here as well. Tools and solutions related to managing containers, including provisioning, deployment, relocating, scaling, or decommissioning these resources can be included here or called out separately if you have a large presence of this type of technology in your environment.

Your list, shown in Table 8.2, should have a line item for each server, storage, and platform in place, along with the requisite asset details, as shown.

**Table 8.2  Server, Storage, and Platform Example**

| Asset Name | |
|---|---|
| **Server 1 (name, serial #)** | Type [processor type, etc.] |
| | Function [server function or purpose] |
| | Acquisition date |
| | Cost or estimated cost |
| | In-service date |
| | Estimated useful life |
| | Annual license cost, if any |
| | Annual support cost, if any |
| | Announced end of support |
| | Announced end of life |
| | Other relevant data, as needed |

# Cloud Technologies

Cloud technologies are evolving so quickly that it's hard for most IT professionals to keep up unless this is specific to their role. In this section, we will touch on key elements to be aware of, but you should certainly spend time researching this topic independently.

Cloud-based solutions can offer numerous benefits, such as reduced costs (certainly the reduction of capital costs to acquire computer hardware), speed to solution (no need to purchase and configure hardware), scalability (get as much or as little computer power as you need at the click of a button), and potentially high performance (faster, newer resources coupled with as much power as you need can produce high-performance solutions). The potential downsides are difficulty in managing these operational costs (users can self-provision and run up the bill), identity and access management, and various security challenges. Cloud solutions are not magic bullets, but they can be the right solution if the need is properly defined. In other words, pushing all your computer power to the cloud without understanding the pros and cons will not turn out well.

If you're using cloud-based servers, for example, it's your responsibility to secure them. If you are using servers provided by a cloud hosting company, it might be their responsibility to secure them. This is one key example of how important it is to understand the specifics of the cloud platform you're using and the contractual agreements around that use.

Additionally, some HIT professionals have limited experience with cloud technologies. If you're dealing with limited skills in this regard, your move to the cloud can cause significant issues such as not managing the solution very well, not following best practices (architecting a mess), or not knowing how to troubleshoot and resolve issues. This generally results in confusion, uncontrolled costs, and security gaps. Be sure your team has the skills and expertise needed to properly manage these complex resources – whether that's hiring the right talent or using third-party managed services temporarily or permanently.

Identity access management (IAM) and privileged account management (PAM) are two areas of security that can be particularly challenging with multiple cloud-based solutions. While there are many ways to address these security challenges, a good resource is the Cloud Security Alliance. You can find more information in the Resources section at the end of this chapter.

Finally, cloud-based resources can significantly reduce costs and speed time-to-solution, but there's a caveat. Poorly managed cloud solutions can sap your budget, your staff's time, and your organization's ability to move quickly to capture market opportunities. It's worth the time and effort to develop a sound cloud strategy and roadmap so you can avoid as many of the pitfalls as possible. Your strategy should include developing clear use cases for Software-as-a-Service (SaaS), Platform-as-a-Service (PaaS), Infrastructure-as-a-Service (IaaS), and the emerging Everything-as-a-Service (XaaS) service options.

# Addressing Shadow IT

This is a good point to pause and discuss shadow IT. Shadow IT is typically defined as IT functions occurring in an organization outside of IT visibility or control. Shadow IT has proliferated in direct proportion to the availability of cloud-based solutions. Cloud services help companies move quickly by provisioning needed IT resources on demand without the costs and timelines related to acquiring and installing those resources. This convenience, however, comes with hidden costs. These include tangible financial costs, security concerns, data inconsistency, and a lack of centralized oversight and management, all of which can impact organizations that have shadow IT.

IT cannot support systems it is not involved with or aware of. If the configuration of the cloud-service doesn't fully support the way the business needs to operate, there's no IT expertise available to assist in resolving that problem. IT systems outside of IT can also pose significant security risks. End users are typically focused on achieving business results and not examining how data is managed, transported, or secured.

With data being generated, stored, and utilized across the organization, the management of data becomes fragmented. This often results in poor-quality data for the enterprise. Trying to stitch together data from these disparate systems can pose a significant challenge to the Business Intelligence (BI) and Data Analytics (DA) teams. Understanding how the source system handles data, how it might be transformed as it moves from one format or one system to another is crucial for managing data quality and security.

Shadow IT leads to another problem called *divergence*. This is when "owners adopt different practices to manage their shadow technologies that lead to weaker management processes. The result can be inconsistent process outcomes and greater potential for control and compliance problems." [8.2] Clearly, in healthcare, control and compliance with critical data are fundamental to running the business.

Finally, when non-IT departments control user access and provisioning, it typically leads to the granting of excessive access or permissions. In addition to the security risks, this environment also increases costs. Unused licenses, overprovisioned services, and a lack of normal IT operational oversight (e.g., auditing, monitoring, and clean up) increase costs, which typically continue to grow month-over-month when not managed.

If you are not confident you can identify and manage the shadow IT in use in your organization, there are software tools that will detect and enumerate your organization's shadow IT. You may consider implementing one of these tools in order to identify and manage your shadow IT. Some of the solutions fall in the category of cloud access security broker (CASB) software. Deploying software to identify, secure, and manage shadow IT is becoming more common as shadow IT has proliferated in recent years. You may consider implementing these kinds of solutions as part of your renovation project or independently, depending on how large a problem shadow IT is in your HC organization.

Shadow IT will not go away any time soon. Rather than try to continually fight shadow IT, you should begin by understanding what's driving end users to take IT matters into their own hands. Has IT been a roadblock in the past? Have IT staff failed to really understand the business challenges users are facing? Has IT tried to steer users toward IT systems that exist (vs. IT systems that meet the business need)? It's important to talk with your end users to better understand their needs. This will help align IT with operations and allow you to begin the conversation about shadow IT. In some cases, the organization has simply allowed end users to implement shadow IT solutions, even when it has a well-functioning and responsive IT department. In this case, shadow IT is an organizational problem.

IT is uniquely qualified to assess and address data security, manage user provisioning, and audit and monitor IT systems. Being able to work closely with your organizational partners to understand the business needs, find the best solutions to those needs, and offer IT support may be your best path forward. Developing solutions that support end-user workflows while maintaining better cost and security controls should be viewed favorably by everyone. End users typically don't want to be in the IT business; they just need a faster, more nimble response to their needs. Through your IT renovation project, you'll be improving much of your IT service and operations, so you also may be able to develop a shared management model that addresses these issues. In essence, you can build IT-as-a-Service for your organization through a shared IT service model. This empowers end users, removes a lot of the frustrations (for IT and the organization), and ensures IT is well-managed to align with the strategic requirements and operational needs. [8.3] Finally, you might consider using a shadow IT detection tool or a CASB solution to help you contain and manage this environment more successfully.

## Network Components

The next section of IT technology to inventory are your network components. This includes network devices such as switches and routers, as well as firewalls, virtual private network (VPN) appliances, voice components (VoIP), fax (FoIP), as well as wireless network components, and security-related network devices such as data loss prevention (DLP) or security information and event management (SIEM) devices.

For wireless (Wi-Fi) networks, there are clearly large components – switches and routers – that manage the wireless network and smaller components, like Wi-Fi antennas, that provide Wi-Fi coverage throughout your facilities. Hopefully you're using a software tool that delineates all of your network

Table 8.3  Network Components Example

| Asset Name | |
|---|---|
| *Network device name* | Type, IP address, location, etc. |
| | Function |
| | Acquisition date |
| | Cost or estimated cost |
| | In-service date |
| | Estimated useful life |
| | Annual license cost, if any |
| | Annual support cost, if any |
| | Announced end of support, if any |
| | Announced end of life, if any |

devices, including every antenna, every repeater, every booster, etc. You
may not choose to document all the details about each of these items in
a spreadsheet, as shown in Table 8.3, but if you have the data, it is worth
documenting. For example, you might be getting ready to refresh an entire
building's Wi-Fi infrastructure, so there is a need to delineate those items. Or
you might have a refresh plan already underway where you're replacing those
items on a rolling basis. If you have these details covered, you can certainly
include them in this inventory process or make a note to address those smaller
details later. The decision is about what level of detail you want to include.
Going down to devices that are in the few hundred-dollar cost range may not
be worth the effort, at least not for the purposes of this renovation plan. That's
your choice based on your organization's asset management guidelines.

## Telcom and Connectivity

This is a huge segment of IT that requires considerable management on
behalf of the organization. Connectivity (standard telephony, VoIP, and
Internet) is a complex set of technologies and services provided by multiple
telecommunication (telcom) vendors. This often is an area that is under-
managed in IT simply because of the specialized knowledge it takes to
understand circuits, routing, and vendor pricing bundles. Many healthcare

organizations end up paying far too much for these services simply because they lack the expertise to understand various vendors' offerings or how to effectively compare the cost or capabilities of the multitude of circuit types available, for example.

As a result, many organizations look to trusted third-party vendors to assist in managing their connectivity arrangements to ensure that they get the best rates from providers and negotiate the best contracts on behalf of the organization. This is a skill rarely found inside HIT departments, so considering outsourcing the procurement and oversight to a trusted third-party can potentially save tens (or hundreds) of thousands of dollars and hundreds of hours of IT management time. For example, many telcom providers bundle circuits in specific ways. Unbundling them can lead to large cost increases. Bundling them in the right way can double your bandwidth while halving your cost, for example. These kinds of changes can be recommended by a third-party vendor, reviewed by the HIT leaders, and implemented for significant cost savings. It also avoids burdening IT staff with remaining up-to-date on telcom offerings that are constantly changing. Most HIT organizations have numerous circuits that are no longer in use but are still being billed monthly. Though a third-party vendor will share in the savings, the net savings to the organization can add up quickly and it's savings you might not otherwise find. The internal connectivity and telcom components are, of course, part of the IT function. Managing access, bandwidth, connectivity, latency, Quality of Service (QoS), etc. are all elements you should be actively managing either through IT technology or through third-party telcom vendors.

You should have a complete list of all your incoming and outgoing circuits to each location, along with providers, formats (MPLS, SD-WAN, SASE, etc.), relevant contractual terms, etc. A list is shown in Table 8.4. You may also choose to include your voice/telephony solution as well as your cellular service provider(s) here.

**Table 8.4  Telcom and Connectivity Example**

| Connectivity Inventory | |
|---|---|
| Location 1...Location n | Circuits |
| | Circuit type (format, speed, etc.) |
| | Provider(s) |
| | Terms |
| | Other |

Before we move on, let's also discuss some of the other telcom elements that might be in your environment. We won't go into detail on these, but we'll mention a few just to spark your thoughts around what you might have in your organization today – or more importantly, what maybe is left of an abandoned project a decade ago. If any of these elements are still connected to your main network, you have a serious, unmanaged risk. If any of these elements are not connected to your network but are still being billed to your organization, you have unmanaged costs. Either way, you need to clean these up as part of your renovation work.

Connectivity Options (*partial list*):

1. Legacy wired network components
2. Legacy wireless network components
3. Legacy wireless mesh network components
4. Bluetooth
5. 4G cellular extenders
6. Telephony (VoIP)
7. Internet connectivity (many variables)
8. Site-to-site connectivity

Also be sure to look for obsolete or unused components so you can pull them out during your renovation project. For example, early generations of enterprise wireless mesh network solutions were often piloted in healthcare to address the issue of spotty Wi-Fi coverage in difficult areas such as radiology suites (with lead-lined walls) or emergency departments (with strong radio signals coming from emergency vehicles). These prior solutions may still be in your racks or in your outlets, so scour your environment. Look at prior projects and initiatives, if you have documentation going back a decade, and see what might be lounging around your environment.

## Enterprise Data Warehouse, Database Systems

Enterprise data warehouses (EDW) and database systems are typically managed by an IT infrastructure team and are considered part of the infrastructure domain. While all electronic health record software solutions rely on large databases as their foundation, we are not including those here. We will discuss those as part of our enterprise application discussion later in this chapter.

Large databases require servers, storage, and database administration to build, maintain, and enhance these functions. Your EDW may be on-premise or in the cloud, or you may have a hybrid solution. Therefore, both the architecture and the hardware/software solutions in use may be a combination of technologies that need to be well-managed for several reasons. The primary one is to ensure data is true and accurate, that the data pulled from these systems is trustworthy. The secondary reason, though equally important as the first, is that data needs to be secure. Since data in EDWs typically includes some of the most sensitive and confidential organizational data, it is a prime target for attack. Ensuring access is tightly managed and monitored and that data is secured and backed up is of the utmost importance. IT's job is to ensure the *confidentiality, integrity,* and *availability* of organizational data, and much of that data resides in these systems. A partial list of attributes is shown in Table 8.5.

Under asset name, you should list each specific asset, by name or designation (however you identify these assets in your environment) and list the attributes shown. Of course, you can add as much detail about these assets as you find useful.

Servers, storage, network, telcom, and databases make up the bulk of your infrastructure services. If you have additional infrastructure elements you want to include, delineate them as we have here.

**Table 8.5   Enterprise Data Warehouse and Databases**

| Asset Name | |
|---|---|
| *Enterprise Data Warehouse* | Location, designation |
| *Database Clusters* | Platform, operating System |
| *Database Systems* | Application |
| | Cost or estimated cost |
| | In-service date |
| | Estimated useful life |
| | Annual license cost, if any |
| | Annual support cost, if any |
| | Announced end of support |
| | Announced end of life |

# Enterprise Applications

Your EHR software is one of the largest and most critical enterprise applications you manage, but there are many supporting applications that allow the business to fully function. Other enterprise applications include document management, finance, human resources, and supply chain applications, to name a few. You might also have solutions such as enterprise faxing, electronic signature software, voice recognition software, and other software applications needed in healthcare that are typically interfaced to the EHR.

Other enterprise applications can include payroll and time reporting, recruitment, training and compliance, workforce management, performance management, benefits management, policy management, employee communication, emergency management, contract management, risk and audit management, case management, patient communications (or Customer Relationship Management, CRM), facilities management, operations and maintenance, fleet management, and food and beverage management. This is still just a partial list of software you might have in your complex healthcare environment, but it's a good list to start with.

If your healthcare organization operates in a specialized space, such as ambulatory surgery, pulmonology, cardiology, or infectious diseases, for example, you may have other specific software used to provide these services. Later in this chapter, we'll briefly touch on medical device management, which may include some of these specialized applications in use.

Table 8.6 shows an example of the data points you might choose to collect. For each asset type, develop the required set of details around the asset.

The details you collect will be specific to each application, but be sure to note whether something is currently managed by IT or outside of IT (shadow IT), as well as where it's hosted (location). This way, you have a clean starting point in your renovation project for determining how to best manage these applications.

## License Volumes, Thresholds, and Budgeting

For enterprise applications and some infrastructure applications, if your licensing is volume-based (such as patient visits, inpatient stays, or the number of transactions per time period, for example), be sure to note your volume thresholds along with the cost for breaching the threshold. For

**Table 8.6 Enterprise Applications**

| Asset Name | |
|---|---|
| *Electronic health record* | Software vendor, current version |
| *Document management* | Platform/operating system/location |
| *Financial management* | IT-managed or non-IT managed |
| *Human resources management* | Operational owner |
| *Supply chain management* | Licensing model (perpetual, subscription) |
| *[insert other key systems]* | Number of licenses |
| | Cost per license or annual cost |
| | Annual support cost |
| | Renewal dates |
| | Software dependencies |
| | Other relevant information |

example, some vendors have soft limits where additional units (users, files, etc.) can be breached and noted, and you true up your costs quarterly or annually. Some vendors have hard stops where you can't add users or files without paying additional fees.

You'll need to track your volumes and ensure you estimate for your next budget cycle, especially if your licensing or volume reviews don't sync up well to your budget cycle. For example, your organization may prepare budgets in July but your volume review is in October, and new fees start in January. If you don't put in an accurate estimate in July, you'll be over budget all year once the increased fees take effect.

## Include All Shadow IT

It's important that when you inventory your systems, you include all electronic systems used by the organization – whether they are currently managed by IT or not. As we've discussed, many IT solutions were provisioned or enabled outside of the IT governance process in the past few years. You should still inventory all IT systems and include them in your renovation plans.

Part of your renovation project will involve looking at all the shadow IT in your organization to determine how to best address the situation. This will require a piece-by-piece approach so you understand why the function moved outside of IT, whether it really does need to come back into IT, and if so, what the best solution looks like. In most cases, the application experts and owners will remain the operational leaders, but IT should ideally manage things like user provisioning, cybersecurity, and the application lifecycle. In almost all instances where applications live outside of IT, these IT-related activities are not being done at all. Every application in use across the enterprise needs to be known by IT. Ensuring data is safe, secure, and well-managed is a requirement for healthcare data in today's environment and one the IT department is uniquely qualified to do.

## IT Infrastructure Applications

These applications include all the software used to manage and monitor your infrastructure. You can include all of your monitoring solutions, such as network monitoring, security monitoring, and access monitoring. You might choose to break out all of your cybersecurity-related solutions into a separate cybersecurity category. Infrastructure applications include things like desktop imaging software, anti-virus/anti-malware solutions, mobile device management, project management, and service management (ITSM, CMDB, ITAM, etc.). Any system that is used by IT to run the IT function should be included in this section.

The reason for performing a thorough inventory of these systems is because during your assessment and renovation phases, you will have the opportunity to see where you have overlaps and where you have gaps. Odds are good you have both, whether you're aware of them not. Overlaps and gaps are almost impossible to avoid because so many solutions expand their capabilities into related areas over time. For example, a service management solution may also provide monitoring or user provisioning or … you name it. Understanding the current and future capabilities of each system you own is the basis for being able to clean up your environment.

This is ground zero for your renovation: cleaning up what you have and what you use to manage your IT environment. When you have a set of organized tools and capabilities at your disposal, you can begin straightening up your processes around managing all these IT assets and elements. Your IT infrastructure application list could look something like that shown in Table 8.7. For each asset type, develop and document the list of related attributes.

**Table 8.7  Infrastructure Applications**

| Asset Name | |
|---|---|
| *Software configuration* | Software vendor, current version |
| *Service management solution* | Platform/operating system/location |
| *Monitoring solutions* | IT owner |
| *Asset management solution* | Licensing model (perpetual, subscription, etc.) |
| *Project management solution* | Number of licenses |
| | Cost per license or annual cost |
| | Annual support cost |
| | Software dependencies |
| | Other relevant information, as needed |

# End User Devices

The category of End User Devices (EUD) includes all the equipment assigned to or used by end users in your healthcare system. This includes obvious devices such as workstations and laptops, monitors, docking stations, printers, scanners, and multifunction devices (MFD). Of course, you should have a good inventory of workstations, laptops, and some printers/MFDs. You may keep high-level track of monitors, knowing how many you buy, how many you install, and how many you remove/replace, but you likely don't track much more than that. For your renovation project, you'll need to know how many, where, and what configuration (operating system, patch level, etc.) you have of devices that require active management. If you don't know where all your desktop or laptop computers are, you can't patch or upgrade them, and they become thousands of little security holes on your network. MFDs can become vectors in cyberattacks, and these devices can also store protected health information (PHI), so they need to be managed as well. Hopefully your desktop team is actively managing these devices, if not, that should be part of your renovation work.

# Cybersecurity

We've broken out cybersecurity into separate chapters (building blocks and assessment), so we won't cover those aspects here. If you choose to, you can certainly delineate your cybersecurity software solutions in this chapter, or you can compile all your cybersecurity elements in the cyber sections. The key is to have a comprehensive and consistent inventory of all your IT solutions, however you choose to approach this work.

# Other IT Technology

Here is a list of software solutions you might have in place that may not have specifically been called out in this chapter. It is not comprehensive but might prompt you to think of solutions that sometimes fly under the radar.

## *Operations Related*

Software testing
System integration
IT vendor management
Enterprise architecture
Load balancing
Virtual private network (VPN) solutions
Remote access solutions
Domain services
File management solutions
Deployment solutions
Capacity management
Event management
Scheduling solutions
Planning solutions
IT analytics solutions
IT finance/cost accounting

## *Support Related*

Application support
Centralized faxing or printing
IT training solutions
Service Desk training solutions
Collaboration solutions

### Security Related

Identity and access management
Security awareness
Incident response
Threat and vulnerability management
Data privacy and security
Governance and risk management
Business continuity and disaster recovery

As you look at each function of your organization, you'll find applications you may be aware of but are not actively managing, or perhaps you'll stumble upon applications in use you had no idea were in your environment. Talk with end users, talk with stakeholders, and run reports on networks and devices to see what's being used to ensure you become aware of every application used in every corner of your organization. You can't manage what you can't see, so this is very valuable work, though it's painstaking and time-consuming.

On the desktop side, you may run a discovery tool to see what is installed on desktops. Often, you'll find things like streaming apps chewing up your network bandwidth or stand-alone productivity tools used by the individual to enhance their work. You need to evaluate if it's acceptable to have these one-off tools and, if so, how they should be managed. Other non-work-related apps are part of your IT governance function and may require an organizational decision at the senior leadership level. Is it OK to stream music? To access social media sites? To access video sites? To access personal email systems? Do you have controls, guardrails, or policies governing how this works? While these are not specific to IT technology and are typically outside IT's authority to manage directly, it's important to consider these elements as part of your renovation plan. Preparing for the future of IT includes knowing how to manage and address these types of technologies and new ones that emerge in the future.

## Medical Device Technology

If you work in a hospital setting and are responsible for medical device management as a part of your IT function, you should perform a similar inventory and assessment of those technologies. Systems like cardiac monitoring systems, advanced imaging systems, hybrid operating room systems, or even nurse call systems are outside the scope of specific IT technology discussion. However, medical device management, or the Clinical Engineering (CE) function, is increasingly managed within the IT function.

Advanced medical systems involve servers, workstations, storage, and network capabilities. As such, they function as IT systems within deeply clinical settings. Managing them within the IT framework helps improve the management of these systems through an integrated approach to device and system administration. This includes ensuring these systems are secure, that data and interfaces are working as expected, and that these systems are patched, updated, and upgraded according to manufacturer's specifications. The maintenance and support of these advanced clinical systems are typically performed by specially trained, dedicated CE staff, not IT staff. However, having CE and IT staff report up through the same chain of command helps ensure these teams are working collaboratively to the benefit of the organization. Additionally, CE and IT staff can help train each other to bring a broader understanding of these unique environments to each team. If you're managing the CE function within IT, ensure that you include this in your overall IT assessment. If this is managed outside of IT, you may want to collaborate with your counterpart to ensure clinical systems are being managed according to current IT standards.

## Summary

IT technologies are clearly the foundation of all you do in healthcare IT. The basic technology components may have changed platforms (installed, virtualized, or X-as-a-Service) or locations (on-premise vs. cloud), but the building blocks are the same. Ensuring you have a full view of all the technology your team is responsible for is a starting point. You can use this chapter as a kick-starter for thinking about all the technology under your IT roof and how well you track and manage it.

## References

[8.1] Iron Mountain, "7 must-do's for secure ITAD," no date, https://www.ironmountain.com/resources/general-articles/7/7-must-dos-for-secure-itad, accessed March 7, 2023.

[8.2] Lawton, George, "Centralized services as a hedge against shadow IT," January 25, 2023, https://www.techtarget.com/searcherp/tip/Centralized-services-as-a-hedge-against-shadow-ITs-escalation, accessed April 5, 2023.

[8.3] Ibid.

## Resources

Cloud Security Alliance, "Security guidance for critical areas of focus in cloud computing v4.0," July 26, 2017, https://cloudsecurityalliance.org/artifacts/security-guidance-v4/, accessed March 3, 3023.

Federal Cloud Computing Strategy, "From cloud first to cloud smart," no date, https://cloud.cio.gov/strategy/, accessed March 3, 2023. [Example of a detailed cloud strategy.]

International Association of Information Technology Asset Managers, no date, https://iaitam.org/, accessed December 17, 2022.

White, Sarah K., "IT asset management (ITAM): Best practices and certs for optimizing IT assets," July 20, 2021, https://www.cio.com/article/217546/it-asset-management-itam.html, accessed December 17, 2022.

# Chapter 9

# IT Service Management and IT Operations Building Blocks

In this chapter, we'll explore the most common elements of IT service management (ITSM) and operations. Some elements might be new, and some may jog your memory, acting as reminders of things to look at in your department. You can also explore resources provided at the end of this chapter.

## IT Service Management (ITSM) and IT Operations Management (ITOM)

Let's start by identifying the difference between ITSM and IT operations management (ITOM). Referring to Figure 9.1, you can see that there are internal IT operations (ITOps) required to manage the IT function, which in turn support the delivery of IT services to the organization. ITOM is essentially part of ITOps.

ITOps are the foundation of excellent service delivery. Both ITOM and ITSM rely on having well-developed processes that are supported by policies, procedures, technology, and training. Delivering great service is rarely applauded, it is simply expected. However, developing mature ITOM and ITSM capabilities is what enables you to get your department out of the "order taker" mode to become a valuable contributor to strategic initiatives.

As we've discussed, everywhere you turn in IT, there's an applicable framework, and this is no exception. To implement ITSM and ITOM, you

DOI: 10.4324/9781003377023-11

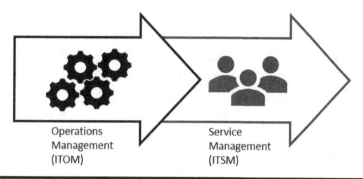

**Figure 9.1   IT service management (ITSM) and IT operations management (ITOM).**

can use the ITIL, the International Organization for Standardization (ISO), Control Objectives for Information Technology (COBIT), or other similar frameworks as the basis for your ITSM efforts. Most healthcare organizations utilize some form of ITIL, either the high-level concepts or the detailed framework.

Regardless of the framework you use, it's important to ensure the framework doesn't become the work itself. Some IT departments rigorously adhere to a framework, which is fine if that adherence doesn't devolve into bureaucracy. Some IT departments adhere more conceptually to a framework and others more rigorously. You can approach this in whatever manner works for you as long as work is conducted in a logical, consistent, and documented manner. In your renovation work, you may need to assess whether your service management function is too rigid, too lax, or appropriate for the size and type of organization you serve.

## Achieving Operational Excellence

While it can be an elusive goal, developing operational excellence in IT is worth pursuing. When operations are well-defined, when staff are well-trained in carrying out those processes, and when effective monitoring and coaching systems are in place, ITOps can generate job satisfaction, lower costs, and improve security. Operational excellence only comes from reviewing each workflow in the department, then analyzing, optimizing, and automating, when feasible/desirable. This is often one of the first steps in the digitization/digitalization/digital transformation process in any IT organization.

If your ITOps are chaotic, nothing is reliable. That creates risks, costs, errors, gaps, and ultimately very poor service delivery for the organization. It also tends to create a challenging environment in which IT staff have to work, creating frustration, confusion, and disengagement. When IT service delivery is of poor quality, it also directly and indirectly impacts patient care. Nurses, doctors, and other care providers focus on issues with technology instead of tending to the patient's needs; support staff deal with printer, network, or access issues instead of supporting the care providers; business staff deal with slow computers or blocked access to resources instead of managing the business of the organization. Each IT issue end users deal with creates friction. Each friction point acts as a multiplier of dissatisfaction with the IT function.

Of course, the opposite is true as well. When users rarely have technology issues because systems are well-maintained, when users are properly provisioned, systems are updated, backed up, patched, and managed seamlessly, and issues that do occur are easily reported and quickly resolved, you have achieved a notable level of service excellence. Perfection in IT is the lack of a problem and that rarely gets noticed or appreciated by the organization. When nothing goes wrong, when systems are simply humming along, end users are satisfied, they rarely will comment on (or compliment) IT for the lack of issues. However, developing and delivering world-class operations and service to your organization is the reward in itself. You'll know you're delivering a great experience; you'll know you've reduced friction for your users, and you may ultimately be able to articulate this great service delivery with key performance metrics (KPIs), data showing adherence to service level agreements (SLAs), end user satisfaction metrics, or other relevant indicators that IT is enabling operations to deliver great patient care.

## Types of IT Operations

ITOM defines how ITOps are managed. This includes how new systems are procured, servers are provisioned or hardened, systems are patched or updated, and systems are monitored for performance or security. ITIL defines four areas of IT functions, we add a fifth to break out infrastructure as a separate functional area: operations, technical, application, infrastructure, and service desk (SD). Cybersecurity is an important topic that has its own domain, and operational elements clearly intersect with both ITOM and ITSM. We'll discuss cybersecurity in this context very briefly in this chapter. You can refer Chapter 12 on cybersecurity for a deeper dive.

# IT Operations Management (ITOM)

ITOps (and ITOM) ensure the IT functions are performed in a consistent, reliable manner. In turn, this helps ensure that business operations are uninterrupted by technology issues. While technology will always have failures, reducing unexpected downtimes is a key function of ITOps through the proactive management of processes such as patching, upgrades, backups, and monitoring.

ITOps is responsible for provisioning, monitoring, and managing infrastructure resources such as servers, storage, and network resources. Operations also manages system workloads and utilization and assesses proposed changes to systems.

## IT Technical Management

Technical management includes managing the many different technologies used in healthcare IT today. That includes things like developing technical roadmaps, defining enterprise architecture, configuring and testing cloud-based platforms (prior to application deployment or user provisioning), and defining technical standards for provisioning of new IT assets or resources. On the other end of the spectrum, it also includes managing end user devices, printers, faxes, bar code scanners, tablets, document scanners, microphones (for dictation), and all other technologies in use by end-users. In some healthcare organizations, technical management may also include the management or oversight of medical devices.

## IT Application Management

Ensuring that applications are highly available, function as designed, and are updated and optimized is the essence of application management. In today's hybrid environment, there may be cloud-based applications that are managed completely outside the IT department. That may or may not be an acceptable arrangement for your organization. As we've discussed, when you assess your capabilities in this area, it will be important to understand which cloud-based systems are in use, where data resides, how security and user provisioning are managed, and what backup, redundancy, and failover solutions exist. You may be under the impression that the software provider or the business unit has all of these elements covered, but often that is not the case.

Though the old "command and control" model for IT is no longer viable, there is still a need for active IT management and engagement for *all* IT solutions a healthcare organization uses. In Chapter 8, we discussed the need to determine where applications are, who's managing them, and what the gaps and risks are, so you can create a plan for addressing those concerns. You'll have the opportunity to address these elements both in your assessment phase and in your renovation plan.

## IT Infrastructure Management

Most healthcare organizations have complex IT infrastructures. From wide area networks connecting regional or local sites to telephony and faxing, from servers and storage in data centers to virtualized solutions, from cybersecurity to network micro-segmentation and more, IT infrastructure management requires a deep technical understanding of all the technologies in use as well as an enterprise view of the architecture and how it supports the enterprise. Since infrastructure is the foundation of IT services, it is important that you have highly reliable infrastructure management. Healthcare organizations rely on an always-available, always-fast, always-secure network and the availability of critical functions needed to provide quality healthcare.

## IT Service Desk Management

In many healthcare organizations, SD and Service Desk Management (SDM) often the most well-defined processes in the IT function. The SD function has evolved from being more like a telephone operator, simply routing calls to one team or another. Today, most organizations have expectations around first call resolution for their SD. This means that SD staff need to be well-trained not only in customer service skills but in a wide variety of basic technical skills, from device management to application troubleshooting and just about everything in between.

There used to be a belief that reporting on how many calls or tickets the SD handled was a measure of success – more was better. Framed differently, every contact with the SD is because an end user has a problem. Therefore, more is definitely *not* better. In fact, the fewer contacts the organization has with the SD, the better the IT function is likely performing. The caveat, of course, is that if your IT function is generally deemed to be unhelpful or nonresponsive, your end users may have simply given up contacting you. If you've fallen into this level of dysfunction, fixing your SD function and regaining your customers trust is a long, slow road. It can be done through consistent processes, solid training for your staff, and honest communication and feedback from the organization.

End users contact the SD for many different types of IT problems – from reporting problems with hardware, software, or connectivity to requesting a new laptop or a replacement cable. However, the common element is this: each time a user has to contact the SD, they are interrupted from doing their own job. So, each SD contact could essentially be seen as a failure. While that's a harsh view, it's good to look at it through that lens so when you assess your SD function, you can find ways to reduce the need to contact the SD such as ensuring technology is well-managed (to avoid failure) and providing options such as self-service portals, automation, monitoring and repairing on the fly, etc. If users do have to contact the SD, make sure each contact is a professional and value-added interaction.

A great example of service management and improving the end user experience is implementing a hardware monitoring solution, which regularly monitors all of the thousands end user computers (workstations, laptops, and printers, primarily) through simple automation. If the memory or hard drive on any device started generating specific error codes, a technician can be dispatched to replace that component in advance of failure. Typically, this can be scheduled at a time that is convenient for the end user or when the end user is out of the office (nights, weekends, etc.). This pro-active replacement of soon-to-fail components reduces SD contact, but more importantly, it reduces downtime and frustration for end users. Then, the thousands of doctors, nurses, patient care techs, case managers, and others directly delivering patient care are less likely to run into a technology issue that would create friction for them.

This example shows the power of innovative thinking and the deployment of a few basic technologies and processes. They can have a significant and positive impact on the environment and on end-user perceptions of IT service quality.

Using a robust ticketing software solution can help by providing actionable data and insights around demand, capacity, and trends. Though some solutions are very comprehensive, some are too complex or resource-intense for healthcare organizations. In some cases, it's just not feasible to have a team of analysts dedicated to supporting the ticketing system, as some of the more complex systems require. The most important element of a ticketing system is ease-of-use for both IT staff and end users and ease-to-configure to meet the unique needs of your IT department. In addition, it's important to have a reasonable cost per user, a flexible licensing model (i.e. there's a difference between an end user reporting a problem and an IT analyst using the ticketing system to manage their day-to-day work), robust reporting capabilities, and a reasonable support model (i.e. doesn't require a team of expensive analysts and doesn't cost a fortune to get support from the vendor).

## Cybersecurity, IT Incident, and Security Management

IT is responsible for maintaining the confidentiality, integrity, and availability of IT systems and data. By definition, then, ITSM includes all the processes for managing the prevention, detection, response, and remediation of any issues that arise.

As we discuss the many available IT frameworks throughout this book, perhaps the most critical framework to have in place is a cybersecurity framework (CSF), which gives you a roadmap to developing and maturing your cybersecurity function. Without these functions in place, very little else matters. You can deliver the most robust applications or the fastest network, but if you don't secure your IT assets to the very best of your ability, those other things won't matter when you experience a breach. Protecting these assets is required by law, so using a framework to ensure you are compliance *and* secure is wise.

Most organizations use a security framework. In healthcare, HITRUST and National Institute of Standards and Technologies (NIST) are two of the most popular. HITRUST is perhaps more comprehensive and pulls in required elements from HIPAA, PCI, and others. NIST is often seen as somewhat less complex and easier to work with. The key is to select a framework and then work within that framework to fill out your cybersecurity capabilities. Given that NIST is suitable for many types of HC organizations (small, large, simple, and complex), we'll focus briefly on the NIST CSF. NIST CSF was created and is managed by the U.S. government. It identifies five key activities:

1. Identify
2. Protect
3. Detect
4. Respond
5. Recover

More recently, the framework was extended to cover three additional dimensions: Core, Tiers, and Profiles. For more on the original NIST CSF as well as this voluntary addition, visit the NIST website referenced at the end of this chapter. [9.1]

Incident and security management are the processes and practices related to monitoring, identifying, and responding to incidents. Security management involves all the activities around security, which overlap with operations, application, and technology management as well as SDM. We'll discuss information security management later in this chapter. We also cover cybersecurity in more detail in Chapter 12.

## *Business Continuity Management*

Business continuity (BC) management is often discussed in tandem with cybersecurity, but it is really its own process. An organization might need to use its BC plan (BCP) if it experiences a successful cyber-attack, but it might also need to invoke the BCP if there is a natural disaster or, as we saw recently, a pandemic.

Most healthcare organizations participate in or use the National Incident Management System (NIMS) as defined by the U.S. government's Federal Emergency Management Agency (FEMA) as the framework for organizational incident response. Under NIMS, there are the Incident Command System (ICS) and the Hospital Incident Command System (HICS). Through these models, HC organizations train their leaders in the use of these systems so that if there is a disaster event, they can easily coordinate with national and governmental resources using an agreed-upon framework (NIMS, ICS, and HICS). These frameworks identify command-and-control functions for coordination across healthcare, law enforcement, emergency services, and governmental agencies. As such, they are not specific to IT but are systems you should be familiar with as they impact your BC planning and response.

In general, BC management is an organization-wide process, of which IT is a portion. However, most HIT departments have their own BCP that covers the myriad of details specific to the IT function. Your organization relies on your team to protect the confidentiality, availability, and integrity of all data, especially patient data. BC management is typically documented in a BCP, which should be based on a business impact analysis. You can assess your IT operational readiness with respect to business continuity and disaster recovery (BC/DR) based on the maturity of your BCP processes. You can also refer to Chapter 11 for more on BCP.

# IT Processes

There are many IT processes you will need to assess and perhaps mature through your renovation project. This section reviews some of the more common IT processes to spark your review.

## IT Asset Management Process

As you recall, we discussed ITAM in Chapter 8, so this is a brief review from the process perspective. ITAM includes the processes of defining, acquiring, provisioning, maintaining, upgrading, and disposing of IT assets, both tangible (hardware) and intangible (software). In many healthcare IT organizations, this process is well-managed and includes defining hardware and software standards, procuring best prices through negotiated pricing contracts, provisioning through automation software that also hardens assets according to standards, and more.

Upgrading software and systems as updates become available is part of the asset lifecycle management process. It also includes creating a reliable and repeatable patching process for all IT assets. Unpatched vulnerabilities are easy targets for hackers. Patching systems is one of the easiest ways to prevent low-level hackers from gaining access to your systems, so your IT asset management process should absolutely have a robust patching process.

Do you have processes for deploying assets and ensuring that asset is actually deployed? Have you had instances of IT staff removing equipment from inventory for support services only to find those assets were never deployed and are unaccounted for? Whether the person brought a laptop home or left it in a data closet by accident, missing assets are a problem. Every asset should be accounted for either in inventory or on the network. Having systems in place to ensure your assets are where they are supposed to be is part of asset management.

As previously discussed, one element often overlooked is the removal of assets no longer in use, whether it's a network device, a server, or an application. When we perform the assessment tasks later in this book, you'll look for all your unused assets and create a plan for removing them from the environment.

## Information Security Management

Information security and cybersecurity are often used interchangeably, but they are not exactly the same thing. Technically speaking, cybersecurity is a subset of information security. At a high level, information security refers to the requirement to maintain the confidentiality, integrity, and availability of electronic information. Cybersecurity generally looks at protecting data and systems from attack or compromise. Typically, information security activities include tasks like hardening servers, turning off unused services, protocols and ports, and managing user provisioning. All of these things contribute to cybersecurity, but they're all internal activities of the IT department to keep assets secure internally and externally.

It's less important to define exactly where the line between information security and cybersecurity is and more important to ensure your IT activities are covering all your information security and cybersecurity needs. Using a framework like NIST CSF or HITRUST, as previously discussed, you can ensure you have a robust security function.

Additionally, healthcare organizations must comply with regulatory requirements, most notably HIPAA Privacy and Security, HITECH Act, and more recently, Information Blocking. [9.2] The HITECH Act was intended to expand the use of electronic health records, but there are additional requirements around privacy and security. More recent information sharing and regulations around data blocking may not seem like a security function, but opening an EHR system to provide data per regulations often brings with it security risks that must be assessed and mitigated.

## IT Project Management

Operations work typically consumes between 20% and 40% of an IT department's time and resources. Project work typically consumes between

60% and 80% of the department's efforts. Therefore, having project management expertise in the IT department is absolutely essential for success. Whether or not you have formal project management structures in place, such as a Project Management Office (PMO) or Project Managers (PMs) on the team, you must have a defined project management process in place to deliver projects on-time, on-budget, and in-scope.

As we discussed in the IT governance chapter, projects should be defined, requested, reviewed, vetted, approved, and prioritized through the IT governance function. In healthcare IT, we often see projects slide in from some hidden side door, and before you know it, project work is underway without proper oversight. The PMO function, in conjunction with the IT governance function, is the most effective way of managing IT demand.

Having a project management process can be as simple as requiring an operational owner, a budget, a charter or scope statement, a task list, and a timeline. You can manage a project using a spreadsheet, a service management system, or a solution specific to project management. The key is to make visible the project efforts so they can be approved, prioritized, and managed, especially when resource contention or project roadblocks arise.

## IT Communication Management

Very often, healthcare IT departments lack any communication management. Information between leaders, among staff, or to/from the organization is fragmented across a multitude of communication channels – email, team channels, text messages, documents, network locations, and individual laptops (spreadsheets, word processing documents, etc.).

Creating and maintaining an IT communication plan and process will help ensure information is correctly communicated to the appropriate stakeholders in a timely manner. There are many ways to accomplish this, but without an intentional plan that is executed with consistency, you will hear your staff (or other staff) complain they don't know what's going on – regardless of how often you communicate. Having a consistent process builds muscle memory, and over time, the complaints about not being informed will subside. For example, sending a link to PMO statistics on a monthly basis or sending a quarterly email to organizational leaders sharing highlights, major accomplishments, and projects underway are common methods used to share IT information with appropriate audiences.

## *Cloud Management*

Cloud management is partially about managing the cloud-based solution itself, which was covered in Chapter 8. However, there's more to managing cloud-based services than the actual technology, which is why we discuss it throughout this book.

Cloud management can include:

1. Selecting cloud solutions
2. Architecting, implementing, and supporting solutions
3. Provisioning and managing user access
4. Managing resource allocation and expansion
5. Managing licensing
6. Managing security
7. Managing data (backups, archives, repatriation at contract termination, etc.)
8. Managing overall costs

If you are like many healthcare IT organizations, you have moved some assets to the cloud, but you may lack cloud technology expertise. Do you have staff on board who are trained, experienced, and/or certified in technologies such as Amazon AWS®, Microsoft Azure®, or Google Cloud®? Moving IT assets to these technologies may (or may not) be the right move for your organization, but without trained and ideally, certified in-house experts, you risk having poorly managed architecture, utilization, data hygiene, cost management, and cybersecurity management, among other things. Cloud-based technologies bring many benefits, but they also bring a host of new challenges that must be addressed.

In your renovation project planning, if you have moved assets to the cloud but you're still stumbling around a bit, you can make plans to improve your expertise in this area or improve your financial management of these engagements, for example. If you have not yet moved to the cloud in any significant way, you can use the renovation phase to plan what skills and capabilities you'll need in order to achieve success in such a migration. This continues to be a rapidly evolving body of knowledge, so you'll need to get current quickly or engage with a trusted third-party vendor to assist you in this process.

## *DevOps/Agile*

DevOps is a combination of development and operations. It's typically used to describe the intersection of software development and ITOps. Though most healthcare IT organizations are not in the business of developing software, almost all are in the business of configuring and managing software. For example, most organizations using an EHR are deeply involved in analyzing end user workflows and building configurations in the system to reflect those desired workflows. Whether that's how a patient visit is structured or how claims data flows out and back, the EHR must be configured to optimize how the organization provides care. In that respect, every healthcare IT organization is involved in the development of systems. The goal of DevOps is to shorten the software delivery cycle time and provide continuous delivery of high-quality software.

DevOps is often used in conjunction with the term Agile. According to software firm, Atlassian, DevOps and Agile relate to each other in this manner:

> "DevOps is an approach to software development that enables teams to build, test, and release software faster and more reliably by incorporating agile principles and practices, such as increased automation and improved collaboration between development and operations teams. Development, testing, and deployment occur in both agile and DevOps. Yet traditional agile stops short of operations, which is an integral part of DevOps." [9.3]

When you're looking at your software management practices, you may want to explore DevOps and Agile methodologies. They can help you deliver better results at a more rapid pace for your customers. For example, one healthcare IT team organized their EHR analysts' work around agile methods and began delivering fixes and new solutions to the organization every two weeks instead of every three months during an upgrade. This more consistent value creation helped end users get what they needed faster and re-enforced IT's reputation as a value-added business partner instead of a department that simply said "wait in line."

## Vendor Management

All IT departments should have a strong vendor management process in place, yet many do not. Vendors come in all shapes and sizes, some reputable and helpful, some less so. Some vendors will give as little as possible and stick to the letter of the contract; others will go above and beyond to help ensure your success. Which vendors do you want to work with?

Having a defined process for finding, evaluating, engaging, contracting, and managing vendors is an important IT function. Knowing who your vendors are, what their expertise is, what their reputation is, and how to best leverage their capabilities will help you get more from each engagement and ensure you're driving value for the dollars spent.

In concert with vendor management is contract management, which should be a core competency for your team. Reviewing contracts, understanding the operational implications, and understanding what remedies are in place in case things go wrong is crucial. Many organizations have found themselves locked into a contract with a poorly performing vendor without any defined remedies for resolution. Contracts should always be written assuming the worst-case scenario will occur. When vendor relationships go well, the contract almost never gets pulled out and referenced. When things do go wrong, the contract is the only legal recourse either party has, so ensuring you have favorable (or at least well-defined) terms in your IT contracts is very important. Even if your legal team reviews all contracts, and they should, they can only tell you what the contract says or intends legally. They can't tell you how it will impact your operations, so you'll need to ensure you've considered how contractual terms could impact your ITOps.

Vendor management also includes consultants, temporary labor, and contractors. Ensuring the terms are clear and enforceable will drive success. When developing Statements of Work (SOWs), you should have clear deliverables, costs, resources, timelines, expectations, scope (what is and is not covered), and acceptance criteria (if applicable) for these engagements. The more specific the SOWs, the greater the likelihood the vendor will deliver exactly what you're expecting.

# IT Service Management (ITSM)

ITOM and ITSM have many common connecting points. Specific to service management are processes and metrics related to providing service to end users, as depicted at the outset of this chapter in Figure 9.1.

## *Service Request Management Process*

We know that having standardized, repeatable processes for ITSM is the key both to providing outstanding service to the organization and keeping your teams organized and productive. Service management applies to requests for applications, software enhancements, hardware upgrades, new user requests, or modifications to user access, for example. Many service requests can be automated. A service request excludes incidents, problems, and projects.

## Service Delivery Metrics

The saying *you can't manage what you don't measure* is very true in IT. Of course, the counterpoint is that you can spend more time managing metrics than doing the work. There is a reasonable middle ground most healthcare IT organizations find. Most often, HIT teams define and monitor key metrics that reflect the quality of the service being provided to the organization. The metrics you select have a lot to do with how your organization runs. A few commonly used metrics include:

1. Percent uptime of key systems
2. Number and duration of unplanned downtimes
3. % assets encrypted
4. % assets patched to current levels
5. Number and percent of issues caused by IT changes
6. End user satisfaction levels
7. First call resolution rates
8. Average time to resolution for key technologies
9. % Service level adherence
10. % of incidents for which root cause is identified
11. % projects received through governance process
12. % projects completed on time, on budget, in scope

Selecting metrics that matter to the organization is important, and these can often be reviewed through the governance process. Bringing forward a set of proposed metrics for monitoring and measuring, much the way HC organizations do with clinical quality metrics, can be a great way to engage your end users and make the work of the IT department more transparent. Measuring progress against defined metrics and reporting those out shows the organization your commitment to improving the work you deliver in much the same way operations does.

## Knowledge Management Process

Knowledge management can be a broad topic, but in this context, we're looking at two specific meanings. First, managing the knowledge of the IT department is crucial. Many healthcare IT organizations still operate with the hero syndrome – one or two really competent people swoop in to save the day when things go wrong – because knowledge is in their heads. It's not documented, and it's rarely shared. This creates a significant risk to an organization and should be eliminated through requiring more senior staff to share knowledge with the team via creating knowledge base articles or through team training sessions.

All modern service management software tools include some form of knowledge management function. Some knowledge articles are intended only for IT technical staff (such as how to harden a server), and some are intended for end users (such as how to reset a password or clear a printer jam). Creating content for both internal and external use should be part of your development of your service delivery capabilities. When end users can resolve basic issues on their own, such as resetting a forgotten password, they can get back to work sooner and don't have to wait on hold or wait for someone to be assigned their request via the ticketing system. Providing a self-service portal as part of your service delivery function can be an excellent way to improve end-user satisfaction (for those who choose self-service) and reduce IT staff effort on basic support tasks.

In addition to technical knowledge management, your team also may be responsible for the organization's intranet, using some form of internal website software. Often, organizations use intranet sites for storing and sharing organization-wide information. Typically, these collections of sites grow organically, are not curated, and end up becoming large, unwieldy, and convoluted sites. It can be challenging for IT to manage the organization's intranet if there are no assigned organizational content owners. Managing your intranet site(s) is beyond the scope of this book, but it is an effort you may want to consider as part of your longer-term IT renovation efforts if there is no other department responsible for managing your intranet.

## Incident Management Process

ITSM defines an *incident* as an unplanned event, such as a service interruption. Multiple incidents are referred to as a *problem*, described next. Effective incident management requires an IT department to have standard, documented, and repeatable processes for addressing incidents. The objective is to restore the element (hardware and software) to its required operational state as quickly as possible without breaking anything else. Given the complexity of healthcare IT environments, the number of failure points rises almost exponentially annually. The use of cloud-based systems adds a layer of complexity to incident management that must be factored into the operational model.

If the incident is related to a cyberattack, you will need to invoke your cybersecurity incident response plan, which is much broader in scope than a standard IT incident. A cybersecurity attack can at first appear to be an isolated incident, so having clear definitions in place around how to identify a single incident from a cyberattack and which steps are appropriate in each scenario is vital. We'll discuss cybersecurity and incident response separately.

## *Problem Management Process*

Multiple incidents are defined as a problem. Problem management is the process of identifying and resolving the underlying causes of related IT incidents. This includes examining root cause via an after-action review (often referred to as a Root Cause Analysis, RCA). Without a retrospective review of problems, IT organizations will fail to grow and improve over time. As an IT leader, there are few things more frustrating or embarrassing than continually 'fixing' something that should have been addressed through an RCA analysis and remediation plan. If you find your team battling the same types of issues and problems repeatedly, you will want to pay particular attention to your incident and problem management processes during your renovation work. You'll get an opportunity to assess your capabilities in this regard in the next section of the book.

## *Change Management Process*

One of the most powerful processes in most healthcare IT departments today is (or should be) the change management process. In this case, we are referring to managing changes to electronic systems vs. organizational change management, which is discussed in Chapter 29. Even if you have challenges with other standardized processes, you should have a rock-solid change management process. In some organizations, all changes to applications go through one change management process, while all infrastructure changes go through another. That can work if there is strong linkage between these two process teams. However, it is also likely that the infrastructure team may approve a change that they think only impacts infrastructure, only to find out they took down a critical interface or application by accident. Therefore, it's wise to have all changes reviewed by one change management body, even if apps and infrastructure changes are reviewed in separate meetings. Wide visibility to changes is critical so errors and unintended consequences of change are minimized.

In addition, the change management process should provide context and transparency so changes are successfully implemented, and if there are issues, changes are backed out quickly and successfully. It is very common for IT changes to cause errors. You know from your troubleshooting experience that when something breaks, the first question everyone asks is, "What changed?" So, having a solid change management process in place can reduce these kinds of errors and speed time to recovery if something does go wrong.

## Summary

We covered a lot of ground in this chapter and reviewed some of the more common elements of ITOps and service management. HIT departments must manage internal operations extremely well in order to deliver excellent service to end users. Ultimately, everything done in IT supports the delivery of patient care. Having a stable, reliable network and EHR, having printers that print and faxes that fax, having working phones, and usable reports are all part of delivering patient care. Understanding how excellence in IT supports and enhances patient care will go a long way in demonstrating the value of IT in your organization. Yet, there are no doubt many opportunities to improve your internal operations and service delivery that will be invisible to your end users. In the assessment chapter, you'll have the chance to look across your IT landscape and identify where you have the biggest opportunities for improvement. You can focus your initial renovation efforts on those and then create a plan for continuous improvement over time.

## References

[9.1] U.S. Government National Institute of Standards and Technologies (NIST), NIST Cybersecurity Framework, CSF Version 1.1, February 12, 2014, https://www.nist.gov/cyberframework, accessed July 21, 2023.
[9.2] National Archives Code of Federal Regulations, Information Blocking, Title 45, Subtitle A, Subchapter D, Part 171, Subpart A, 171.103, "Information blocking," last updated February 2, 2023, https://www.ecfr.gov/current/title-45/subtitle-A/subchapter-D/part-171/subpart-A/section-171.103, accessed February 5, 2023.
[9.3] Hall, Tom, "DevOps vs. Agile," no date, https://www.atlassian.com/devops/what-is-devops/agile-vs-devops, accessed February 5, 2023.

# Resources

Fruhlinger, Josh, "HITRUST explained: One framework to rule them all," May 31, 2021, https://www.csoonline.com/article/3619534/hitrust-explained-one-framework-to-rule-them-all.html, accessed February 5, 2023.

Holtsnider, Bill, Brian D. Jaffe, IT Manager's Handbook: Getting Your New Job Done, San Francisco, CA, Morgan Kaufmann Publishers, 2001.

U.S. Government, Federal Emergency Management Agency (FEMA), last updated November 29, 2022, https://www.fema.gov/emergency-managers/nims, accessed February 5, 2023.

Wager, Karen A., Frances W. Lee, John P. Glaser, Health Care Information Systems: A Practical Approach for Health Care Management, Fifth Edition, Hoboken, NJ, John Wiley & Sons, Inc., 2022.

# Chapter 10

# Business Intelligence and Data Analytics Building Blocks

The ultimate goal of business intelligence (BI) and data analytics (DA) is to provide a comprehensive set of organizational data to enable better, faster, more accurate decisions for all facets of the business. It means being flexible and agile, being well-governed to ensure the confidentiality, integrity, and availability of organizational data, and providing viable end-user self-service options.

A detailed discussion of BI is outside the scope of this book. This section is intended only as a brief overview of the BI function in healthcare. We've included a diverse list of references you can review in the Resources section at the end of this chapter.

## Data in Healthcare

Data is becoming increasingly important in the competitive landscape. According to a recent Forrester Consulting study, "businesses that rely on data management tools to make decisions are 58% more likely to beat their revenue goals than non-data-driven companies. And data-driven organizations are 162% more likely to significantly surpass revenue goals than their laggard counterparts." [10.1]

Reliable, secure data in healthcare is vital to delivering care. From analyzing population health metrics for value-based care reimbursement to analyzing workloads or emergency room demand patterns, all healthcare organizations need to become proficient in the use of data. Using data,

DOI: 10.4324/9781003377023-12

however, is only part of the equation. Ensuring data is reliable, secure, and actionable is equally important. That's where BI, DA, and data management come in. For more on IT and data governance, you can refer to the material in Chapter 5. We'll touch on artificial intelligence (AI) and machine learning (ML) only briefly. A full discussion of those technologies in healthcare is outside the scope of this book. However, the renovation work you do will set a solid foundation for the implementation and management of AI and ML in your organization going forward.

Broadly speaking, BI is the collection of methods, tools, and technologies that support business and DA. There are generally four major types of DA: *descriptive, diagnostic, predictive,* and *prescriptive. Descriptive* identifies trends and relationships using historical data and describes a current (or prior) state. *Diagnostic* analytics describes processes used to query data to ask why something happened or an event occurred. *Predictive* uses historical and current data and extrapolates data to predict possible future outcomes. *Prescriptive* uses historical and current data and helps answer the question, "what *should* we do?" In essence, you're asking the data to help guide your future actions.

The market has evolved and many cloud-based solutions currently can provide analytics, visualization, and cloud-based infrastructure to accelerate the development of advanced BI solutions.

On the more technical side, there are three segments: *content creators, consumers,* and *managers.* Content is generated by individuals in the organization (or sometimes through pulling in external data via an interface). Consumers are those individuals in the organization who use the data. Managers, in this context, are typically those in the IT department who create and manage various data storage solutions such as enterprise data warehouses (EDW) and data marts that present data to the consumers in a usable manner. The IT team typically is responsible for pulling data in from many sources and storing it in a usable manner. This process is referred to as extract, transform, and load (ETL). BI can be as simple as an end user having access to data they pull into a spreadsheet and format into a pivot table, or it can be as complex as creating a large report from multiple data sources into an intermediate database so it can be further transformed to meet a regulatory reporting requirement, for example.

The primary activities related to stored data are:

1. Access and view data
2. Interact with the data
3. Validate the data

4. Analyze and develop insights
5. Share
6. Govern

Ideally, the BI function in healthcare leads to faster, more accurate answers to questions such as "What's driving up our average length of stay?" or "Which patient populations are under-represented in our vaccination program?" The BI function can also be used to leverage data sets to identify trends or even predict outcomes that might benefit from an intervention. For example, looking at which patients have A1C blood glucose levels that have risen over the past 12 months and which interventions have proven most effective at reducing those levels in various demographic groups could provide actionable insights for modifying patient outreach programs. These types of insights can be found through effective data analysis using various BI tools.

As healthcare continues to generate massive volumes of data, it will be increasingly important to have a strong BI/DA function, including data governance, to collect, curate, and secure the data. Much of that data will become the source of key organizational decisions that ultimately drive your digital transformation initiatives, so getting this right is very important. Assessing and developing your capabilities along these lines will help support your long-term success.

# Centralized BI vs. Decentralized BI

A centralized BI function is one in which all data is managed through a single function, usually the IT function. This means that all data is centrally managed, including user's access to reports. Often, this means the BI team will develop reports, both as projects and as ad hoc requests, to supply the data needed by the organization. Decentralized BI is where some or all of the reporting functions reside outside the central group (IT). End users create, store, and manage data independently.

## *Centralized BI*

A centralized model has strengths and weaknesses. The strengths are that the data and data sources are managed through a single team that has expertise in the management of data. That team is responsible for implementing software solutions to properly manage data (especially the storage and management of that data) and for using the data to create reports for the organization. These reports may be related to large, complex initiatives where the reporting function may take months to create and fulfill the need. These reports could be recurring regulatory reports or operational reports that, once built, are automatically generated, and distributed to end users. Examples include month-end financial reports, encounter reports, length-of-stay trends, and just about anything else a healthcare end user might need to track and measure. Finally, these reports could be simple ad hoc reports a user needs on any given day. Getting data from a dedicated data team helps ensure data definitions are standardized, that data is clean, reliable, and accurate, and that reports are generated in a manner that lends credibility to the end result (i.e. reports are trusted to be accurate).

This can also reduce redundancy, reduce costs, and improve the security of the data. When all enterprise data is stored in systems that have been specifically built for this purpose, data typically is better managed. The cost of centralized data repositories is typically less expensive and more secure than having a lot of little pockets of data housed across the organization.

The downside of centralized BI is that everything has to flow through a single team, which makes it a potential bottleneck. Report requests have to be validated and prioritized by the team, which sometimes causes less critical reports to get pushed back and delayed repeatedly. This creates a poor experience for the end user who "just needs a simple report," but who can't seem to get their need prioritized against the many other reports needed across the organization. If the BI team is large enough, this may not be an issue, but it often ends up being one of the primary complaints of this model. These delays and frustrations are often one source of the proliferation of shadow IT. When end users cannot get the data they need, they often take matters into their own hands. A slow, bureaucratic, centralized function will invariably lead to IT functions happening outside of IT.

## *Decentralized BI*

A decentralized BI function is one in which the data is created, stored, and managed by teams or departments across the enterprise. For example, HR might maintain their own data repositories and run their own reports related to compensation, benefits, paid time off, etc. The supply chain function might have their own data stores; clinical leaders might set up their own databases in order to run reports related to functions in their areas.

The upside to this is end users often know exactly what data they need, so defining their data needs doesn't have to go through an IT team that might need to learn the details of that request. End users also have real-time access to data and can often get their ad hoc reporting needs met very quickly, resulting in higher end-user satisfaction.

The downside, of course, is that these systems are not centrally managed, so there's the risk of duplication of data as well as data disparities. Imagine a scenario where two departments are tracking the same metric but they're measuring it differently. For example, hospitals always monitor average daily census data. Perhaps the Emergency Department is tracking it from midnight to midnight, but the ICU, which might transfer patients to step-down units at 11 in the morning tracks it from noon to noon. Both will report their data, and those metrics will be accurate for that department, but it does not sync up across the organization. This is one of the primary risks of a decentralized BI function. As an executive at a HC organization, having a single, verified source of data is of utmost importance, especially when reports are provided to a Board of Directors, to regulatory agencies, or to governmental agencies.

As enterprise EHR systems, along with other enterprise applications such as finance, supply chain, and HR, grow in capabilities and complexity, there is some danger in decentralizing BI. If BI is managed in individual departments, it can be difficult to get consistent data across the enterprise. Additionally, data may be redundant, poorly sourced, or out of sync with master data stores. This is the issue of *divergence* discussed previously. When a healthcare CEO asks for a report and gets two different answers from two different sources, it calls into question the entire data set. In addition, redundancy often leads to higher costs as server, storage, and compute needs are spun up across the enterprise without IT oversight.

Finally, and just as important, data decentralization can create significant security risks if data sets are not properly managed in terms of users' access, storage, backups, interfaces, encryption, and monitoring.

Another consideration is that most end users are not experts at setting up database structures, ensuring data is well-defined and managed. As data proliferates to the far corners of the organization, the risk of data loss, data breach, and data theft increases exponentially – not because end users are bad but because the security and monitoring mechanisms needed to keep that data secure are often completely absent from these decentralized solutions. Data that flows to different storage solutions across the enterprise may also drift outside the organization, creating potential legal and regulatory problems.

## *Hybrid BI Model*

Perhaps the more ideal model is a semi-centralized BI function where the EDW is managed by IT and access to business analysts is provided through data access tools. These tools are full-featured and allow analysts to easily analyze, aggregate, share, and visualize data sets. This method ensures business data analysts have full access to needed data while enterprise data is managed by the IT team. It can also help control data quality and consistency as all groups pull data from the same verified and validated sources. It can also reduce costs and improve security across the enterprise.

In healthcare, where there are significant regulatory and financial implications related to the management of data, having a centralized approach to managing the data and a decentralized approach to providing access to those analyzing the data may be the most optimal.

As you examine your organization's BI environment, you'll need to look at your EHR and other enterprise applications to determine if your current structure is the best solution for the way you operate. You'll need to assess the creation, management, access, and security of these data sets to ensure you meet regulatory (HIPAA, etc.), cybersecurity, and organizational data needs effectively.

In Chapter 22, where we discuss the assessment of these capabilities, we'll discuss methods for evaluating how well your company uses analytics, how mature your BI function is, and what you'll need to do to advance these capabilities.

# Collections of Data

There are a number of different ways data are collected and managed. In particular, the terms "data warehouse," "data lakes," and "data hubs" are often used interchangeably, but they are not the same. Each has specific use cases. As you renovate your BI function, you may want to take a deeper dive into this area of knowledge because it continues to evolve rapidly. We'll briefly discuss three of the commonly used structures here.

## *Enterprise Data Warehouse*

An EDW is designed to contain structured, well-defined historical data. It's most often used for running analytical queries and should be designed for fast, repetitive work. Because the data is well-structured, an EDW supports complex queries, often using SQL, often for common business reporting needs.

In order for reliable data to be added to an EDW, you need to spend a fair amount of time ensuring your data is cleaned and transformed through the ETL process. This takes time and effort on the front-end, but facilitates fast, accurate reporting on the back-end. For this reason, EDWs are not well-suited for business process reporting that relies on real-time data.

## Data Lakes

Data lakes hold large volumes of data, both structured and unstructured (lacking defined structure or schema), from a variety of sources. Data in a lake is usually less strictly managed (i.e. not curated) than EDW data. As a result, data may be duplicated or lack the structure of an EDW. The best uses of data lakes typically include things like discovery or initial analysis. Since the data is unstructured and unfiltered, it's not a reliable source for final data. Data in a data lake typically needs to be cleaned up before use in analysis and decision-making, but a data lake can be a good sandbox environment.

## Data Hubs

Data hubs are collections of data from many sources, including EDWs, data lakes, streaming data sources, or operational data stores, for example. Data is highly structured and has been improved through the ETL process. The ETL process ensures that data from multiple sources is combined, transformed into a common format, and loaded (stored) in a storage solution such as an EDW. Data hubs are typically used by one or more business applications. A digital integration hub (DIH) aggregates subsets of data from multiple sources and systems. It can also synchronize changes made to data back to the connected applications. Essentially, DIH is a very powerful data access layer that supports real-time business data processing.

Most healthcare organizations are using some form of EDW, some may be using data lakes as well. The use of data hubs and the underlying technologies (in-memory data grids, or IMDG) are less common and may be found more often in academic or research medical settings for now.

## Using the Right Technology

Understanding the way data and data management technologies are evolving is important as you build your BI function. You may have built various capabilities over the past decade and now find they are not purpose-built or suitable for your current or future needs. So, you may need to renovate these before you are ready to evolve the function. In some cases, you may have to rip-and-replace so you don't keep patching a solution that ultimately is not well-suited to your data needs. As you likely know, every database type has its strengths and weaknesses, which is why specific types are used for different purposes. Big data essentially follows a similar pattern. Each format or structure has specific use cases, and if you don't have the correct structures in place, you'll struggle to meet the data demands of the organization.

## Data Management

We discussed data management briefly in Chapter 5, but we'll dig down into a bit more detail here. Data management is the body of knowledge around managing all aspects of organizational data, from data architecture to storage, security to data dictionaries, and more. As mentioned, BI is more than just data management, but data management is at the heart of having a robust BI function. In essence, a strong BI function relies on a sound data management function. Data analysts and end-user report writers can become very frustrated with the BI function if the data are not well-managed. It can waste valuable time and resources and what's lacking in data management is often made up for in reporting "work arounds," which is the least efficient and highest-risk way to address data needs. For example, pulling data from a less suitable source and 'massaging' it to meet a specific reporting need is not uncommon, but it's also not an ideal scenario for all the reasons we've discussed in this chapter.

Once data quality is assured through strong data management processes, the BI function can really begin to deliver significant value to the organization.

The Data Management Association International (DAMA) has created a Data Management Body of Knowledge (DAMA-DMBOK2) that provides excellent detail around managing data, much the same way the well-known Project Management Book of Knowledge (PMBOK) details process excellence around project management. We'll briefly touch on the DAMA elements here. For more information, refer to the References section at the end of this chapter.

The Data Governance wheel, from DAMA, shown in Figure 10.1, depicts the key elements of data management and provides a good high-level view of

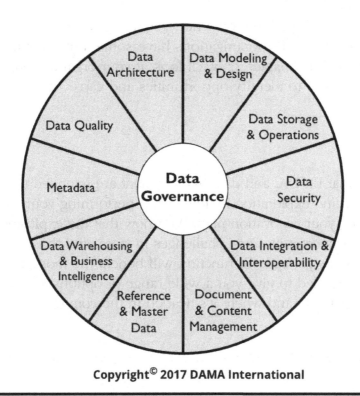

Copyright© 2017 DAMA International

**Figure 10.1   DAMA DMBOK2 wheel image (10.2).**

the required elements. There's an updated version that is a bit more complex, so if you're interested, visit the DAMA website listed in the Resources section at the end of this chapter to review their most current materials.

The data governance process includes these ten elements:

1. Data architecture
2. Data modeling & design
3. Data storage & operations
4. Data security
5. Data integration & interoperability
6. Document & content management
7. Reference & master data
8. Data warehousing & BI
9. Metadata
10. Data quality

From data architecture to storage and operations; from security to content management; from data dictionaries to metadata, all aspects of data management must be addressed when you're working with enterprise data. Many healthcare IT organizations have some, but not all, of these elements in place. In Chapter 22, we'll look at your organization and your management of data to identify opportunities and gaps.

## Summary

This brief look at BI, DA, and data management are intended to prompt further inquiry and exploration in advance of performing your assessment and developing your renovation plan. We know that the explosion of data has both opportunities and challenges in store, and those who can develop a rigorous yet agile BI function will benefit the most. The Resources included are intended to give you a wide range of options for exploring where BI/DA is today and where it's headed in the coming years.

## References

[10.1] Papudesu, Chandra, Vice President of Product Management, Catalog, and Lineage at Collibra, "How a data catalog can help your business reach new heights," January 7, 2021, https://www.dbta.com/Editorial/Trends-and-Applications/How-a-Data-Catalog-Can-Help-Your-Business-Reach-New-Heights-144574.aspx, accessed February 4, 2023.

[10.2] DAMA Wheel Image, https://www.dama.org/cpages/dmbok-2-wheel-images, accessed November 28, 2022.

## Resources

Ackerman, Beth and Paul Christensen, "Define your data strategy," https://www.ibm.com/garage/method/practices/think/define-data-strategy/, accessed October 29, 2022.

Averdunk, Ivan, "Clarify roles and responsibilities by using a RACI matrix," https://www.ibm.com/garage/method/practices/manage/raci-matrix/, accessed July 18, 2023.

Data Management Organization, no date, DAMA.org, accessed November 28, 2022.

Davenport, Thomas H., Randy Bean, and Shail Jain, "Why your company needs data-product managers," October 13, 2022, https://hbr.org/2022/10/why-your-company-needs-data-product-managers, accessed October 29, 2022.

Desai, Veeral, Tim Fountaine, and Kayvaun Rowshankish, "A better way to put your data to work," July-August 2022, HBR.org, https://hbr.org/2022/07/a-better-way-to-put-your-data-to-workorg), accessed October 29, 2022.

Earley, S., & Henderson, D., Sebastian-Coleman, L (Eds.). The DAMA Guide to the Data Management Body of Knowledge (DAMA-DM BOK). Bradley Beach, NJ: Technics Publications, LLC. 2017.

Fishman, Neal, "Establish data governance," no date, https://www.ibm.com/garage/method/practices/manage/establish-data-governance, accessed October 29, 2022.

Ivanov, Nikita, "Digital transformation and the role of data hubs, data lakes and data warehouses," August 21, 2020, https://www.forbes.com/sites/forbestechcouncil/2020/08/21/digital-transformation-and-the-role-of-data-hubs-data-lakes-and-data-warehouses/, accessed January 4, 2023.

Natarajan, Prashant, John C. Frenzel, Detlev H. Smaltz, Demystifying Big Data and Machine Learning for Healthcare (HIMSS Book) 1st Edition, Boca Raton, FL, CRC Press, 2017.

Sainam, Preethika, Seigyoung Auh, Richard Ettenson, and Yeon Sung Jung, "How well does your company use analytics," July 27, 2022, https://hbr.org/2022/07/how-well-does-your-company-use-analytics, accessed January 28, 2023.

Sebastian-Coleman, Ph.D., Laura, Navigating the Labyrinth: An Executive Guide to Data Management, Technics Publications, Basking Ridge, NJ, 2018.

Wager, Karen A., Frances W. Lee, and John P. Glaser, Health Care Information Systems, A Practical Approach for Health Care Management, Fifth Edition, Hoboken, NJ, John Wiley & Sons, Inc., 2022.

*Chapter 11*

# IT Business Continuity and Disaster Recovery Building Blocks

Business continuity (BC) and disaster recovery (DR) are the plans and processes to ensure the enterprise can run in the event of a disruptive occurrence such as a fire, flood, or cyberattack. BC from an organizational perspective includes things like how to run a hospital in the midst of a pandemic or how to continue operations if there's a supply chain problem, a burst pipe in the ceiling of a patient care area, or an extended EHR downtime due to a network malfunction or cyberattack.

BC includes DR as one element. Some organizations refer simply to BC to include the entire spectrum of disruptions and recovery plans; others have separate BC and DR plans. So, you may see references to a BC plan (BCP) or a BC/DR plan. In both cases, scenarios that can disrupt operations are assessed, mitigation plans are developed, and the plan contains the detailed information to guide the organization through potential disruptive events.

From an IT perspective, we are focusing on how we keep the business running in the face of various disruptive events, some of which may be disasters, some of which may not be. A successful cyberattack that takes down key infrastructure is a disaster event. An Internet connection from one Internet service vendor going down is typically viewed as a disruptive event. In order to ensure business operations can continue to run without interruption, such an event might require network traffic to be rerouted to prevent an overload of existing circuits, for example.

DOI: 10.4324/9781003377023-13

BC refers to all events that could potentially disrupt business operations, from minor to major events.

The high-level elements in every BCP are:

1. Risk assessment
2. Business impact analysis (BIA)
3. Risk mitigation strategies
4. BC/DR plan development
5. Emergency response and recovery
6. Testing, training, and auditing
7. Plan maintenance

We will discuss each very briefly here and use these elements when we perform our assessment in Chapter 23.

## Risk Assessment

The first step in developing a BCP is to understand your current state. Typically, you perform a risk assessment specific to IT to understand the environment in which you are operating. A hospital or hospital system has different IT risks than a large provider group or a community health center with thirty clinics across three states. This assessment includes threats and vulnerabilities. Threats are typically defined as things that could harm the organization. Vulnerabilities are typically defined as the weaknesses an organization has, often specific to identified threats. When threats and vulnerabilities line up, attackers have a much higher chance for a successful attack. For example, phishing is a universal threat. End users who are not trained to spot phishing emails could be considered a vulnerability. So, too, could email systems that are not up-to-date or those that lack any sort of spam/phish blocking automation. By identifying threats and then looking at whether the organization is vulnerable to those threats, you can focus your efforts on things that are most likely to impact the organization.

Incidents or events that can damage or impair IT functions can have adverse impacts on the organization. Typically, once risks are identified, they are assessed in terms of the likelihood for that risk to occur and the impact should it occur. For example, a tsunami is a catastrophic event, but the likelihood of that occurring in areas that are far from any ocean would be zero. So, if you're working in Kansas, you would not consider the risk of tsunamis, but you would consider other natural disaster scenarios such as the risk of tornadoes. In the risk mitigation strategy activity of BC planning (later in this chapter), you can use the likelihood and impact assessment to determine which risks you need to plan mitigation strategies around and which ones you can accept or omit.

## Business Impact Analysis

Next, you perform a business impact analysis (BIA), which starts with understanding all the electronic systems in place. This document is really the backbone of your BCP, so you should spend adequate time and effort on it as it will pay dividends later.

In Chapter 8, we reviewed IT technology systems, so we won't repeat that here. However, you should include all the technology components in your list. We've talked about creating and maintaining a full inventory of systems and this is yet another reason that supports such an effort. Once you have a list, you assess the criticality of the item along with the required recovery time. For example, if your network is down or one of your security systems is down, that might be considered Priority 0, which means no other work is done until these core infrastructure components are recovered. Enterprise applications, including the EHR (or perhaps only the EHR), would be considered Priority 1. This would mean that if infrastructure is up and running, nothing has a higher priority for recovery.

A thorough BIA should contain these elements at a minimum:

1. Identify all critical systems and processes.
2. Identify the operational owner of each system.
3. Understand the criticality of the system.
4. Identify the backup strategy (location, frequency, security, encryption, verification, and recovery).
5. Based on risk assessment, identify mission-critical, important, and minor business functions.
6. Identify system dependencies.
7. Identify potential upstream and downstream losses.
8. Identify the maximum tolerable data loss.
9. Identify the maximum tolerable recovery time.
10. Identify alternatives (can payroll be processed manually, is there a vendor to whom calls could be routed, etc.).

11. Identify mitigation strategies for all critical and important systems, where possible.
12. Identify the priority of recovery for all systems with associated financial and operational impact.
13. Identify the location of technical information about each system.
14. Identify the IT subject matter experts responsible for recovering the system.
15. Identify the method for validating the recovery (data, operations, etc.).

These elements are incorporated into your BCP.

## Risk Mitigation Strategies

Expanding on your risk assessment, you should develop strategies to minimize organizational risk related to the risks identified. The likelihood and impact of each identified risk should drive your efforts around mitigation. More effort should be expended identifying risk mitigation strategies for the most likely and highest impact risks. Figure 11.1 shows

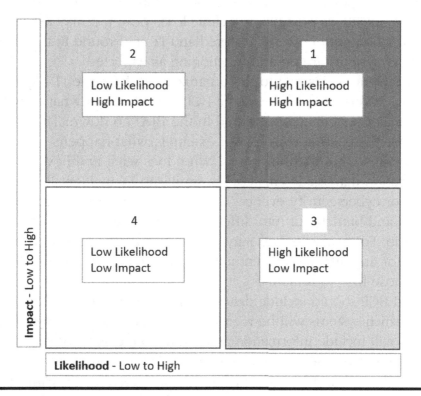

**Figure 11.1    Likelihood/impact matrix.**

a likelihood/risk matrix. Risks can be mitigated, avoided, transferred, or accepted. Your risk mitigation strategies should document decisions around these risk management activities for identified risks.

Most organizations prioritize creating risk mitigation strategies for Box 1 then Box 2 and 3. Some organizations choose not to identify risk mitigation strategies for items in Box 4, focusing instead on the highest likelihood and impact items only. How you approach it is a matter of organizational risk management philosophy and policy. From an IT perspective, you are best positioned to assess potential IT risks and address them through a variety of mitigation strategies.

# BC/DR Plan Development

A good healthcare IT BC plan should tie into the organization's BCP. If the organization has plans for what they would do if a building floods or a clinic loses power, IT should have plans for how IT systems would be managed in those same scenarios. For example, if an area of a building floods, the main power should be shut off, and all IT systems should be removed as quickly as possible. If a clinic loses power, it may require no specific IT action until power is restored and IT staff round in the clinic to ensure all IT systems are on and functioning as expected.

Beyond the activities tied to the organization's BCP, the IT department should have a very clear and specific BCP that identifies what IT will do when major systems (as identified in the BIA) go down. This should include specific timeline metrics. For example, what happens in the first 30 minutes? The first four hours? Who does what and how is communication managed? This is very similar to IT Incident Response planning for cybersecurity events. The plan can leverage the same workflows and branch out into different decision trees depending on the scenario. For example, you may choose to set 30 minutes as the first threshold for any disruptive event and define the specific actions to be taken in those first 30 minutes.

A sound BCP should include detailed information from the BIA that indicates which systems will be recovered, in what order, and by what method. It will include information about how to recover systems and how to resume work. Recovery is not just an IT function. In healthcare, especially, recovery must be a coordinated effort between IT, clinical, and operational leaders to ensure the tight coordination and sequencing of system recovery, testing, validation, data entry (or catch-up work), and resumption of normal operations.

For disaster scenarios, such as a cyberattack or a major system outage, a clear plan for invoking an incident response plan should be defined. Once a disaster or incident is declared, there should be a very clear and well-documented set of steps IT will take to begin to assess the situation, get it under control, notify the organization (and possibly law enforcement agencies), and develop remediation plans.

## Emergency Response and Recovery

Regardless of how well your plan is written or how well you assess your options, no event will ever go to plan. That is why it's critical to ensure you have both a well-documented plan and a practice schedule. Drills should include the most likely disruptive events called out in your BCP or BC/DR plan. This may include practicing various incident response scenarios related to cyber events. When the disruptive or disaster event occurs, you should have a well-practiced response. If you have ever talked with first responders, they always say that they just do what they are trained to do. While it does not make their actions any less heroic, it's true that they train these scenarios over and over to make their actions almost second nature. So even when things don't pan out exactly the way they did in the drills, a well-rehearsed team will have practice experience that helps them make better decisions if they need to deviate from the plan.

## Testing, Training, and Auditing

Your BIA and BCP can be somewhat time consuming to compile, and for that reason, many healthcare IT departments have very basic plans or no plans at all. Once you have a plan, put it to the test through tabletop drills, training sessions and auditing both the plan and the response. Check that your assumptions are correct and that your plan is workable. You can test your plan in conjunction with organization-wide BC drills as well. Some organizations use an IT event as the basis for their enterprise BC drills at least annually to ensure everyone knows what to do in a downtime event, whether from an outage or a cyber-attack. Auditing the plan entails ensuring the plan is current and reflects actual state. Auditing also involves ensuring your team can recover key systems in the timeframes and via the methods outlined in the BCP. The technology landscape in every HC organization is constantly changing so auditing the BCP is an important activity to ensure the plan remains viable.

## Plan Maintenance

Finally, review and update your plan regularly. The plan should be updated any time you make a substantial change to your IT systems. For example, if you acquire a new hospital, open a new clinic, implement a new enterprise software solution, or re-configure your network architecture, your plan should be updated to reflect these changes. Adding a task to your change management process to review/revised the BCP, when appropriate, can help remind your team of major changes that should prompt review of the BCP.

Barring any new IT elements, you should review your plan at least annually. You will find that it is much easier to update the plan annually than to allow it to become outdated. At that point, you'd have to basically start over again, so maintaining the plan is the more effective approach. In the annual review, you'll add the new features or functions you've implemented, remove the old systems you've decommissioned, and verify the existence of current backups, encryption, security controls, etc. This process should take fewer than 20 hours per year and it's a small investment for a large security measure.

In the BC/DR assessment chapter, we'll use these elements to assess the capability maturity of your BC/DR plans so you can add specific improvement tasks to your renovation project as needed.

## Cloud Solutions

Many organizations use cloud solutions, in part, to mitigate risk. Having cloud-based solutions enables companies to rely on vendors to manage redundancy, high-availability, backups, recovery, and security among other things. However, it is important as an IT leader to be extremely clear about what your cloud solutions include and exclude. For example, some cloud solutions simply rent you hardware and possibly the operating system. You're responsible for configuring, deploying, maintaining, and securing your environment. If that's the case, your BC/DR planning should include how you'll manage unexpected downtimes within this solution or platform. Alternatively, you may be purchasing a complete end-to-end solution from a vendor that includes the hardware, operating system, software, backups, redundancy, and security. If that is the case, you may be set. Be sure to have every contract for every solution on hand. Read each contract and all Statements of Work (SOWs) carefully to determine what is included and what you can expect in the way of vendor response times. If you have a cyber event, what are the vendor's responsibilities? What are yours? Do you know? For each vendor, you should have a very clear summary document that spells these things out. This should be included in your BC/DR plan and should be regularly reviewed as your cloud solutions evolve over time.

## Summary

BC and DR planning have been part of healthcare and healthcare IT for decades. The increasing use of electronic systems and the complexity of those systems make BC/DR planning that much more critical. The use of cloud technologies can both help and hinder BC/DR planning. Ensure you have a very comprehensive, current BCP or BC/DR plan to manage the IT risk on behalf of the organization. In Chapter 23, we'll assess BC/DR capabilities, and if you have gaps, you can develop a plan to address those. Business continuity planning, along with cybersecurity, are two healthcare IT competencies that are required by regulation and must be well-developed to protect the organization at its most fundamental level.

## Resources

Gundurao, Arun, Jorge Machado, Rut Patel, and Yanwing Wong, "IT Resilience for the Digital Age," May 11, 2021, https://www.mckinsey.com/capabilities/mckinsey-digital/our-insights/tech-forward/it-resilience-for-the-digital-age, accessed November 27, 2022.
Snedaker, Susan, Business Continuity and Disaster Recovery for IT Professionals, 2nd Edition, Waltham, MA, Elsevier, Inc., 2015.

## Chapter 12

# IT Cybersecurity Building Blocks

The purpose of this chapter is to look at the key components and major milestones along the path toward maturing your cybersecurity capability. The assumption is that you have a robust and well-defined cybersecurity program in place and that your renovation project will help you improve those capabilities. A full discussion of healthcare cybersecurity is certainly outside the scope of this chapter and this book. You can check the References section at the end of this chapter if you are looking for more detailed guidance on this topic.

This chapter and Chapter 24 cover the top-level items that you should assess as part of your renovation project. That said, you should ensure you have undertaken a full cybersecurity risk assessment and developed very strong policies, processes, and technical controls in this area. Since HIT continues to be at the center of the target for cyber criminals, having a strong program is simply a baseline requirement now. This chapter and the associated assessment chapter will help you improve your overall capabilities, but they are not intended to guide you through developing or managing a detailed cybersecurity program.

## Overview

Statistics about successful healthcare breaches regularly make headlines, and sometimes these constant headlines can serve to dull us a bit to the reality of the threat. However, the damage done by each serious breach

DOI: 10.4324/9781003377023-14

is significant. From patient data (medical, financial) being exposed to EHR downtimes (disruption to care) to loss of revenue and reputation, successful cyberattacks have a large, negative, and lasting impact on patients, staff, and the organization. Recovering from the damage can take years. It can be costly for individuals to recover identities, and it can be costly for healthcare organizations on numerous fronts (ransom payments, loss of revenue, loss of cyber insurance, loss of reputation, loss of providers/staff, etc.).

Although attacks have become more sophisticated, many attack methods still rely on a handful of basic vulnerabilities – open ports, unpatched systems, simple passwords, and uneducated users among others. Ensuring your cybersecurity fundamentals are fully addressed goes a long way in reducing risk of successful attack. These include maintaining encrypted (inviolable) backups and regularly testing those backups, scanning your network for vulnerabilities, and addressing those in a timely manner, setting alerts for account irregularities (such as a user account being elevated to an Administrator account), regularly patching and updating systems in a timely manner, and training employees to avoid falling for phishing and social engineering attacks. Often, cybersecurity teams want to focus on sophisticated solutions, which have their purpose, but ensuring all the basic measures are in place will create a solid foundation upon which to build a more robust capability.

Every HIT organization must have a comprehensive cybersecurity program in place – both by regulation and by necessity. We know hackers are increasingly targeting healthcare organizations. With techniques such as double-barrel ransomware attacks and Ransomware-as-a-Service, the cyber threat landscape is ever-changing. The stakes could not be higher and they increase each year as the valuable troves of data continue to grow in healthcare.

At their most fundamental, security functions are intended to protect the confidentiality, integrity, and availability of an organization's electronic data. We'll begin by discussing the elements of any successful cybersecurity program and end with a few notes about managing cloud security. Of course, this is just a cursory review of cybersecurity as part of a renovation plan. Many elements of cybersecurity are addressed when you renovate your IT function. Removing unused hardware and software, shutting down unused ports, and hardening existing infrastructure, for example, are all part of renovation and all shore up your cybersecurity stance.

## Cybersecurity Program Elements

The key aspects of any cybersecurity program include these:

1. Select a framework.
2. Focus on basic security hygiene.
3. Develop policies and procedures around cybersecurity.
4. Evolve your cybersecurity solutions.
5. Educate your end users.
6. Develop and practice incident response.
7. Grow your cybersecurity capabilities.

1. **Select a framework.** Many U.S.-based healthcare organizations use the U.S. government's National Institute of Standards and Technology (NIST) Cybersecurity Framework (CSF) because it is relatively straightforward and can be applied to a wide variety of organization types. There are other frameworks suitable for healthcare, including HITECH, Center for Internet Security (CIS), and ISO. The key is to select and use a framework so you have a roadmap both for developing your program and assessing your capabilities and progress.
2. **Focus on basic security hygiene.** Many successful attacks leverage some very basic security holes. For example, attackers exploiting unpatched operating systems or open firewall ports. Developing strong processes, policies, and documentation around basic security functions will go a long way toward reducing risk. Timely patching of operating systems and applications, training on hardening network-connected devices (network, server, storage, and end devices), and data encryption, for example, are things every IT department should be doing anyway, and these actions come at no additional cost. Adding sophisticated software solutions can certainly improve security, but they are far less effective if the foundational elements are not in place.
3. **Develop policies and procedures around cybersecurity.** Policies should be in place that define how cybersecurity will be implemented and supported in the organization. Some policies are required by regulation, including HIPAA. Some policies are required to maintain best practices or to minimize financial risk. For example, PCI (Payment Card Industry) rules stipulate requirements around the security of credit card data. These are not regulations and an organization does not *have*

to comply, but failure to do so can compromise the organization's ability to collect credit card payments and will negatively impact the cost of processing those transactions. In other words, if you are not compliant, it will impact your ability to collect credit card payments, but you will not be violating any regulations.

Procedures define how policies will be carried out. Procedures also define how various activities will be conducted. They help standardize work and reduce risk in the organization. For example, procedures should include everything from how computer equipment is evaluated and selected to how systems are hardened, patched, and maintained to how incident response activities will proceed.

It can be challenging in HIT to set aside focused time to develop a useful set of policies and procedures, but it is important to step away from daily demands and get this done. Whether you are complying with regulations or with organizational risk management requirements, you must have these in place.

4. **Evolve your cybersecurity solutions.** Evolving your cybersecurity function means fully leveraging the solutions you have in place and continuing to assess how well these are meeting your needs. As cybersecurity solutions continue to change in the marketplace, you should keep an eye on how they are shifting. For example, several years ago, the standard anti-virus and anti-malware solutions used data files to identify malicious software. These data files had to be periodically updated in order to keep pace with the malicious software being propagated by attackers. Inevitably, attackers would find a vulnerability and exploit it before software companies could update the data files. This meant a lot of organizations were vulnerable to a particular exploit for days, weeks, or even months before they could close that gap. Eventually, the industry moved to a different model that utilized ML to identify and stop malicious activity. This was a significant evolution in anti-malware solutions. Clearly, in healthcare, we cannot implement the latest and greatest solutions every time something shows up in the market. At the same time, we cannot sit back and keep propping up legacy solutions as they become obsolete and inject more risk into the organization over time. The rising use of AI will certainly influence the next generation of solutions and no healthcare organization can afford to be too far behind the curve.

In addition, evolving cybersecurity solutions means evolving the methods, processes, and procedures you use for managing your cyber risk. As your IT architecture changes, as you move to hybrid cloud solutions, for example, you need to assess your environment to see how cyber risk is impacted. Assessing your activities, your progress, and your gaps on a periodic basis (weekly, monthly) will help ensure you continue to grow and evolve. Every healthcare organization has gaps and risks – it's virtually impossible to close all gaps and address all risks. Instead, you should actively work on closing the highest priority gaps and monitoring risks. Evolving your capabilities ensures you maintain forward progress.

5. **Educate your end users.** It only takes one person to click a malicious link to introduce harmful software into an organization, so relying on end users always doing the right thing is not a viable plan. That said, when every end user is educated on how to avoid falling victim to phishing and similar attacks, the organization's risk is reduced. The added benefit to this is that employees bring this knowledge and these behaviors home, helping to protect personal computers and personal accounts outside of work.

6. **Develop and practice incident response.** Putting in place the fundamental controls is the first step, but it is as important to have a very well-developed incident response plan. You cannot try to figure out how to respond on a Saturday night at 10pm when files are starting to be encrypted across the network. Instead, you should develop a simple but effective incident response plan. There are ample resources available online to develop a good plan. The plan should include things like contact information for IT leaders, by team; contact information for legal counsel, insurance carriers, and security vendors; response steps; and a timeline for decision points. For example, when do you declare a disaster or serious event? Who gets notified and when? When do you call your CEO, your insurance company, your cybersecurity vendor, or the FBI?

   The key is to think through what you should do when the bad thing happens. You can be guaranteed of only one thing. When the event occurs, the stress of the situation will cause you to have very limited critical thinking skills. A cyberattack is a time for planned and precise responses, not shoot-from-the-hip reactions.

   Having a documented plan (that is kept up-to-date) and training your team on using that plan are your best bets for having an effective response when a serious incident occurs. Remember, it's a matter of when, not if, something will happen on your network.

7. **Grow your cybersecurity capabilities.** In today's environment, the competition for skilled cybersecurity analysts is fierce. Healthcare organizations are competing for the same cyber experts that everyone else is. There will continue to be growing competition for these high-end technical skills across all industries. Healthcare organizations cannot compete on salary in some cases and are often unable to fill key cybersecurity vacancies. While there is no substitute for a skilled, experienced cyber expert, the next best step is to build that capability internally. Finding staff with the right attitude and aptitude for cybersecurity within your own ranks (or across the organization) can be a very effective approach at growing the capability. You may need to hire a third-party organization to shore up your capabilities for a few years until your internal resources gain the skills needed, but it beats the alternative – which is to have key vacancies for years on end or rely solely on expensive external support.

Of course, there's far more to a strong cybersecurity program, but if you cover these basics, you'll be on track to continue to improve your cybersecurity stance over time. We'll use these high-level capabilities as the basis for assessing your cybersecurity capabilities later.

# Cloud Security

We discussed cloud technologies throughout this book thus far. As you are aware, with the growing sophistication of cloud-based solutions, there's a growing cybersecurity risk to organizations that do not properly manage the security of these solutions. In some cases, the vendor provides all the security controls; in other cases, the organization is expected to manage security controls as if these resources were in their own on-premise data center. In some cases, IT staff are not well-trained in cloud architecture, technologies, and solutions. Unfortunately, the speed at which these resources can be provisioned often outpaces IT staff's ability to become proficient with these technologies. It is vital to ensure you have the skills on your team to manage cybersecurity for all technologies, including SaaS, Platform-as-a-Service (Paas), and Infrastructure-as-a-Service (Iaas), as well as any new or emerging solutions, such as Everything-as-a-Service (Xaas).

## Summary

Cybersecurity in healthcare should be one of your strongest capabilities. From strategy to architecture, ITOps to user management, and all aspects of IT in between, cybersecurity should be your foremost consideration. This brief chapter is intended to remind you of the fundamentals to assess for your own cybersecurity program. However, you should have in place a very robust cybersecurity program that includes frequent assessments, audits, and remediation plans. As part of your renovation plan, you need to determine whether your cybersecurity capabilities are where they need to be for your organization. If not, this renovation project is the perfect time to put these priorities front and center.

## Resources

Adkins, Heather, Betsy Beyer, Paul Blankinship, Piotr Lewandowski, Ana Oprea, and Adam Stubblefield, Building Secure and Reliable Systems: Best Practices for Designing, Implementing, and Maintaining Systems 1st Edition, North Sebastopol, CA, O'Reilly Media, Inc., 2020.

Chaput, Bob, Stop the Cyber Bleeding: What Healthcare Executives and Board Members Must Know About Enterprise Cyber Risk Management (ECRM), Bob Chaput and Clearwater Compliance, Nashville, TN, 2020.

Cloud Security Alliance, "Cloud security alliance (CSA) cloud controls matrix and CAIQ v4," June 7, 2021, https://cloudsecurityalliance.org/research/cloud-controls-matrix/, accessed March 3, 2023.

Cloud Security Alliance, "Security guidance for critical areas of focus in cloud computing v4.0," July 26, 2017, https://cloudsecurityalliance.org/artifacts/security-guidance-v4/, accessed March 3, 2023.

Fitzgerald, Todd, Information Security Governance Simplified: From the Boardroom to the Keyboard, Boca Raton, FL, CRC Press, 2012.

Gorge, Mathieu, The Elephant in the Board Room: Cyber-Accountability with the Five Pillars of Security Framework, ForbesBooks, Charleston, SC, 2021.

HIMSS, "Cybersecurity in healthcare," no date, https://www.himss.org/resources/cybersecurity-healthcare, accessed March 4, 2023.

IBM, "What is cybersecurity," no date, https://www.ibm.com/topics/cybersecurity, accessed November 29, 2022.

ISACA, Certificate of Cloud Auditing Knowledge (CCAK), Seattle, WA, Cloud Security Alliance and Schaumburg, IL, ISACA, 2021.

NIST, "Cybersecurity framework overview," May 24, 2016, updated April 19, 2022, https://csrc.nist.gov/Projects/cybersecurity-framework/nist-cybersecurity-framework-a-quick-start-guide, accessed November 29, 2022. For a downloadable PDF version, use this link: "Getting Started with the NIST Cybersecurity Framework: A Quick Start Guide," August 2021, https://nvlpubs. nist.gov/nistpubs/SpecialPublications/NIST.SP.1271.pdf

Pino, Lisa, "Improving the cybersecurity posture of healthcare in 2022," February 28, 2022, https://www.hhs.gov/blog/2022/02/28/improving-cybersecurity-posture-healthcare-2022.html, accessed February 6, 2023.

US Department of Health and Human Services (HHS), "Health industry cybersecurity practices: Managing threats and protecting patients, 2023 Edition," https://405d.hhs.gov/Documents/HICP-Main-508.pdf, Tech Volume I: https://405d.hhs.gov/Documents/tech-vol1-508.pdf, Tech Volume II: https://405d.hhs.gov/Documents/tech-vol2-508.pdf, accessed April 18, 2023.

# Chapter 13

# IT Staffing Building Blocks

One of the key building blocks of any IT function is staffing. As we have seen in recent years, the demand for talented IT staff across all business sectors has been very strong and healthcare has been competing with big tech, finance, and cybersecurity companies for IT talent. Since people are so critical to the long-term success of the IT function, we need to develop plans for shoring up the gaps and challenges we see in HIT today. While there is no one-size-fits-all solution, we'll look at some foundational aspects of successful IT staffing in this chapter. When we perform the staffing assessment later, we'll use these building blocks to assess where your staffing is currently and your opportunities for improvement. During the renovation stage, you'll develop plans to build the team of the future.

In Chapter 8, we discussed a wide array of technologies. Clearly, your team needs to have the requisite technical skills for both current and future technology solutions. This typically involves upskilling existing staff after you've determined what the most likely future technology demands will be for your company. We'll discuss some aspects of the technical skills staff will need, but we'll also take a wider look at IT staffing in healthcare today.

For most HIT organizations, staffing (and total Full Time Equivalents or FTEs) has grown organically over time, just like many of the systems we support. People may have been pushed into roles because they were available vs. being the right person for the role. Many IT managers must deal with teams they inherit and often those teams have a wide range of skills and abilities.

IT staffing should be based on the demand of the organization, the technologies in use, the projects planned and underway, and the desired

DOI: 10.4324/9781003377023-15

future state. That almost never happens in HIT, but it's worth setting as the goal. In many organizations, IT staffing is sometimes decided as total headcount or percent of total headcount, such as "IT will have $X$ FTEs in the next budget year" or "IT is allocated $Y$ percent of total organizational FTEs." Other times, staffing is a process of asking for staffing you need and negotiating to some middle ground the organization feels it can afford. Unfortunately, it's not uncommon after some sort of IT crisis, such as a key server outage, network failure, or successful cyber-attack, IT will get the requested approval for additional staffing. However, after the crisis resolves, the downward pressure on IT staffing resumes. This is not an implied criticism of healthcare leadership; it is a description of the dynamic economic realities all organizations face in this industry.

Organizations must find the right level of IT staffing to support the needs of the organization. Unfortunately, because IT is complex and because IT expertise often commands higher salaries in the marketplace, IT can be seen as simply a very expensive function for the organization. As we'll discuss throughout this book, working with organizational leaders to build a better understanding of the value IT delivers to the organization can assist both in demand management and in staffing requests. When you have others outside of IT supporting the hiring of IT skills to support enterprise initiatives, the discussion around staffing and FTE levels is somewhat easier.

Regardless of how your organization approaches staffing in general and IT staffing more specifically, there are several things that are true.

## Key Principles

1. **You are not a wizard.** You cannot magically get three people to perform the work of six. You cannot magically get people without a specific skill to become experts in a new skill overnight. Trying to be a magician with respect to skills and staffing will only wear you out, it will not help you succeed. Keep this in mind as you look at IT demand, project requests and current skills, capabilities, and staffing levels. It is a tough conversation to have with the organization, but sometimes a necessary one. You can use parallel examples to help drive your point home. A doctor is not a substitute for a case manager, and a medical assistant cannot perform surgery. The right person with the right skills in the right job is how we build competent organizations. That is true clinically, and it is just as true in IT.

2. **You cannot control organizational demand.** You can only *manage* organizational demand and IT capacity. The better you know what your teams are doing, how productive they are, where there are bottlenecks and/or lack of skills holding you back, the better you can articulate demand vs. capacity. You can work to anticipate and manage organizational demand through an effective governance process. Additionally, leveraging automation can increase IT capacity and/ or reduce IT demand. This should be part of your renovation project planning and falls under the heading of digitalization efforts, discussed in Chapter 2.

3. **The skills your team needed last year are not the skills they will need next year.** As technology rapidly continues to evolve and solutions become increasingly sophisticated and complex, your team likely does not have the right skill mix to successfully navigate the changes on the horizon. When you assess your teams, you will need to look at what you need today to carry out the work of the organization and what you'll need tomorrow to ensure you are prepared for what's next. Managing today's work while preparing for tomorrow's needs can be challenging, but once you assess your staff's current skillset, you can develop a roadmap to achieve these goals.

## Staffing Sources

As healthcare budgets are challenged in today's environment, IT costs will continue to come under pressure. As we discuss more fully in the chapters on IT value creation (Chapters 15 and 27), moving the dialog from IT as a cost center to IT as a source of innovation and value creation can help reduce these difficult conversations about IT costs, but they will never go away completely. As a leader of your IT function, you know that you must balance cost vs. value and you must be a good steward of the budget you are allocated.

This certainly applies to IT staffing as well. Your options, of course, are to hire full-time employees, hire contractors, hire consultants, or outsource a function. In almost all cases, you will use a mix of these options. The costs involved vary greatly. Employees come with benefits and training costs. Contractors and consultants come at a premium hourly rate and are not always available when you need them. Outsourcing can add a layer of management, and therefore, distance between organizational values and service delivery. In other words, an outsourced employee's loyalties are to their employer and not necessarily to your organization.

If you are interested in reading up on this topic, the article in the Resources section at the end of this chapter by Aaron De Smet, et al. from McKinsey titled "The Great Attrition is Making Hiring Harder" is an excellent overview of some of the hiring trends emerging and where you might creatively source your future talent.

## Staffing Locations

Currently, in addition to staff counts, there are conversations around location. During the pandemic, the bias against work from home (WFH) or work from anywhere (WFA) seemed to diminish. However, as things have normalized, this topic has become the center of the conversation with many organizations, including healthcare. With IT, requiring staff to work on-site can be a limiting factor in hiring, especially with some of the more in-demand technical roles. Many healthcare organizations are currently working through some sort of hybrid approach, but it will likely evolve to allow IT to hire the staff it needs, regardless of where those staff physically reside. True, having out-of-state employees can be a challenge in terms of making them feel as though they are really part of the team and in terms of the legal elements of employment (insurance plans, benefits, taxes, etc.), but this requires our management and leadership skills to evolve. This also has the potential to create a divisive environment because certain roles in healthcare require one to be on-site. Providers, nurses, medical assistants, phlebotomists, and many others have to be where the patient is. Working from home is not an option. For IT, certain jobs required presence, such as desktop or network services. Other jobs can be fully remote. The challenge for all business leaders is to navigate this evolving landscape in a way that serves our patients, our organizations, and our staff to the greatest degree possible. While it can be a difficult situation to manage, it will continue to be part of the hiring landscape for years to come.

## Staffing Schedules and On-Call

Every healthcare organization must schedule staff to meet the needs of the organization, and IT is no different. Depending on the type of healthcare organization you're in, you may have IT staff working both regular shifts and evening/weekend shifts to meet demand. The other thing we've seen is more flexible work schedules in some settings. Are your staff working the traditional Monday through Friday, 8AM to 5PM (or similar) schedule, or have they flexed their days and hours? Some organizations have moved to four-day work weeks, others allowing 36-hour weeks over four, five, or six days. Some have been able to accommodate part-time or less-than-full-time. Others have looked at staffing regular hours during nights and weekends to reduce overtime and improve service levels for the organization. Finally, most HIT departments require some manner of on-call staffing so emergency issues can be triaged in a timely and effective manner. All these variables come into play as you assess your capabilities today and your needs for tomorrow.

## Leveraging Automation

There are numerous tasks within IT that are well-suited to automation. From user provisioning to remote access authorization to system imaging and beyond, many tasks in IT are routine and predictable. These tasks are excellent candidates for automation. Automation may increase your application/license costs, but those costs should be more than offset by increased efficiency, reduced cyber risk (or risk of errors), and increased availability of IT staff time to focus on more value-added tasks. Your level of automation is part of your staffing equation moving forward, and we'll include this in the staffing assessment work in Chapter 25.

## Technical Skills

The list of technical skills is long and changes constantly. In Chapter 25, when you perform your IT staffing assessment, you can develop a specific list of technology capabilities needed by your teams today and in the future. For now, these high-level categories serve to prompt thought around your skill mix on your teams.

1. Data center, server, and storage clusters (and related virtualization solutions)
2. Cloud data center, cloud platforms, cloud server, and storage clusters
3. Networking, network security, and network architecture

4. End user and mobile device centralized management, configuration, and support
5. Data management (storage, encryption, security, definitions, validation, and management)
6. Cybersecurity monitoring and management (SIEM, DLP, event logs, etc.)
7. Business intelligence (reporting, data engineering, analytics, etc.)
8. Enterprise application management
9. Clinical application management
10. IT application management

From understanding operating systems, network protocols, and interface technologies to knowing how to talk with operational users to understand business requirements, IT skills need to evolve. Your team needs to be well-positioned for the future by having the requisite technical skills to manage and secure the environment.

As cloud-based solutions continue to evolve and expand, you should ensure you pay special attention to your team's cloud-based skills. This includes everything from hardware-only solutions to full-service cloud solutions. Your team not only needs the skills to manage these technologies, but they also need to understand the larger architecture, the interconnections, and the entire universe of your organization's cloud, hybrid, and on-premise solutions. They also need to know how to manage the operational implications, such as user provisioning, cost per unit, contractual terms, and more. Many healthcare organizations today would not be able to claim that level of expertise across all the cloud domains currently in use in their company.

## Business Skills

Skills needed by IT staff have evolved over the years. In today's environment, having deep technical skills is only one element. Developing business skills like critical thinking, business process analysis, and effective, professional communication are increasingly needed competencies in successful IT departments. Well-rounded staff who will drive results in your department have a wider mix of skills that include:

1. **Active listening.** IT staff must interact with a wide variety of stakeholders across the organization and need to be able to actively listen to understand the needs of these stakeholders. Working to

understand sometimes nuanced needs is vital to delivering exactly what is needed vs. what the IT staff person might think is needed.

2. **Collaboration and teamwork.** No one can act as a lone wolf in IT and expect to be successful over the long run. Being able to successfully work with others to find solutions will ensure the results are the best they can be.

3. **Communication.** This is a basic skill, but it is the most common source of issues in almost all organizations. Communication encompasses both verbal and written modes. Some IT people are the type who will "tell you how the watch is made" when you ask them the time. Others are the type who are rather blunt because the world is very black-and-white to them. Bluntness may be perceived as being rude or hostile. These different types of communication styles have strengths and weaknesses, and having a team with well-rounded communication skills will yield faster, better results with fewer angry escalations to you. Having staff who can really listen to end-user needs and identify the root causes of issues will be invaluable, no matter their role.

4. **Business analysis.** More and more roles in IT require staff to understand how the business operates. Investing in business analysis skills for the team can be beneficial as it provides a framework for standard business analysis, resulting in standardization and streamlined work. Check out the Resources section for more on this topic.

5. **Critical thinking.** Critical thinking is a key business trait as well. Being able to conceptualize, analyze, synthesize, evaluate, and apply information to a situation are the key components of critical thinking. This also includes being able to keep an open mind, ask questions, and challenge assumptions. While you do not want staff who push back constantly, you also don't want staff who blindly take orders and work by rote. Using critical thinking and challenging assumptions, when appropriate, will help reduce risk and improve results.

6. **Time management.** Being able to manage oneself and one's deliverables is a fundamental skill for success in any job.

7. **Project management.** Understanding how projects work and how to manage a project is a valuable skill for all IT staff, even if they are not directly managing a project. For example, as a participant on a project team, it's valuable to understand why timelines, deliverables, and dependencies matter, as well as the downstream impact of these project elements.

8. **Curiosity and creativity.** These two traits help staff ask, "what if?" These are the core elements of innovation, and if you are going to transform your IT function after you renovate it, you will need to seek out those who demonstrate curiosity and creativity. Not all IT staff will have these traits and that's fine as long as you have core staff or leaders who do. They can paint a vision of the future and allow others to fill in the details.

9. **Perseverance.** Being able to persist through challenges and setbacks is another important trait for anyone in business, but especially in IT. Not all solutions, projects, or technologies involve a straight path forward. Being able to persist calmly in the face of these setbacks is important. However, there is a difference between persistence and being unwilling to admit that something isn't successful, when further effort will not change the result. This leads us to the next important trait.

10. **Ability to fail fast.** At some point, a pilot project or an experiment will be a complete failure. Maybe the initial assumptions were flawed, maybe the situation shifted quickly, or maybe the implementation was a mess. Regardless, there are times when things are off the rails, and the best course of action is to stop. Being able to fail fast, or stop something from continuing, and move on is an important trait that is the flip side of perseverance. Unfortunately, sometimes it is only in hindsight that we realize we should have persisted or quit earlier. Understanding both sides of this equation helps you figure that out the best path sooner.

11. **Honesty and ability to self-assess.** Clearly, expecting complete honesty from IT staff is fundamental. Honesty is fostered by creating a safe environment where people trust that honesty will be honored. The ability to self-assess is about personal honesty. You clearly want people who are able and willing to say they are weak in an area or don't understand something or made an error. This has much to do with leadership, the environment you create, and the expectations you set. However, if you have staff who chronically hide errors or misrepresent the truth, you are better off without them. They generally create far bigger problems, such as undiscovered errors, unremedied risks, and overall divisiveness than their technical skills are worth.

These are important traits because, as IT moves faster and becomes more complex, no one person can be the expert anymore. Everyone needs to continually learn, unlearn, and relearn technical skills, and it's a constantly evolving process. The team needs to be woven together in a way that creates flexibility and strength. Fostering these traits in your team in tandem with their technical skills will ensure you have a team that will continue to grow and meet the needs of the organization.

## Making Work Fun

The subject of this section might have caught you by surprise. Fun? In HIT? An article titled "Designing Work that People Love," is a very worthwhile read and describes the benefits of designing more enjoyable jobs. [13.1] The article's bottom line is this: What if you made everyone's job more fun or more enjoyable by 20%? What would that do to productivity, morale, and retention? It's worth asking because it's relatively easy to do. You may well choose to make this part of your IT staffing renovation plan.

The easiest way to increase job enjoyment is to identify what people are good at and enjoy in their current jobs and what they are not good at and do not enjoy. Let's say you have ten people on a specific team. Some of them love working on routine break-fix tickets; some love interacting with end users; some thrive on the gnarliest, most difficult technical problems; and some enjoy organizing and leading the work. If you increase the work they love and hand off the work they don't really like to someone who *would* enjoy it, everyone wins. For example, maybe Loren thrives on solving the most difficult problems, and Jose really loves the rhythm of daily break-fix activities. Why not give Loren more of the hard problems to solve and give Jose more of the break-fix tickets? According to Buckingham, if each can do just 20% more of what they love, their job satisfaction increases exponentially.

This contradicts the old notion that you need to ensure people work on their areas of 'weakness' in order to become well-rounded. While you can't have someone avoid certain competencies required for the job, you can emphasize the parts they enjoy most and minimize those they dislike. On every team, there's usually a good enough mix of people so that shifting tasks around to some degree will work. Part of building a strong team is building a diversity of talents, temperaments, and technical skills. Designing and managing jobs in a more flexible and adaptive way should certainly be part of your renovation plan. As staffing continues to be a challenge, finding ways to fully leverage the best of each person will drive their job satisfaction, higher retention, quality deliverables, and ultimately, your organization's success.

# Diversity, Equity, and Inclusion (DEI)

We won't spend too much time on this topic, but it's important to include this in your staffing assessment and planning. Though you might think that DEI initiatives are something that happen at the corporate level or are solely the domain of your Human Resources department, it's important that you understand the value in diverse teams. When you look at your staffing, you should try to hire and foster diversity, not because it's a hot topic at the moment, but because numerous studies have proven diverse teams are stronger [13.2]. Having different points of view and different backgrounds makes teams smarter and more effective than non-diverse teams. With the challenges of finding IT talent these days, there is a growing trend to develop internal capabilities by hiring younger or less experienced staff and training them. As you're doing this, you open the door to hiring more diverse candidates and enhancing the team structure. There is sometimes the fear that if we train staff, they will leave. There is a larger risk if we don't train staff and they stay. Do you really want untrained staff working on your critical systems, or are you willing to invest in your staff knowing some will choose to leave at some point in the future? Look at hiring people who have potential, who have the right attitude and aptitude, and you will develop very strong teams able to meet the evolving demands of HIT.

In Chapter 25, we will walk through an IT staffing assessment and incorporate these traits so you can assess where your staff's capabilities are along these various dimensions.

# Summary

Staffing critical IT functions will continue to be a challenge going forward. Developing strong IT staffing capabilities and getting creative about how to meet the staffing demands of your healthcare organization will be key to your success.

Building great teams takes thought, planning, and effort. As you retool your teams for the future, you'll need to understand all the elements that make up strong individual contributors and strong teams. Building well-rounded, diverse, and collaborative teams is hard work, but some of the most important work you'll do in your IT career.

# References

[13.1] Buckingham, Marcus, "Designing work that people love," May-June 2022, https://hbr.org/2022/05/designing-work-that-people-love, accessed December 2, 2022.

[13.2] Rock, David and Heidi Grant, "Why diverse teams are smarter," Harvard Business Review, November 4, 2016, https://hbr.org/2016/11/why-diverse-teams-are-smarter, accessed December 31, 2022.

# Resources

Bernstein, Ethan, Michael Y. Lee, and Joost Minnaar, "How companies are using tech to give employees more autonomy," January 28, 2022, https://hbr.org/2022/01/how-companies-are-using-tech-to-give-employees-more-autonomy. accessed December 21, 2022.

Buckingham, Marcus and Ashley Goodall, "The power of hidden teams," Mary 14, 2019, https://hbr.org/2019/05/the-power-of-hidden-teams, accessed December 2, 2022.

Buckingham, Marcus, "What great managers do," March 2005, https://hbr.org/video/5335748697001/what-great-managers-do, accessed December 2, 2022.

Business Analysis Body of Knowledge (BABOK), no date, https://www.iiba.org/career-resources/a-business-analysis-professionals-foundation-for-success/babok/, accessed December 3, 2022.

De Smet, Aaron, Bonnie Dowling, Bryan Hancock, and Bill Schaninger, "The Great Attrition is making hiring harder. Are you searching the right talent pools?" July 13, 2022, https://www.mckinsey.com/capabilities/people-and-organizational-performance/our-insights/the-great-attrition-is-making-hiring-harder-are-you-searching-the-right-talent-pools, accessed January 2, 2023.

Dukach, Dagny, "How technology is transforming work," November 7, 2022, https://hbr.org/2022/11/research-roundup-how-technology-is-transforming-work, accessed December 2, 2022.

Indeed Editorial Team, "How to design a skills matrix," July 17, 2022, https://in.indeed.com/career-advice/career-development/skills-matrix, accessed October 11, 2022.

Nelson, Bob, "Why work should be fun," May 2, 2022, https://hbr.org/2022/05/why-work-should-be-fun, accessed December 21, 2022.

*Chapter 14*

# IT Management and Leadership Building Blocks

In this chapter, we examine the management and leadership skills needed for leading healthcare IT in the future. As you contemplate your future digital transformation efforts, you will need to ensure your team has the right mix of skills. That means the right people leading the right teams as well as the right people driving innovation and change. John P. Kotter, a prominent business and change leader, said that management is about dealing with complexity, and leadership is about dealing with change. Clearly, we need both capabilities in our ranks. In a 2001 article that's still relevant today, Kotter said, "Of course, not everyone can be good at both leading and managing. Some people have the capacity to become excellent managers but not strong leaders. Others have great leadership potential but, for a variety of reasons, have great difficulty becoming strong managers. Smart companies value both kinds of people and work hard to make them a part of the team." [14.1]

## Managers and Leaders

We need both managers and leaders to be successful, and these traits are not always found in the same people. That means you'll have to assess both leadership and management skills, capabilities, competencies, and potential. You can then develop each individual's skills to their fullest. An excellent eBook by Matt Gavin [14.2] delineates these elements well. These are shown in Table 14.1.

DOI: 10.4324/9781003377023-16

**Table 14.1  Management vs. Leadership Traits**

|  | Manager | Leader |
|---|---|---|
|  | *Manager* | *Leader* |
| **Focus** | Complexity | Change |
|  | Tactical | Strategic |
|  | Present | Future |
| **Actions** | Plan | Vision |
|  | Manages staff | Builds relationships |
|  | Manages processes | Articulates vision |
|  | Organizes work | Aligns work |
| **Traits** | Consistency | Innovation |
|  | Stability | Movement |

When you look at these differences, you can see that some people are very good at dealing with complexity, sorting things out, and simplifying processes or situations. Others are very good at creating a vision, navigating change, helping others cope with uncertainty, and making decisions with partial or rapidly changing data. In some cases, you might know individuals who perform very well in both arenas.

However, you can probably think of a few people who have a manager title who aren't good at planning, managing staff, setting accountability, or organizing work. In those cases, you either have a person unsuited to management or someone who needs coaching and training. It's fairly common for highly competent technical staff to be promoted into management simply because they excelled technically. However, being an excellent technician does not necessarily translate into being a good manager or leader. As you look at your team, you can probably identify the people who fall into these areas. Maybe they've learned the requisite skills through coaching, education, or experience...but maybe they haven't. This is the work you'll do when you undertake your assessment in Chapter 26 and something you'll need to address in your renovation plan.

Also, we are now facing a generation of managers and leaders who are getting ready to retire, making way for new leaders to emerge. However, as leadership changes, so too do cultures, norms, and expectations. That means staff will have to deal with change on many fronts – technology, business, and leadership. Having a plan in place to replace those who are retiring through developing internal talent or hiring fresh faces from outside the organization will be an important aspect of assessment and planning. It also means change will be the norm. Preparing for these changes through pro-actively identifying and developing a range of management and leadership skills will be vital to long-term success. We discuss managing organizational change in depth in Chapter 29. You can use the material from that chapter to develop an effective approach for managing this type of change as well.

As you assess your IT leaders, you'll look at the standard leadership traits such as innovation, engagement, perseverance, calmness under pressure, transparency, honesty, accountability, and more. You may also begin to look at your team with an eye toward how they handle complexity and change. This will give you additional options when developing your team and looking at the future to determine what sorts of managers and leaders you'll need.

The digital transformation underway requires the ability to manage both complexity and change. The renovation project you'll undertake also requires the ability to manage those two dimensions. As we've seen, not everyone is good at both. As a leader in your IT organization, though, you need to be able to understand the differences and see those traits in the managers and leaders you select. If you hire only those with strong management skills, your teams will lack the vision needed for innovation. If you hire only those with strong leadership skills, your teams will lack the basic management of the thousands of details needed to keep daily operations running smoothly.

In the assessment chapter, you'll be tasked with taking a close look at each of your leaders in your department (we'll call them leaders here to indicate they have a leadership title – Lead, Supervisor, Manager, Director, etc.). You'll also be tasked with determining if you have the necessary management and leadership skills in your department for the long run. For example, you might have a mix of very seasoned and very new managers. You probably have some managers who excel at managing people but struggle with other managerial aspects of the job (prioritization, finance, etc.). You likely have others who are excellent with managerial aspects but are very rough around the edges with their staff. You may have others who can see three steps ahead but can't organize their workday effectively. Your renovation plan can take these factors into account, and you can create a plan for each leader to gradually improve their capabilities so they become the best leader they are able to be.

# Key Capabilities

So, what do you need to be a successful IT leader in today's world? These are a few elements you should look for and develop in your team. Of course, there are many more, but this is a good list to start with.

1. Managing and improving daily operations
2. Leading change, innovation, and transformation
3. Emotional intelligence, communication, and collaboration
4. Accountability, perseverance, honesty, and transparency
5. Critical thinking, strategic thinking, and strategic planning
6. Staff development (including diversity, equity, and inclusion) and engagement (building trust, engaging the team) and development
7. Decision-making
8. Negotiating positive outcomes (internal and external to IT) through effective collaboration
9. Change management
10. Financial management
11. Vendor and contract management

The world has changed dramatically in the past few years, and the needs of IT staff have also changed. Tomorrow's leader will need to be able to address things like flexible work schedules, flexible work locations, and upskilling and reskilling staff for a rapidly evolving technology landscape. Many of these are new challenges that lack clear definitions or solutions. Today's leader needs to be able to manage both complexity, change, and uncertainty in almost equal measure. A leadership team that has a mix of these capabilities is much more likely to be successful.

We mentioned this in the IT Staffing chapter, but it's worth repeating here. As an IT leader, you should actively be looking for ways to leverage your staff at their very best. This means increasing the type of work they most enjoy (and therefore, are usually most competent in) and minimizing the work they enjoy the least. While we cannot completely re-work jobs and roles, we can tweak them to make everyone a bit more satisfied with their work. As we look at how to manage with continued staffing shortages and the ever-changing hiring challenges, retaining the competent staff we have is the best strategy. Successfully retaining those staff means ensuring they have work that brings them fulfillment and enjoyment while adding value to the organization. This is as true for leaders as it

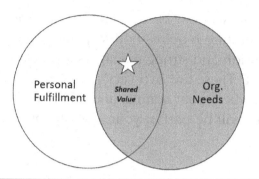

**Figure 14.1    Intersection of fulfillment and productivity.**

is for front-line staff. Figure 14.1 depicts the intersection that generates consistently positive results.

Of course, the larger the overlap area, the better the person is suited to the overall role. If you find a small sliver of overlap (very little "shared value"), you may have hired someone into the wrong role, and that may need to be part of your assessment as well. Again, managers and leaders not only need to assess this with their staff, but you also need to assess your managers and leaders along the very same lines. What do they enjoy? What are they good at? What do they naturally gravitate toward? These are their areas of strength to be fully leveraged. What do they avoid? What do they struggle with? These are the areas of their job they will never love and might only have moderate proficiency. Minimizing the impact of these imbalances is a better approach than trying to change people's basic likes and dislikes. While some might find this approach a bit too accommodating, it's similar to having a toolbox full of tools and pulling out a hammer to pound a nail and a saw to cut a board. Using the right tool for the job is always the most effective approach. So it is with staff and leaders. Ensuring you have the right people in the right roles with the right skills for the work at hand will always yield better results.

## Summary

As we look at IT transformation, these traits and skills will be very important in driving the type of change needed to meet the demands of tomorrow. IT transformation, as we discussed earlier in this book, is not about just digitizing the work we do, but about coming up with completely new ways of doing business leveraging the latest technology. As technology continues to evolve, so will our business models and approaches to delivering care. This future requires both capable leaders who can see and articulate a future vision and strong managers who can organize the work once the vision is set. These are two very necessary traits in healthcare IT's future, so assessing where your team is and what you'll need to develop a well-rounded team will be part of your assessment and then your renovation plan.

## References

[14.1] Kotter, John P., "What leaders really do," December 2001, https://hbr.org/2001/12/what-leaders-really-do, accessed December 3, 2022.

[14.2] Gavin, Matt, Harvard Business School Online, October 31, 2019, https://online.hbs.edu/blog/post/leadership-vs-management, eBook "How to Become a More Effective Leader," accessed December 4, 2022.

## Resources

Broadbent, Marianne, and Ellen S. Kitzis, The New CIO Leader: Setting the Agenda and Delivering Results, Gartner, Inc., 2005. *[Note: While this book is now more than fifteen years old, it still contains some of the best information for CIOs and IT leaders available. A timeless resource for all IT leaders]*.

Buckingham, Marcus, "Designing work that people love," May-June 2022, https://hbr.org/2022/05/designing-work-that-people-love, accessed December 5, 2022.

Garrad, Lewis, Tomas Chamorro-Premuzic, "How to make work more meaningful for your team," August 9, 2017, https://hbr.org/2017/08/how-to-make-work-more-meaningful-for-your-team, accessed December 5, 2022.

Lane, Dean, The Chief Information Officer's Body of Knowledge, Hoboken, NJ, John Wiley & Sons, Inc., 2011.

Snedaker, Susan, Leading Healthcare IT: Managing to Succeed, Boca Raton, FL, CRC Press, 2017.

Tulane University blog, "The importance of healthcare leadership," October 5, 2021, https://publichealth.tulane.edu/blog/healthcare-leadership/, accessed December 4, 2022.

Wager, Karen A., Frances W. Lee, and John P. Glaser, Health Care Information Systems: A Practical Approach for Health Care Management, 5th Edition, Hoboken, NJ, John Wiley & Sons, Inc., 2022.

*Chapter 15*

# IT Value Creation Building Blocks

The topic of value creation in IT is one that is not frequently included in IT discussions. However, it is increasingly necessary in order to justify IT expenditures and to articulate exactly what value the organization is receiving from IT. If IT continues to be seen simply as a necessary expense, investments in innovation will always be hampered. Conversely, if IT is seen as a value-added service, the organization will look to maximize the return on the investment. You want IT to be seen as a really sound and necessary investment. You also want IT to be seen as a strategic business partner and source of innovation rather than just a break/fix shop.

It's well-known that things that are thought to be 'free' are typically undervalued compared to things that are not. A *free* app, a *free* lunch, a *free* anything is seen as being worth less than something you have to pay for. At the same time, we've all become accustomed to the fact that free things almost always come with a cost. *Free* apps scrape your data or your browsing history. *Free* meals come with a sales pitch, a marketing message, or the gathering of your customer data. IT costs are no different. Nothing is free, there is always a cost, but end users don't always see the cost of IT services. What they see is free – more laptops, more applications, more storage, more you-name-it. If all it takes to get more IT is to submit a ticket or a requisition, the organization simply sees IT as order takers. Free means the products and services

DOI: 10.4324/9781003377023-17

IT provides are destined to be undervalued. It is also difficult for end users to be responsible stewards of organizational resources when they don't understand (or have access to) what IT actually costs. When someone suggests adding 1,000 users to an app, do they understand the cost per user? Costs include not only the licensing and maintenance costs for each user license but also the training and potentially the expansion of the infrastructure (storage, compute capacity, etc.) that go along with every new user license. Does the requester see all of this? Probably not. These are the kinds of business conversations IT needs to have more often.

On the other hand, IT is also often viewed by organizational leaders as a large, expensive hole into which people and technology are tossed. An ever-expanding operational budget, ever-expanding staff rosters, and a never-ending stream of requests for more money and more resources will eventually lead to the organization push back and reduce budgets. Often, these actions come at the worst possible time – when you are in the middle of a key infrastructure upgrade or a critical deployment of a new technology.

The question for HIT leaders is how to avoid being seen as free by end users and as too expensive by organizational leaders. The short answer is found by researching, documenting, and articulating IT value.

How do you articulate the value of IT in your organization today? You might respond by saying you share project outcomes or IT achievements with senior leaders, via committee reports, etc. But those don't tell the story of IT value, they are simply outcomes of IT investments and efforts. That's not a bad start, but that's not where your efforts should end.

## Seven Elements of IT Value

According to a report by Gartner, Inc., there are seven key elements to IT value creation. These are:

1. Value is always determined by the stakeholder.
2. Not all outcomes are equally valued.
3. Build two value narratives: change and run.

4. Measure IT's impact on stakeholder outcomes, not on IT effort.
5. Align IT costs to the business services they enable.
6. Communicate IT value in the stakeholder's language.
7. Those funding IT must understand the value and impact of IT to stakeholder objectives. [15.1]

Let's walk through each of these.

1. **Value is always determined by the stakeholder.** IT is often focused on delivering the technology, the platform, or the capability, but that is not what resonates with stakeholders. Instead, IT should focus on meeting stakeholder expectations by delivering on objectives and outcomes. The technology solutions are secondary to the business outcomes.

2. **Not all outcomes are equally valued.** Your organization will usually value efforts that drive business outcomes and grow revenue far more than cost reductions or cost avoidance. Partner with business leaders to identify and prioritize business outcomes, then map your technology solutions to those. Many IT departments work in the opposite manner, and the discussion becomes about technology instead of business outcomes.

3. **Build two value narratives: *operating* and *transforming*.** Value is derived differently from operational (run) vs. transformational (change) efforts. These two should be measured differently so that clear distinctions can be made. For example, metrics for operational value would include things like cost per $x$, percent reduction in cost per $y$, or reduction in time to $z$ (better performance at a lower cost). Transformative efforts will include metrics like return on investment (ROI), percent revenue increase, percent market share increase, and other investment-laden language to reflect the benefit received from an IT investment (vs. IT cost). Framing information in this way helps highlight the value of IT investments.

4. **Measure IT's impact on stakeholder outcomes, not on IT effort.** Your stakeholders care about outcomes, not what it takes IT to deliver those outcomes. While internal discussions on IT effort are certainly appropriate, discussing platforms, technology, and IT effort with stakeholders does not communicate value. These are IT production tools, in a sense, and are simply the mechanisms by which business

objectives are accomplished. As much as IT staff may want to talk about technology, keep those discussions internal and ensure your business conversations focus on business outcomes, not IT effort. That said, it's also important to discuss IT's contribution to business outcomes. Focus IT metrics on business outcomes; avoid language that reflects effort or technical output.

5. **Align IT costs to the business services they enable.** When discussing IT costs, it is preferable to link them to business objectives. For example, licensing might be on a per-seat or per-user basis. Use this language to discuss costs. Everything IT enables is in support of the business, so reflecting the cost and benefit to the organization in business terms helps drive the concept of IT value. For example, your Service Desk software and Service Desk staff support the business, they don't exist for IT's sole benefit. In this case, you could indicate that support of the business costs $X per employee and reduces time to resolution for issues that would otherwise impact the end user's productivity. While it is also true that the Service Desk software and staff enable better triage of IT issues and facilitate the tracking of issue resolution, none of that matters to end users. Focus on what adds direct value to the business when discussing IT services.

6. **Communicate IT value in the stakeholder's language.** Whenever possible, avoid deep discussions about technology, platforms, and capabilities. Avoid using IT language, especially jargon, with end users. Instead, talk in business terms that tie to outcomes and drive informed decisions. It can be easy to fall into tech-speak, so be sure to run important communications past a trusted non-IT colleague so they can help you weed out any jargon.

7. **Those funding IT must understand the value and impact of IT to stakeholder objectives.** Partnering with business leaders for IT funding discussions will improve your odds for success. When business leaders are on board with IT spending because they are passionately advocating for the project and its business outcomes, the IT cost is generally better received by those making funding decisions, including the CFO and the CEO. Often, business leaders overlook key cost components in their proposals, and IT often overlooks key business outcomes in their proposals. Working together on joint proposals to ensure adequate funding and support will drive better results.

# Measuring IT Value in Healthcare

There are numerous methods for measuring the value of IT in healthcare, though it can be challenging in some scenarios because benefits are both tangible and intangible. For example, you can measure the ROI of an imaging system based on acquisition and ongoing costs, the number of images generated, and reimbursement per image. Conversely, it's not easy to measure satisfaction with the ease-of-use of the patient portal in financial terms. So, you are often faced with having to use different methods for different situations.

You can calculate ROI when financial data is easily obtained. You can look at total cost of ownership (TCO), business impact (how IT solutions support business strategies), or Key Performance Indicators (KPIs) in other situations. For less tangible areas, you can perhaps measure user adoption, user engagement, or overall satisfaction with IT solutions. Ultimately, the business determines what is of value and what is not, so ensuring you are closely aligned with business strategies, objectives, and outcomes is what will drive value.

# Business Relationship Management

You might be wondering how you get these valuable conversations going. How do you link up with your counterparts to shift from the traditional IT function to a more innovative, value-creating function? You accomplish this, at least in part, through business relationship management (BRM).

When business partners feel that IT understands their needs and objectives, they are more likely to see the value IT delivers to the organization. As you develop your BRM capabilities, you move from order taker to trusted adviser to strategic partner.

BRM is not just about developing strong, trusted lines of communication between IT and business leaders. It is about managing these relationships to help shape IT demand, deliver value, and find ways to innovate through collaboration. For more on BRM, see the Resources section at the end of the chapter.

# Technology Business Management

Another element of generating, managing, and articulating IT value is through a technology business management (TBM) framework. TBM is the body of knowledge around managing IT as a business. The TBM Council defines a taxonomy that you can use to develop your own TBM initiative within your organization or to guide you in developing a solution that works best for your organization. Since TBM can be used in any industry, viewing solutions from other industries than your own can help you see how it might be implemented very simply or at a more advanced level. For more information about formal TBM, see the Resources section at the end of this chapter.

A presentation by Kevin Coyne, Director of Technology and Services, Bureau of Industry and Security at the U.S. Department of Commerce explains TBM well. In 2017, he presented "Technology Business Management (TBM) Overview." He made three key statements:

1. TBM defines a business model and decision-making framework that enable IT to run as a business.
2. TBM provides IT organizations with the solutions—strategies, methodologies, and tools—to manage the cost, quality, and value of their IT services.
3. TBM was instituted by CIOs, CTOs, CFOs, and other technology leaders. Founded on transparency of costs, consumption, and performance, TBM gives technology leaders and their business partners the facts they need to collaborate on business-aligned decisions. [15.2]

The TBM framework allows you to manage IT more like a business. It helps you to manage and articulate cost, quality, and value. As with any framework, you can keep it quite simple or make it quite detailed. For the purposes of our IT renovation work, we're going to stick to the basics to provide some ideas about how you can begin to implement a TBM framework in all the IT work you do. This will enable you and your IT leaders to better articulate the value IT provides to the organization in every conversation.

TBM has been widely adopted by various branches of the U.S. government. A document from the U.S. General Services Administration (GSA) and the U.S. Department of Education titled "Technology Business Management Playbook," describes a very practical approach to implementing TBM. It outlines seven steps, listed here. [15.3]

1. **Identify key players and stakeholders.** An effective TBM program involves IT, operations, and finance stakeholders.

2. **Determine current state.** It's necessary to understand the current state, including operational needs, projects, strategic initiatives, and current state of all IT systems.
3. **Identify measurable desired outcomes.** Identify how you can deliver the right IT services for the best possible price (cost) as you work with your stakeholders.
4. **Start aligning data.** Based on the current state and desired outcomes, start working with financial data.
5. **Look for insights.** Once you start mapping IT systems and costs to business functions, what does your data tell you? Where does it lead you? Follow your data.
6. **Rollout and adoptions.** Once you have finished a first pass at TBM, start integrating additional TBM methods and concepts to foster value conversations across the organization.
7. **Keep maturing the TBM implementation.** Assess your maturity and identify opportunities to maximize the TBM mindset and implementation. Metrics might include cost of IT service per user, per service line, per location, (etc.) per year, or cost vs. target or cost vs. budget. You may also want to track infrastructure costs (those IT investments required for all IT functions) as a percentage of total IT costs or as a percentage of total revenue and track those changes over time.

This is just one approach to implementing TBM, but you can see from this example, the elements are universal and can apply to any business or industry.

Ideally, using TBM, you can work to optimize IT costs so they are well-aligned with the objectives of the organization. You can better focus your IT efforts on the things that bring value to the organization, and you can invest in innovation that drives the business forward. This happens in large part because IT costs and investments become more transparent and business partners engage in discussions about IT and what will drive the most value for the organization.

TBM addresses the needs of multiple stakeholders across the organization. Coyne identifies these key outcomes from TBM: [15.4]

1. **Strategic alignment** through service and project portfolio management

2. **Value delivery** through portfolio, financial, and asset tracking
3. **Performance measurement** through metrics and reporting
4. **Resource management** through labor, software, and hardware tracking
5. **Risk and compliance management** through policies, procedures, and contracts tracking

You can see that by aligning with organizational strategy, you will deliver value. If you measure performance and manage resources, you'll deliver value. While this is a vast oversimplification of TBM, it is the foundation and a viable approach to improving the alignment of IT to the business, to enable renovation and later, transformation.

## TBM Components

This section is not intended to give you a full grasp of TBM. Rather, it's intended to give you an overview of the elements of TBM so you can determine how, when, or whether you'll go down this path. The good news is that even modest TBM efforts can help improve the IT discussions at your organization.

Fundamentally, TBM looks at IT through three different filters: IT, Finance, and Business.

### *The IT Perspective*

The IT view aligns closely with the information we covered in Chapter 8. These elements include having an inventory of hardware and software systems as well as the costs of those systems as a starting point. This includes the data center, compute (servers), storage, network, printers, (etc.), end user devices, applications, service delivery, security & compliance, and IT management. These are the technology functions supported by IT spending in support of the organization.

These can be further delineated into platform services, infrastructure services, delivery services, security services, business applications, clinical applications, and end-user services. These are the products and services delivered by IT and consumed by the organization.

## The Finance Perspective

These elements are ones you are quite familiar with. The finance perspective describes the types of assets and services purchased to deliver the IT function to the organization. For example, it would include hardware, software, telcom, utilities, internal labor (labor, benefits), external labor, outside services (contractors and vendors), and others. These are typically line items or expense categories in an IT budget.

## The Business Perspective

This perspective includes the business domains and describes the capabilities of the organization supported by the technology spend and resources described in the IT and Finance perspectives. Business domains in healthcare might include inpatient, outpatient, patient engagement, business intelligence, billing, quality, and regulatory, for example.

Some of the items that would be included in the business section are financial systems, including general ledgers and fixed assets. Human Resources systems might include employee management systems, benefits, and compliance systems. Operational or clinical systems, of course, include the EHR along with all the software systems interfaced with the EHR. Some of those systems, such as document management or electronic faxing, are usually considered IT systems whereas systems used for clinical treatment, such as hybrid operating room (OR) systems, or advanced imaging systems (PET, MRI, and CT), are considered clinical systems. These systems are rarely included in the general IT category because the business value and ROI of these systems are tied to clinical care and are generally easier to calculate.

# Beginning with TBM

IT systems are very different from clinical systems. We can't easily calculate the cost per case or the cost per use because things like the network are simply pervasive, always-on infrastructure elements required for the basic functioning of the business. Still, there are ways to talk about the value of IT systems in a way that makes sense for operational leaders. For example, if your organization has 5,000 employees and your EHR annual license and maintenance fee is $5,000,000, quick math says that the cost is $1,000 per employee. Of course, not all employees use the EHR in their roles, but it is a quick way to show cost. Perhaps your organization has 3,800 employees in jobs related to clinical care (providers, care coordinators, medical records, quality, business office, etc.). Then the cost of the EHR on a per person basis is $1,316. In a pure sense, there is no real context or value in doing this, but what if you did that for every application, every system, every network component? What if you said, in essence, "we spend $8,500 per employee for computer systems that enable us to provide patient care." That starts getting attention from business leaders.

Now, suppose you take it a step further and calculate the cost of providing basic business tools for all employees, such as email, word processing, spreadsheets, an intranet, Internet connectivity, desk phones (and telephony circuits), cell phones, etc.

Add in the cost of required licensing for these solutions for each employee as well as any supporting infrastructure (i.e. if you need to buy or rent servers for a function, include the total cost of that as well).

Pretty soon, you're able to say, "Every time we add a new employee, we add $4,500 of software licensing to our annual costs. These include: [list]."

You can begin to see how you can use this data at a very basic level to express the IT cost per employee, per job function, per location, per specialty, etc. This begins to help contextualize IT costs and move you away from the perennial conversation about what you're doing to control or reduce IT costs. You might still feel that pressure, but then the conversation can shift to the cost of systems per employee or what systems the organization might like to scale back or decommission in order to meet this cost reduction initiative. It is really about making all of these usually hidden costs visible so better business decisions can be made and business leaders begin to see IT costs as their costs.

TBM at its core, is about cost transparency, but having this IT cost data enables you to perform effective IT benchmarking against standards, industries, or peer organizations. It can drive business insights, and it certainly enables more effective IT planning. When individuals stop seeing IT as "free" and when leaders stop seeing IT as "an expense," IT will be better able to meet the strategic needs of the organization.

### TBM Software Solutions

There are software tools that can be purchased to assist with TBM. There are also software solutions you may have already deployed that have elements of TBM built into them or have features that will help you with TBM. As is often the case, the bare-bones solution is to just start out using a spreadsheet to begin your journey.

## Summary

IT is a vital and strategic component in today's healthcare environment. The conversation must necessarily shift from one of cost/expense to one of value and investment. The topics covered in this chapter are just the starting point for you to explore these concepts further. Every organization will approach this slightly differently. The key is to begin moving the conversation to how IT contributes to the achievement of organizational objectives. When operational leaders begin to understand and articulate the IT costs associated with their business units or their strategic projects, the entire discussion of the IT function is elevated to a more strategic level. As you perform your assessments and develop your renovation plan, keep these value conversations in mind and begin the work of articulating the value of IT in every interaction and every conversation.

## References

[15.1] Naegle, Robert, "7 rules for demonstrating the business value of IT," August 24, 2022, https://www.gartner.com/en/articles/7-rules-for-demonstrating-the-business-value-of-it, accessed January 28, 2023.

[15.2] Coyne, Kevin, "Technology Business Management (TBM) Overview, 2017 Financial Management Conference, U.S. Department of Commerce," May 12, 2017, https://www.nist.gov/system/files/documents/2017/05/12/doc2017financialmanagementconference-tbm.pdf, accessed December 7, 2022.

[15.3] U.S. General Services Administration and U.S. Department of Education, "Technology Business Management Playbook," February 2010, https://tech.gsa.gov/playbooks/tbm/, accessed December 9, 2022.

[15.4] Coyne, "Technology business management."

# Resources

BRM Capability, no date, https://brm.institute/category/brm_capability/, accessed January 28, 2023.

CIO.gov, "IT spending transparency maturity model whitepaper," September 30, 2020, https://www.cio.gov/assets/files/IT-Spending-Transparency-Maturity-Model-Whitepaper.pdf pending-Transparency-Maturity-Model-Whitepaper.pdf, accessed December 9, 2022.

CIO.gov, "Meeting IT priorities with TBM: How IT cost transparency helps you meet your IT goals," July 2020, https://www.cio.gov/assets/resources/MIPT-draft-5.0-Final-2020_08.pdf, accessed December 9, 2022.

Technology Business Management Council, "TBM Taxonomy Version 4.0," December 16, 2020, https://www.tbmcouncil.org/learn-tbm/tbm-taxonomy/, accessed December 9, 2022.

# IT ASSESSMENTS

# Chapter 16

# IT Strategy Assessment

In Chapter 4, we discussed the building blocks of IT strategy. As you recall, we reviewed the HealthIT.gov strategy document to better understand how goals, objectives, and strategies relate to one another. Briefly, one of the goals was to "promote health and wellness." Three objectives were identified, and under each objective, and strategies to achieve each objective were discussed. Using that same approach, we'll begin by assessing your IT strategy.

## Assessment Approach – The CMMI Model

We use the Capability Maturity Model Index (CMMI) model for our assessments in all chapters. This model is useful because it helps articulate the relative maturity of a capability within a domain. As such, you can develop definitions that map with the CMMI model in a way that meets your specific needs.

CMMI maturity levels are:

1. Initial – unpredictable, poorly defined
2. Managed – some processes may be in place to manage the dimension
3. Defined – a defined set of processes are in place and generally utilized
4. Quantitatively managed – processes are more refined; data is used to measure and improve the dimension
5. Optimized – continuous improvement and innovation occur at this level

DOI: 10.4324/9781003377023-19

We also use the rating of zero when a capability is not present at all. In each dimension, we will define capability levels zero through five. These statements map to the five defined levels of CMMI plus our added zero rating.

Capability statements are written to reflect the preferred or optimal end state. As you work through your assessments, you'll compare your current state to optimal end states so you can evaluate the maturity of your capabilities. If you choose to develop alternative capability statements, you can do so using this method. Identify the ideal end state, write your capability statement, then define the maturity levels from zero through five using the CMMI model as your guide.

No organization has all capabilities at the highest CMMI level (Level 5), nor should they aspire to achieve that level for every capability. The effort it takes to bring a capability to an ideal or optimized state may not be valuable to your organization. Your goal should be to assess and then prioritize. Which capabilities, if improved, will provide the greatest benefit? Which ones, if left in their current state, will most impair your ability to improve? These are the value judgments you will have to make as you assess your current state.

## Strategy Assessment Overview

We begin by reviewing the dimensions of the strategy domain to explore the various capability levels of IT strategy look like. From there, we develop capability statements and walk through the assessment of each. These statements are intended to get you started. The key elements at the top level are those that are universal to all organizations, so you can use these as-is. However, the capability statements and the defined levels can be tailored to your specific use case. Every organization is different, so you may want to define your levels of capability maturity accordingly.

## Define the Dimension

Every organization has stated goals and objectives, and every organization develops plans to meet those objectives. As such, every organization has strategic plans, even if they are not visible or formalized. If an organization wants to improve metrics for length-of-stay (LOS) or quality metrics for hypertension control, for example, it will list objectives and metrics. Those might be then translated into statements such as reduce LOS by x% or improve hypertension screening by y%. The next step is to identify how you'll accomplish the stated outcomes. How will you reduce LOS or improve hypertension control? The strategy lies in those answers.

The same holds true in IT. You will define goals and objectives for your department and then define how you'll achieve those goals. That is your strategic plan. Recall that the *how* in this case is the high-level *how* and not the detailed, tactical *how*. That means that you might identify a goal to "improve patient experience." You might create an objective to "increase the use of the patient portal." One strategy you might select would be to "identify and implement five key features patients want in a portal." That is the high-level *how*. The tactical *how* would describe exactly how you would find patients willing to provide their perspectives, how you would go about gathering their insights, and how you would implement those changes.

The key capabilities in IT strategy are definition, execution, alignment, and engagement.

**Definition** is used here to describe how well the IT strategy is defined and documented.

**Execution** describes how well IT is performing those strategic functions. This is not a place to discuss all the mitigating reasons your strategy is *on* or *off* track, it is simply a rating of how well this is performed on a consistent basis.

**Alignment** describes how well the IT strategy is aligned with the business objectives or business strategy. Again, these are short statements of fact, not defenses or explanations. Those will be considered when you develop your renovation plan.

**Engagement** describes how well the IT department and the organization engage with IT strategy. You might choose to focus only on IT engagement with IT strategy or you could tie this to overall organizational engagement with IT strategy, which will also surface when you assess your governance process.

## Write Capability Statements

The four elements of this dimension have been expanded here to reflect what a fully implemented or optimized dimension might look like. For example, under "Definition," we provide three statements that reflect what a well-defined strategy might entail. You are encouraged to modify these statements to reflect your own organization, if desired. In the next section, we'll develop the capability statements reflecting the CMMI rating.

1. **[DEFINITION]** A well-defined and detailed strategy has been created and clearly articulated.
   a. IT strategy has been identified and clearly articulated by IT leadership.
   b. IT strategy has defined elements with associated metrics to measure achievement.
   c. IT strategy is documented, and a plan to achieve these objectives has been created.
2. **[EXECUTION]** Specific plans have been created and implemented to execute on the strategic plans.
   a. IT strategy project plan(s) have been implemented.
   b. IT strategic project work is consistently prioritized along with other IT work.
   c. IT strategic project work is documented and measured against planned milestones.
   d. IT strategic project work is modified or adjusted, as needed, to address unexpected events.
   e. IT strategic project metrics are evaluated during and after implementation.
3. **[ALIGNMENT]** The IT strategic plan has been developed in conjunction with organizational stakeholders to ensure alignment with the overall goals of the organization.
   a. IT strategy is developed in conjunction with organizational stakeholders.
   b. IT strategy is used in the governance process to ensure IT work remains aligned with the organization.
   c. IT strategy projects are evaluated periodically against IT and organizational strategic objectives.
4. **[ENGAGEMENT]** IT leaders and staff engage in the development, implementation, and review of IT strategy.
   a. IT leaders and staff are engaged in the development, review, and implementation of IT strategy.
   b. IT leaders engage organizational leaders in the IT/business strategic alignment process.
   c. Organizational stakeholders are informed on a periodic basis about the progress of IT strategic initiatives.

# Assess the Capability

Each capability is stated along with five levels of capability statements. We've added 0 to indicate the capability does not exist. These are provided to be used as-is or as a starting point for your own customized set of statements. Each of the levels, C0 through C5, represents a statement reflecting the capability maturity of the item. This is a combination of qualitative and quantitative assessment, suitable for assessing your IT function across all dimensions. As a quick reminder, CMMI levels are 1 – initial, 2- managed, 3- defined, 4- quantitatively managed, and 5 – optimized. We will use the same model for all assessments.

*Note: You are welcome to create much more detailed assessments. For example, for each dimension listed here (definition, execution, alignment, and engagement), you could develop several capabilities statements, breaking down each into additional layers of detail. The danger in developing such a granular assessment is that you may get bogged down either in creating the elements or performing the assessment. If you are tempted to add more detail, you might consider taking a first pass with less detail and see how that works. You can always swing back through and break elements into additional levels of detail later. This is just your first assessment. There are twelve assessments in total, so give some thought to how much detail you want in each assessment. You may choose to define more elements in some assessments than others. A flexible approach will ensure the results are actionable for you and your team.*

1. **[DEFINITION] A well-defined and detailed strategy has been created and clearly articulated.**
   **C0** – An IT strategy does not exist.
   **C1** – An IT strategy has been discussed or attempted, but never completed.
   **C2** – A draft or initial IT strategy has been developed, but strategic activities have not been defined.
   **C3** – IT strategy is not tied to organizational strategy. Strategic activities are managed at the IT leadership level in a proactive manner but there is little or no organizational engagement.
   **C4** – Strategy aligns at the organizational level. Strategic activities are well-defined and initiatives are well-controlled and well-executed.
   **C5** – Strategy aligns at the organizational level. IT strategy is a well-crafted plan to achieve objectives and includes key performance metrics. The strategy document is kept current.

2. **[EXECUTION] Specific plans have been created and implemented to execute on the strategic plans.**

   **C0** – No IT strategy exists.

   **C1** – An IT strategy exists, but no specific plans have been created.

   **C2** – An IT strategy exists, some plans have been created, none have been implemented.

   **C3** – An IT strategy exists, plans have been created and implemented, with mixed results. No key performance metrics have been identified or discussed.

   **C4** – An IT strategy exists, plans have been created and well-implemented, with generally positive results. Key performance metrics are in development.

   **C5** – An IT strategy exists, plans have been created, well-implemented and optimized. Key performance metrics have been established and met.

3. **[ALIGNMENT] The IT strategic plan has been developed in conjunction with organizational stakeholders to ensure alignment with the overall goals of the organization.**

   **C0** – An IT strategic plan does not exist.

   **C1** – An IT strategic plan is in initial stages of development. No stakeholders have been engaged in the process. IT governance has not been leveraged for this purpose or does not exist.

   **C2** – An IT strategic plan exists in draft stage. Some stakeholders have provided input. The IT governance process is not being leveraged for strategic discussions.

   **C3** – An IT strategic plan exists. Stakeholders provided input to varying degrees. The IT governance process is used to maintain strategic alignment of IT initiatives.

   **C4** – An IT strategic plan exists and is used. Stakeholders have been engaged at all stages. The IT governance process is used to maintain strategic alignment of IT initiatives.

   **C5** – An IT strategic plan exists and is used. Stakeholders have been very engaged at all stages. The IT governance process is used to maintain strategic alignment and the process has been optimized.

4. **[ENGAGEMENT] IT leaders and staff engage in the development, implementation, and review of IT strategy.**

   **C0** – There is no IT strategy.

   **C1** – The IT strategy is in draft stage and has not yet been deployed.

**C2** – The IT strategy has been created and deployed by IT leaders.

**C3** – The IT strategy has been created in conjunction with IT leaders, staff, and stakeholders. It is in the process of being deployed.

**C4** – The IT strategy has been created in conjunction with IT leaders, staff, and stakeholders. It has been deployed, with varying results.

**C5** – The IT strategy has been created in conjunction with IT leaders, staff, and stakeholders. It has been deployed with very strong results. The strategy and processes have been optimized.

# Chart Current State

As we will do in all assessment chapters, we'll take your initial ratings of each capability statement and graph them using a radar-style chart. The scale should be set from zero to five to mirror the CMMI model we're using. Once you have assessed your capabilities, your chart will give you an excellent visual depiction of your current state.

Table 16.1 shows an example of the dimensions, a brief description, and a hypothetical rating to give you an idea of how you can document the data. Figure 16.1 shows the associated radar-style graph. Based on the chart, you can easily see where your opportunities for maturing capabilities are.

If you want to develop more detailed assessments, you can drill down into the second level. In this chapter, we show that second level of detail, but in subsequent chapters, we keep it at the top level. If you want to use additional levels in any subsequent assessment, you can refer to this model.

**Table 16.1 IT Strategy CMMI Ratings Matrix**

| Dimension | Rating | Description |
|---|---|---|
| **Definition** | 3 | A well-defined and detailed strategy has been created and clearly articulated. |
| **Execution** | 1.2 | Specific plans have been created and implemented to execute on the strategic plans. |
| **Alignment** | 2 | The IT strategic plan has been developed in conjunction with organizational stakeholders to ensure alignment with the overall goals of the organization. |
| **Engagement** | 2.5 | IT leaders and staff engage in the development, implementation, and review of IT strategy. |

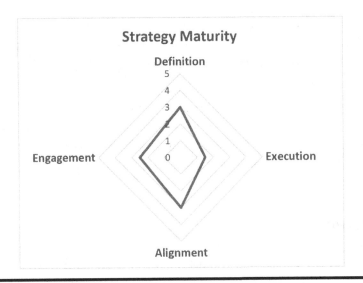

**Figure 16.1  Strategy capabilities radar-style chart.**

You can see the statements provided at the beginning of this chapter have statements a, b, c, etc. To assess these, you could use the same types of capability statements. This level of assessment would yield a matrix similar to that shown in Figure 16.2 and four separate charts that might look like those shown in Figure 16.3. We've used abbreviations to help organize the sub-items.

You may choose to delve into this level of detail for some areas of your assessment, but perhaps not for all of them. While it can be helpful to have this level of assessment in some areas, the risk is that you can easily

| Symbol | CMMI | Definition | | |
|---|---|---|---|---|
| DE1 | 4 | | a. | IT strategy has been identified and clearly articulated by IT leadership. |
| DE2 | 3 | | b. | IT strategy has defined elements with associated metrics to measure achievement. |
| DE3 | 2 | | c. | IT strategy is documented and a plan to achieve these objectives has been created. |
| | | Execution | | |
| EX1 | 2 | | a. | IT strategy project plan(s) have been implemented. |
| EX2 | 0 | | b. | IT strategic project work is consistently prioritized along with other IT work. |
| EX3 | 2 | | c. | IT strategic project work is documented and measured against planned milestones. |
| EX4 | 1 | | d. | IT strategic project work is modified or adjusted, as needed, to address unexpected events. |
| EX5 | 1 | | e. | IT strategic projects metrics are evaluated during and after implementation. |
| | | Alignment | | |
| AL1 | 2 | | a. | IT strategy is developed in conjunction with organizational stakeholders. |
| AL2 | 2 | | b. | IT strategy is used in the governance process to ensure IT work remains aligned with the organization. |
| AL3 | 1 | | c. | IT strategy projects are evaluated periodically against IT and organizational strategic objectives. |
| | | Engagement | | |
| EN1 | 3 | | a. | IT leaders and staff are engaged in the development, review, and implementation of IT strategy. |
| EN2 | 2 | | b. | IT leaders engage organizational leaders in the IT/business strategic alignment process. |
| EN3 | 3 | | c. | Organizational stakeholders are informed on a periodic basis about the progress of IT strategic initiatives. |

**Figure 16.2  Second-level CMMI ratings matrix.**

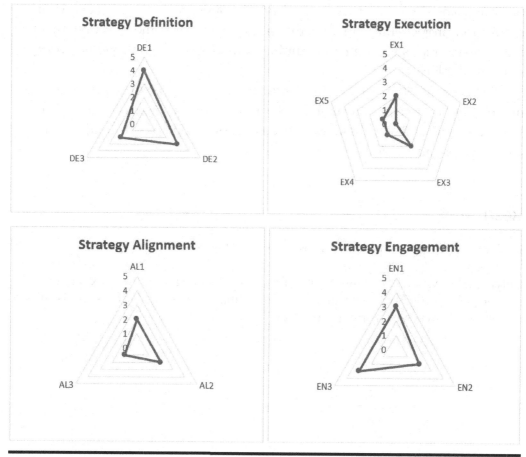

**Figure 16.3    Second-level ratings on radar-style charts.**

overwhelm your teams with this level of detail. You might choose to go into this level of detail in areas that have been particularly troublesome or resistant to change. In those cases, digging down further might help you uncover the root causes of issues that you can remediate through your renovation project. Otherwise, it's advisable to stay at the top level on the first pass. You can always use an iterative approach to your assessment work to get into more detailed assessments later.

## Summary: Future State Notes

In each assessment chapter, we will pause to reflect on what we have learned in this section of the assessment. It is important to take a moment to think through what you have learned, what things may have surprised or disappointed you, and what elements you feel are most critical to your renovation project. Take notes at the end of each assessment to document these observations so you can compile them when you put together your renovation plan.

IT strategy is often elusive in healthcare, but it is possible to develop and implement IT strategy at a basic level and mature the capability over time. Engaging staff and stakeholders in the process will help assure alignment and drive engagement.

## Resources

ISACA CMMI Institute, no date, https://cmmiinstitute.com/, accessed March 18, 2023.

Saltyko, Alexey, "11 key components of a great IT strategy with real examples," no date, https://burniegroup.com/4-most-important-aspects-of-a-successful-it-strategy/, accessed February 6, 2023.

## Chapter 17

# IT and Data Governance Assessment

Using the framework we developed in the prior chapter, we can create an assessment for IT and data governance. For context, let's begin with information that will help inform your assessment of these domains.

## IT and Data Governance Overview

There are several things that negatively impact both IT and data governance in organizations. A 2022 CIO.com article lays out seven overlooked elements. [17.1] These are:

1. Not keeping pace with changing business priorities
2. Poor risk planning
3. Poor operational visibility
4. Failure to align IT or data governance with enterprise governance
5. Using lagging performance indicators
6. Treating data like a byproduct
7. Overlooking insider threats

If a process, particularly related to IT or data governance, fails to keep up with evolving business priorities, it will quickly lose relevance and fall out of sync. To avoid this, IT and data governance must have a strong tie-in to the overall enterprise governance efforts and maintain operational visibility.

While many IT organizations rely on retrospective performance or service level metrics, these alone will not guarantee future success. According to Prashant Kelker, partner for digital strategies and solutions at ISG, "Leading indicators include revenue growth, revenue per client, profit margin, client retention rate, and customer satisfaction." [17.1].

According to Egnyte CSO Kris Lahiri, taking a holistic approach to IT and data governance is important. Elements such as data security, network security, and end-user cyber education should ideally be part of the overall IT/data governance process. Lahiri also recommends "centralizing data views to understand what content is being accessed, and by whom. This will enable the organization to detect malicious activity by recognizing commonplace user behavior and patterns." [17.1]

## IT Governance

We will begin with assessing the IT governance function. Later in the chapter, we'll follow the same process for assessing your data governance function. If you choose to work on them together due to the way in which your teams operate, that's fine. If you choose that approach, be sure to include all the elements that differ between IT and data governance functions.

## Define the Dimension

The function of IT governance is to ensure IT initiatives support and align with the organization's mission, vision, objectives, and strategies. It should be a structured, repeatable process that is well-defined, well-documented, and consistently reviewed.

## Write Capability Statements

The capability statements define the optimal future state. These are used to assess your current capabilities and define a path toward improvement and optimization.

The IT governance function includes these items.

1. **[FRAMEWORK]** Utilizes a framework or defined methodology.
2. **[STRATEGIES]** Reviews and aligns IT initiatives against organizational priorities and strategies and prioritizes accordingly.

3. **[REQUIREMENTS]** Reviews proposed solutions against requirements including scope, timeline, cybersecurity requirements, and cost, among others.
4. **[PRIORITIES]** Prioritizes IT initiatives to provide a roadmap for IT projects keeping visible the work of the IT department.
5. **[SUBJECT MATTER EXPERTS]** IT governance involves organizational subject matter experts (SMEs) such as legal, compliance, and risk management to ensure IT initiatives remain aligned with requirements.
6. **[LESSONS LEARNED]** Results from IT initiatives are reviewed through the IT governance function to gather lessons learned.

## Assess the Capability

Each capability is stated along with five levels of capability statements. These are provided to be used as-is or as a starting point for your own customized set of statements.

1. **[FRAMEWORK] Utilizes a framework or defined methodology.**
   **C0** – There is no IT governance process.
   **C1** – There is an IT governance process, but it does not use any defined method.
   **C2** – There is an IT governance process, the defined method is not fully formed or framework partially implemented.
   **C3** – The IT governance process uses a defined method, which is documented and used periodically.
   **C4** – The IT governance process uses a defined method, which is documented and used consistently.
   **C5** – The IT governance process uses a defined method, which is documented, used consistently, and process improvement is data driven.
2. **[STRATEGIES] Reviews IT initiatives against organizational priorities and strategies, and prioritizes accordingly.**
   **C0** – There is no IT governance function.
   **C1** – The IT initiatives are reviewed at IT governance, but they are often not fully formed and are not reviewed against organizational priorities.
   **C2** – The IT initiatives are reviewed at IT governance; they are sometimes fully formed but are not reviewed against organizational priorities.

**C3** – The IT initiatives are reviewed at IT governance, they are usually fully formed and often reviewed against organizational priorities.

**C4** – The IT initiatives are reviewed at IT governance, they are always fully formed and always reviewed against organizational priorities.

**C5** – The IT initiatives are reviewed at IT governance, decisions are data driven and initiatives are very well formed and reviewed against organizational priorities. New innovative ideas often come from this review process.

3. **[REQUIREMENTS] Reviews proposed solutions against requirements including scope, timeline, cybersecurity requirements, and cost, among others.**

   **C0** – There is no IT governance function.

   **C1** – Proposals are rarely well formed and lacking required elements.

   **C2** – Proposals are sometimes well-formed and typically have all required elements.

   **C3** – Proposals are usually well-formed and often have all the required elements.

   **C4** – Proposals are always well-formed and almost always have all the required elements.

   **C5** – Proposals are always well-formed and always have all the required elements.

4. **[PRIORITIES] Prioritizes IT initiatives to provide a roadmap for IT initiatives to keep visible the work of the IT department.**

   **C0** – There is no IT governance function.

   **C1** – IT initiatives are reviewed; there is no prioritization function.

   **C2** – IT initiatives are reviewed; the method of prioritization is ad hoc and not documented.

   **C3** – IT initiatives are reviewed; the prioritization method is documented and sometimes followed.

   **C4** – IT initiatives are reviewed; the prioritization method is documented and always followed.

   **C5** – IT initiatives are reviewed; the prioritization method is documented and always followed. The process has been optimized, and results reflect this optimization.

5. **[SUBJECT MATTER EXPERTS] IT governance involves organizational SMEs such as legal, compliance, and risk management to ensure IT initiatives remain aligned with requirements.**

   **C0** – There is no IT governance process.

   **C1** – The IT governance process does not involve organizational experts.

**C2** – The IT governance process occasionally involves organizational experts on an ad hoc basis.

**C3** – The IT governance process frequently involves organizational experts on an ad hoc basis.

**C4** – The IT governance process frequently involves organizational experts based on defined criteria.

**C5** – The IT governance process always involves organizational experts when needed based on well-defined and well-understood criteria.

6. **[LESSONS LEARNED] Results from IT initiatives are reviewed through the IT governance function to gather lessons learned.**

**C0** – There is no IT governance process.

**C1** – The results of IT initiatives are not documented and not reviewed.

**C2** – The results of IT initiatives are sometimes documented, but rarely reviewed.

**C3** – The results of IT initiatives are often documented and sometimes reviewed. Lessons learned are infrequently reviewed or incorporated in the IT governance process.

**C4** – The results of IT initiatives are always documented and almost always reviewed. Lessons learned are often reviewed and often incorporated in the IT governance process.

**C5** – The results of IT initiatives are always documented and always reviewed. Lessons learned are always reviewed and incorporated in the IT governance process.

# Chart Current State

Document the elements of the dimension and their associated description and rating in a table, like that shown in Table 17.1. The summary of the capabilities assessment might look like that shown in Figure 17.1, a sample

**Table 17.1    IT Governance CMMI Ratings Matrix**

| Dimension | Rating | Definition |
|---|---|---|
| **Framework** | 3 | Uses a framework. |
| **Alignment** | 3 | Aligns with organizational priorities. |
| **Requirements** | 2 | Reviews initiatives against requirements. |
| **Priorities** | 1 | Ranks initiatives to reflect organizational priorities. |
| **SMEs** | 1 | Appropriately involves SMEs. |
| **Lessons Learned** | 0 | Results are reviewed, lessons learned incorporated. |

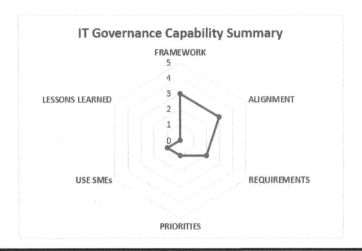

**Figure 17.1  IT governance capabilities radar-style chart.**

radar-style graph. In this case, you have not developed the practice of gathering lessons learned, so you've rated it "0." Your lowest-rated item is not necessarily going to be your highest priority in your renovation project. If you were to decide how to best advance your IT governance capabilities, you might work on prioritization first, then focus on better involving SMEs, then look to develop a lessons learned process. Assess where you'll get the most benefit from expending effort to improve a particular capability.

## Summary: Future State Notes

Based on the chart shown in Figure 17.1, you might decide to focus on improving the capabilities of the prioritization efforts since that may drive better results initially. The goal is always to move each of the dimensions toward more mature capabilities. Sometimes you might choose to build a capability incrementally and focus on efforts that will have the biggest impact first. You can decide when you get to your renovation project plan what you need to improve first in your governance process.

## Data Governance

In Chapter 10, we discussed the value of data governance in a healthcare organization. In this section, we define data governance dimensions, develop capability statements, and assess the capability. If you do not have data governance in place, you can create plans to develop your data governance capability when you develop your IT renovation plan.

## Define the Dimension

Data governance should pull together all relevant stakeholders in the organization who interact with data in a strategic manner. This might include informatics or quality analysts who look at patient, provider, or financial data to provide actionable insights for the organization.

The function of data governance is to ensure data initiatives support and align with the organization's mission, vision, objectives, and strategies. It should be a structured, repeatable process that is well-defined, well-documented, and consistently reviewed. You also should have a defined data management plan that includes elements such as data owners, data definitions, and data sources, among others.

If you have an IT governance function in place, you can model your data governance structure in a similar manner.

## Write Capability Statements

The capability statements define the optimal future state. These are used to assess your current capabilities and define a path toward improvement and optimization.

The data governance function:

1. **[FRAMEWORK]** Utilizes a framework or defined methodology. This includes data ownership, management, quality, validation, retention, security, and other dimensions.
2. **[STRATEGY]** Reviews data initiatives against organizational priorities and strategies, and prioritizes accordingly.
3. **[REQUIREMENTS]** Reviews proposed data requests against requirements including scope, timeline, cybersecurity requirements, and cost, among others.
4. **[PRIORITIES]** Prioritizes data requests to provide a roadmap for data initiatives to keep the work visible.
5. **[SMEs]** Data governance involves data SMEs including data analysts as well as organizational SMEs.
6. **[LESSONS LEARNED]** Results from data initiatives are reviewed through the data governance function to gather lessons learned.

## Assess Capability

Each capability is stated along with five levels of capability statements. These are provided to be used as-is or as a starting point for your own customized set of statements.

1. **[FRAMEWORK] Utilizes a framework or defined methodology.**
   **C0** – There is no data governance process.
   **C1** – There is a data governance process, but it does not use any defined method.
   **C2** – There is a data governance process, the defined method is not fully formed.
   **C3** – The data governance process uses a defined method, which is documented and used periodically. Data management is in initial stages.
   **C4** – The data governance process uses a defined method, which is documented and used consistently. The data management function is maturing.
   **C5** – The data governance process uses a defined method, which is documented, used consistently, and periodically revised to improve the overall process. The data management function has been optimized.
2. **[STRATEGY] Reviews data initiatives against organizational priorities and strategies, and prioritizes accordingly.**
   **C0** – There is no data governance function.
   **C1** – The data initiatives are reviewed in data governance, but they often are not fully formed and they are not reviewed against organizational priorities.
   **C2** – The data initiatives are reviewed in data governance; they are sometimes fully formed but are not reviewed against organizational priorities. Data owners and other responsibilities (RACI) are not identified.
   **C3** – The data initiatives are reviewed in data governance, they are usually fully formed and sometimes reviewed against organizational priorities. RACI matrices are typically created.
   **C4** – The data initiatives are reviewed in data governance, they are always fully formed and always reviewed against organizational priorities. RACI matrices are always created, ownership is clear.
   **C5** – The data initiatives are reviewed in data governance, they are very well formed and always reviewed against organizational priorities. RACI matrices are always created and are used effectively.

3. **[REQUIREMENTS] Reviews proposed data requests against requirements including scope, timeline, cybersecurity requirements, and cost, among others.**

   **C0** – There is no data governance function.

   **C1** – Proposals are rarely well formed and therefore lacking required elements.

   **C2** – Proposals are sometimes well formed and sometimes have all required elements.

   **C3** – Proposals are usually well formed and often have all the required elements.

   **C4** – Proposals are always well formed and almost always have all the required elements.

   **C5** – Proposals are always well formed and always have all the required elements.

4. **[PRIORITIES] Prioritizes data initiatives to provide a roadmap for data initiatives to keep visible the work of the Business Intelligence/Data Analytics department.**

   **C0** – There is no data governance function.

   **C1** – Data initiatives are reviewed, but there is no prioritization function.

   **C2** – Data initiatives are reviewed; the method of prioritization is ad hoc and typically not documented.

   **C3** – IT initiatives are reviewed, the prioritization method is often documented and sometimes followed.

   **C4** – IT initiatives are reviewed, the prioritization method is always documented and followed.

   **C5** – IT initiatives are reviewed, the prioritization method is documented and always followed. The process has been optimized and results reflect this optimization.

5. **[SUBJECT MATTER EXPERTS - SMEs] Data governance involves organizational SMEs such as legal, compliance, quality, and risk management to ensure data initiatives remain aligned with requirements.**

   **C0** – There is no data governance process.

   **C1** – The data governance process does not involve organizational experts.

   **C2** – The data governance process occasionally involves organizational experts on an ad hoc basis.

   **C3** – The data governance process frequently involves organizational experts on an ad hoc basis.

**C4** – The data governance process frequently involves organizational experts based on defined criteria.

**C5** – The data governance process always involves organizational experts when needed based on well-defined and well-understood criteria.

6. **[LESSONS LEARNED] Results from data initiatives are reviewed through the data governance function to gather lessons learned.**

**C0** – There is no data governance process.

**C1** – The results of data initiatives are not documented and not reviewed.

**C2** – The results of data initiatives are sometimes documented, but rarely, if ever, reviewed.

**C3** – The results of data initiatives are often documented and sometimes reviewed. Lessons learned are infrequently reviewed or incorporated in the data governance process.

**C4** – The results of data initiatives are always documented and almost always reviewed. Lessons learned are often reviewed and incorporated in the data governance process.

**C5** – The results of data initiatives are always documented and always reviewed. Lessons learned are always reviewed and incorporated in the data governance process.

## Chart Current State

The matrix of capabilities and CMMI ratings might look like that shown in Table 17.2. The resulting radar-style chart would then look like that shown in Figure 17.2. Your strategic approach and use of SMEs, in this example, look

**Table 17.2   Data Governance CMMI Ratings Matrix**

| Dimension | Rating | Definition |
|---|---|---|
| Framework | 2 | Uses a framework. |
| Strategy | 3 | Aligns with strategic priorities. |
| Requirements | 2 | Reviews initiatives against requirements. |
| Priorities | 1 | Ranks initiatives to reflect organizational priorities. |
| Use SMEs | 3 | Appropriately involves SMEs. |
| Lessons Learned | 0 | Results are reviewed, lessons learned incorporated. |

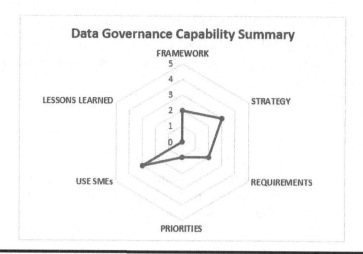

**Figure 17.2    Data governance radar-style chart.**

to be in pretty good shape. Your priorities, framework, and lessons learned could use some focused improvement, so you would likely select one of these dimensions for your renovation plan.

## Summary: Future State Notes

As with IT governance, there are clear opportunities for improvement based on this example. If you were to select one area for immediate improvement, you might target the prioritization function. Ensuring data initiatives align with and support organizational strategies is crucial for the data function to be both effective and valuable. Otherwise, that lack of alignment will eventually lead to people taking data into their own hands outside of any structured methods (shadow data management, in essence), which leads to organizational risk on many fronts. Therefore, improving prioritization might be more important than improving the lessons learned function, which currently does not exist.

Both IT and data governance functions are central to managing IT demand in healthcare. The infinite number of project and data requests can grind IT to a halt if not managed well. As we have discussed in earlier chapters, IT work (including data work) is often perceived by the end user as "free." The governance process requires end users to really think through their requests and helps make visible the amount of effort these requests take – both for IT and for the operational owner. Of course, it also helps ensure projects are aligned with organizational objectives and that these projects and associated costs are approved and prioritized. This drives operational ownership.

# Reference

[17.1] Edwards, John, "7 IT governance mistakes - and how to avoid them," June 21, 2022, https://www.cio.com/article/401388/7-it-governance-mistakes-and-how-to-avoid-them.html, accessed January 7, 2023.

# Chapter 18

# IT Architecture Assessment

Many healthcare organizations lack a formal enterprise architecture (EA) or even a formal IT architecture. The reasons for this are several. First, many healthcare IT (HIT) departments have grown organically over time before some of the more structured methods of managing IT gained popularity. Many HIT departments are running at full capacity just managing break-fix-operations and haven't spent any time evaluating the role of EA in their environment. Still other organizations simply lack the technical expertise to engage in EA design, implementation, and management. That said, every enterprise using technology has EA and IT architecture, whether it's accidental, ad hoc, or formal.

For example, let's look at a small healthcare provider organization running on a very tight budget. The PCs might be all different versions of the Windows operating system – some new, some obsolete, some patched, some not. The network was originally configured by a person who really didn't know much about networking, but managed to get computers communicating with a server sitting under someone's desk. There was no formal or documented structure to Active Directory, so it's a mess. Over the years, IT staff came and went, everyone added on and upgraded as needed. Now, looking back over ten- or twenty-years' worth of IT operations, there's literally a chaotic mess of network configuration, operating systems, access control, and user accounts. Historically, these issues arose because there was no plan, design, expertise, or clear vision for those IT systems, and the day-to-day fires always took priority over planning.

This current state describes many HIT organizations and is not intended as a criticism. This is the reason so many HIT departments need to

DOI: 10.4324/9781003377023-21

undertake a renovation project. It is impossible to move forward with digital transformation on a foundation of technical chaos.

Whether you decide to consider developing your EA via a formal EA framework or simply decide to bring a bit more structure to your environment is your choice. Increase your capabilities incrementally. Using the information in this chapter, you can assess where you are with EA, what additional capabilities might look like, and what approach might benefit your organization most.

## Define the Dimension

EA describes the systems of systems used by the organization to achieve business objectives. As discussed in Chapter 6, EA encompasses IT architecture. If EA is too large to tackle, scale down and start with IT architecture first.

An organization that has an EA in place has a defined, systemic way of identifying and documenting the entire architectural configuration. Many companies implement software programs to help discover, document, and organize the architectural components. EA can help define how information, business processes, and technology interact at an organizational level to deliver results. Because it looks at business processes along with technology, EA can be a useful foundation for a digital transformation.

We will look at the four architecture dimensions discussed in Chapter 6: business, application, data, and technology. If you are using a model that includes other dimensions, you can modify your assessment to include those.

## Write Capability Statements

The capability statements define the optimal future state. These are used to assess your current capabilities and define a path toward improvement and optimization.

1. **[FRAMEWORK]** An EA framework or model is used.
2. **[BUSINESS PROCESSES]** EA activities evaluate business and operational processes to develop IT solutions.
3. **[PROCEDURES]** EA policies, procedures, and guidelines are established and followed.

4. **[PRIORITIZATION]** EA governs the selection, prioritization, and implementation of IT systems.
5. **[ROADMAPS]** EA drives the development of technology roadmaps and digital initiatives.

## Assess Capability

Each capability is stated along with five levels of capability statements. You can modify the statements to suit your needs. These are provided to be used as-is or as a starting point for your own customized set of statements.

1. **[FRAMEWORK] An EA framework or model is used.**
   **C0** – No EA framework or model is used.
   **C1** – No formal EA framework is used, but there is awareness of the need for an enterprise-wide approach to business and IT systems.
   **C2** – No formal EA framework is used, but an enterprise-wide view of business and IT systems is often considered.
   **C3** – A formal EA framework has been selected and is sometimes used.
   **C4** – A formal EA framework has been selected and is always used.
   **C5** – A formal EA framework has been selected, and the processes have been optimized.

2. **[BUSINESS PROCESSES] EA activities evaluate business and operational processes to develop IT solutions.**
   **C0** – No EA framework is used.
   **C1** – No EA framework is used, but business processes sometimes inform IT decisions.
   **C2** – No formal EA framework is used, but business processes often inform IT decisions.
   **C3** – A formal EA framework is used; business processes usually inform IT decisions.
   **C4** – A formal EA framework is used; business processes always inform IT decisions.
   **C5** – A formal EA framework is used to evaluate business processes to develop optimized IT solutions.

3. **[PROCEDURES] EA policies, procedures, and guidelines are established and followed.**
   **C0** – No EA framework is used.
   **C1** –No EA framework is used; EA related policies and procedures have not been developed.

**C2** – An EA framework has been identified, policies and procedures are not fully developed. Work is still ad hoc.

**C3** – A formal EA framework is used; policies and procedures are fairly well-developed. Work is more structured.

**C4** – A formal EA framework is used; policies and procedures are well-developed and consistently used. Work is well-structured and predictable.

**C5** – A formal EA framework is used; policies and procedures are very well-developed and always used. Policies and procedures continue to evolve and are optimized.

4. **[PRIORITIZATION] EA governs the selection, prioritization, and implementation of IT systems.**

**C0** – No EA framework is used.

**C1** – No EA framework is used; selection and prioritization of IT systems is unstructured.

**C2** – No formal EA framework is used; selection and prioritization of IT systems is somewhat structured.

**C3** – A formal EA framework is sometimes used to govern the selection and prioritization of IT systems.

**C4** – A formal EA framework is almost always used to govern the selection and prioritization of IT systems.

**C5** – A formal EA framework is always used and has been optimized to govern the selection and prioritization of IT systems.

5. **[ROADMAPS] EA drives the development of technology roadmaps and digital initiatives.**

**C0** – No EA framework is used.

**C1** – No EA framework is used; technology roadmaps are rarely created.

**C2** – No formal EA framework is used; technology roadmaps are sometimes created but without a view of the EA.

**C3** – A formal EA framework is sometimes used to guide the development of technology roadmaps.

**C4** – A formal EA framework is almost always used to guide the development of technology roadmaps.

**C5** – A formal EA framework is always used and is used to develop technology roadmaps that optimize business and IT initiatives, supporting or creating digital transformation.

# Chart Current State

If your organization is like many in healthcare, you may have minimal EA capabilities. The examples shown in Table 18.1 and Figure 18.1 depict a sample of where many healthcare organizations might map their EA capabilities today.

**Table 18.1  Enterprise Architecture CMMI Ratings Matrix**

| Dimension | Rating | Definition |
|---|---|---|
| **Framework** | 2 | Uses an EA framework or defined methodology. |
| **Business process** | 2 | Evaluate business/operations processes to develop IT solutions. |
| **Procedures** | 0 | EA policies, procedures are established and followed. |
| **Prioritization** | 1 | EA governs selection, prioritization of IT systems. |
| **Roadmaps** | 1 | EA drives development of tech roadmaps, digital initiatives. |

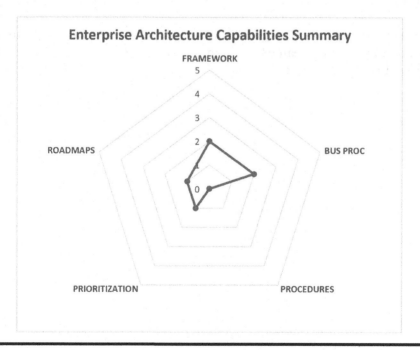

**Figure 18.1   Enterprise Architecture capabilities radar-style chart.**

## Summary: Future State Notes

You may choose to omit EA from your assessment if it does not seem feasible or beneficial to you and your organization at this time. In some respects, EA is a more mature capability, so it might not be right for you as part of this renovation project, but you should keep it on your radar. As you continue to build your IT capabilities, you may choose to add this to your list of competencies.

Your organization would probably benefit from at least reviewing an EA framework and perhaps incorporating some of the basic elements. For those concerned this may place too large a burden on your organization, you can take a very basic approach to EA or simply reserve EA efforts for a later phase of renovation or early stages of your digital transformation. Trying to take on too much, to improve the IT function too fully all at once, could derail your efforts. So, use this information to inform your choices without getting bogged down in yet another framework or another set of processes if it doesn't serve you at this time.

## Resource

Info-Tech Research Group, "Design an enterprise architecture strategy," https://www.infotech.com/research/ss/design-an-enterprise-architecture-strategy, accessed February 8, 2023.

# Chapter 19

# IT Finance Assessment

In Chapter 7, we reviewed numerous aspects of IT finance, including operational and capital expenditures, budgeting challenges, and more. In this section, we will define various elements you can use to assess your IT finance function. Granted, some elements may be managed outside of IT, such as capital funding or depreciation expenses. Regardless of where these elements are managed, you can assess your IT finance capability both based on the IT function itself as well as the finance functions outside of IT.

## IT Finance Views

You can begin by documenting your total expenses for various operational items (OpEx). An example is shown in Table 19.1. A basic list of OpEx items, by category, spend, and percent spend, can be powerful in its simplicity. You can also create a chart like the Treemap style shown in Figure 19.1, which can be helpful in visualizing your expenses, both for internal IT purposes and for the organization. Of course, you can modify this approach as needed, especially if you want to reflect how much of that OpEx cost is hosted on-premises (OPs) and how much is in the cloud. We won't go into the many variations you might consider, but this should give you a good starting point.

Capital expenditures for servers, storage, and network components, as well as any other capital IT investments planned for the budget year, are another element of the IT budget. Often, this is simply a list of projected capital needs along with associated operational expenses. For example,

DOI: 10.4324/9781003377023-22

**Table 19.1  IT OpEx Budget Example**

| *OpEx* | | *In thousands* | *Percent* |
|---|---|---|---|
| **Infrastructure** | Network | 2,700 | 58 |
| | Storage | 640 | 14 |
| | Servers | 475 | 10 |
| | Telephony | 325 | 7 |
| | Cybersecurity | 245 | 5 |
| | End-user computer | 310 | 6 |
| | | **$4,695** | **100%** |
| **Applications** | EHR | 4,600 | 83 |
| | Finance | 265 | 5 |
| | Human resources | 185 | 3 |
| | Supply chain | 200 | 4 |
| | Other | 315 | 5 |
| | | **$5,565** | **100%** |

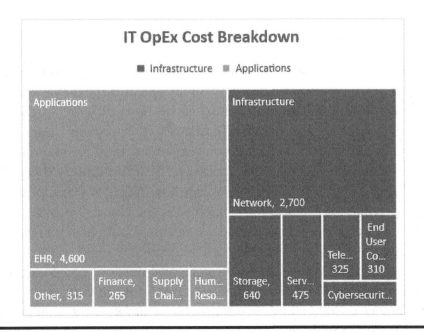

**Figure 19.1  IT OpEx budget example – Treemap style.**

acquiring a new storage cluster and associated software licensing is generally a capital expense, while the ongoing support and maintenance costs for the hardware and software are considered operational expenses. Of course, this is the older model, where hardware is purchased and deployed in a company-owned (or company-controlled) data center. As infrastructure moves to the cloud, these capital expenses go down and operational expenses go up, so you might visualize that trend using data and charts as shown in Table 19.2 and Figure 19.2, respectively. OP represents an on-premise solution vs. a cloud-based solution.

You undoubtedly have a handle on your IT finances, but these examples might give you ideas on how to show the data differently in order to help support your messaging about the need for the business to invest in appropriate IT solutions if it wants to achieve its stated goals and objectives.

**Table 19.2   On-Premises (OP) vs. Cloud – CapEx and OpEx Impact**

|  |  | *CapEx* | *OpEx* | *OP/Cloud* |
|---|---|---|---|---|
| **Infrastructure** | Network | $ 435,000 | $ 65,000 | OP |
|  | Servers | $ - | $ 355,000 | Cloud |
|  | Cybersecurity | $ - | $ 128,000 | OP |
| **Applications** | New Software 1 | $ 285,000 | $ 35,000 | OP |
|  | New Software 2 | $ - | $ 128,000 | Cloud |

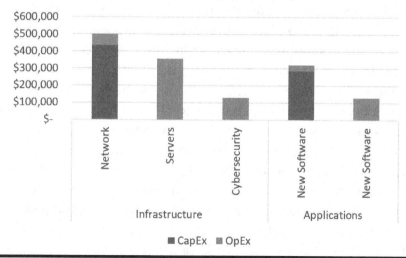

**Figure 19.2   IT finance CapEx and OpEx chart example.**

Figure 19.2 shows how you might create a chart comparing CapEx and OpEx by category. This sort of stacked chart can really help identify spending patterns across various aspects of your IT infrastructure and applications.

You can also detail costs by line, such as network hardware, network hardware maintenance, network software, network software maintenance, application software implementation, license, support, and maintenance costs, etc. The easier you make it to understand your financials visually (at-a-glance), the easier it will be to articulate spending trends.

Additionally, it will be easier to develop your renovation plan if you have compiled the key elements of your financial picture. We'll get into more detail in the next chapter when we work on assessing the technology building blocks. You may choose to swing back through this assessment to add detail after you have gone through other assessments. The clarity these assessments bring will be valuable and may inform your overall financial planning activities.

## Define the Dimension

What does a strong IT finance capability look like? While it varies across organizations, one of the most important aspects is that IT spending is tied to organizational goals and strategies. Not all IT spending is strategic – keeping the network running or the phones ringing are operational tasks required to enable strategic activities. However, large new expenditures or upgrade initiatives should certainly be aligned with organizational strategies.

It's also safe to say that a strong budgeting function must exist. Ideally, IT creates the budget based on current run rates and projected IT needs in the coming year, but often a budget is prepared and presented to IT leadership. In either case, the operational elements must be clearly documented, and changes from year-to-year should also be noted. There should be an internal review of variances on a monthly, quarterly, or annual basis to track how business needs are driving changes to IT spending. Some healthcare organizations may review their budgets and variances on a monthly basis, but they may not provide this data back to IT (or anyone else). That is not an ideal arrangement since it's hard to manage costs you can't see. In these cases, IT leaders typically create shadow books to monitor their expenditures. Like shadow IT, shadow *anything* in an organization is undesirable. It creates separate data sources and generates various forms of risk. If you do not have a budget file or a periodic review, using a spreadsheet to track expenses and variances is a good practice, even if it is a shadow function initially. Having details around your financials will help if you are audited, questioned about expenses, or simply want to create the subsequent year's budget.

Most capital expenditures should be approved through a governance process, and project plans should be created to manage the process from acquisition through implementation and operational turnover. One notable exception is often the IT infrastructure required to provide basic services such as network, security, and access to resources. As we discussed in Chapter 5, these projects can be brought forward for information and visibility or to ensure the timing of major upgrades does not conflict with other organizational initiatives. Operational approval of infrastructure projects is usually not needed since these are required to maintain core IT functions.

The operational expenses related to capital projects should be captured and noted. Often, the operational costs of projects are not made visible, and this creates unbudgeted variances in the IT budget for projects outside their control. The governance and project approval processes should be used to ensure any unbudgeted expenses are properly attributed.

In a more ideal state, using a flexible budget process where changes are reflected throughout the year gives a more accurate picture about the IT investments and value generated from those investments. This is a function of the organization's finance department and its processes around managing budgets, cash flow, and variances.

You will notice there are no benchmarks against industry or other similar healthcare organizations included here. While having these may appear helpful at first glance, there are often so many nuances that without a deep dive on the underlying data, it can paint a false picture. Take the example where HIT departments compare staffing levels, or "staff costs." Does the comparison data include only full-time employees or does it include part-time, contractor, and outsourced staff as well? If you cannot compare 'apples to apples,' you should avoid these kinds of benchmarks when creating your IT budget. No other organization has the same strategic objectives, new initiatives, numbers/types of locations, etc. as yours does. In some cases, comparisons may be useful for the number of staff required to support an enterprise application (like your EHR), for example, but in general, you should use these data points with caution.

Other benchmarking data can be valuable for activities that help your IT function grow and mature, such as IT budget as a percentage of organizational revenue or IT spend on cybersecurity as a percentage of revenue. This is more a comparative measure than a budgeting tool. If your organization uses these kinds of benchmark data, you can add capability statements to reflect that.

You can add or modify these statements to reflect the financial situation at your organization. The key elements that must be present are methods for preparing, reviewing, and managing both operational and capital budgets in your environment.

## Write Capability Statements

The capability statements define the optimal future state. These are used to assess your current capabilities and define a path toward improvement and optimization.

1. **[STRATEGIC]** IT budgets (CapEx, OpEx) are driven primarily by the strategic objectives of the organization.
2. **[VALUE]** IT value assessments or statements are presented to the organization.
3. **[BUDGET]** An operational budget is prepared in collaboration with IT/ Finance leaders and reviewed periodically.
4. **[CHANGE]** Operational budget changes are documented in detail to reflect the source of the changes.
5. **[CAPITAL]** Capital budget requests are strategically aligned, fully documented through a formal project plan, and include relevant data (strategy, costs (CapEx, OpEx), timelines, project charters, etc.).
6. **[VARIANCES]** Variances to IT budgets are reviewed, explained, and documented to reflect the reason for and the source of the variance.

## Assess the Capability

Each capability is stated along with five levels of capability statements. You can modify the statements to suit your needs. These are provided to be used as-is or as a starting point for your own customized set of statements.

1. **[STRATEGIC] IT budgets (CapEx, OpEx) are driven primarily by the strategic objectives of the organization.**
   **C0** – There is no IT budget process.
   **C1** – There is an ad hoc budget process, but there is no alignment with strategic objectives.

**C2** – There is a budget process, there is occasional alignment with strategic objectives, typically when an executive champions a large IT project.

**C3** – There is a budget process, there is regular alignment with strategic objectives, typically through executive champions or IT governance processes.

**C4** – There is a formal budget process, there is strong alignment with strategic objectives, typically through an evolving IT governance process.

**C5** – There is a formal and effective budget process, there is strong alignment with strategic objectives through a mature IT governance process.

2. **[VALUE] IT value assessments or statements are presented to the organization.**

   **C0** – No IT value statements are created.

   **C1** – IT value statements are rarely created or presented to the organization.

   **C2** – IT value statements are created in an ad hoc manner, but not presented to the organization.

   **C3** – IT value statements are created in an ad hoc manner and presented to the organization. IT value is sometimes recognized.

   **C4** – IT value statements are created in a formal manner and presented to the organization. IT value is recognized.

   **C5** – IT value statements are created in a formal manner and presented to the organization in a planful manner. IT value is recognized and supported. Data is used to support value statements.

3. **[BUDGET] An operational budget is prepared in collaboration with IT/Finance leaders and reviewed periodically.**

   **C0** – No IT budgets are created or reviewed.

   **C1** – IT budgets are created by finance but never provided to IT. Individual expense items may require discussion or explanation in an ad hoc manner.

   **C2** – IT budgets are created by finance and provided to IT. Variance explanations are only required for significant variances and only in an ad hoc manner.

   **C3** – IT budgets are created in collaboration between finance and IT. There is a periodic review of IT financials, either structured or ad hoc.

   **C4** – IT budgets are created in collaboration between finance and IT after organizational prioritization of IT efforts has occurred. Variance explanations are a required on a periodic basis.

**C5** – IT budgets are created in collaboration between finance and IT based on organizational priorities and budget item approvals through a governance process. IT expenses are categorized by run-grow-transform (or similar) to strategically optimize IT spending.

4. **[CHANGE] Operational budget changes are documented in detail to reflect the source of the changes.**

**C0** – IT operational budgets do not exist.

**C1** – IT operational budgets exist but are not detailed. They include only high-level categories.

**C2** – IT operational budgets exist and are detailed by category; they do not reflect sources of change.

**C3** – IT operational budgets exist and are detailed by category and sub-category. They sometimes reflect sources of change.

**C4** – IT operational budgets exist and are detailed by category and sub-category. They often reflect sources of change along with the rationale for the change.

**C5** – IT operational budgets exist and are detailed by category and sub-category. They reflect sources and rational of change as well as review of the effectiveness of those changes. Data is analyzed in preparation for budget cycles.

5. **[CAPITAL] Capital budget requests are strategically aligned, fully documented through a formal project plan, and include relevant data (strategy, costs (CapEx, OpEx), timelines, project charters, etc.).**

**C0** – There is no IT capital budget process.

**C1** – There is an ad hoc capital budget process where capital expenditures are requested on an an-needed basis.

**C2** – There is an ad hoc or informal capital budget process where capital expenditures are requested and approved without reviewing strategic alignment.

**C3** – There is a formal capital budget process where capital expenditures are requested, approved, and associated operational costs are captured. Strategic alignment is often considered.

**C4** – There is a formal capital budget process where capital expenditures are requested, approved, and strategic alignment is attained through the IT governance process. Strategic alignment is always considered.

**C5** – There is a formal capital budget process where capital expenditures are requested, approved, and strategic alignment is attained through the IT governance process. Strategic alignment is required. New, innovative initiatives are prioritized, using relevant data, in collaboration with business leaders.

6. **[VARIANCES] Variances to IT budgets are reviewed, explained, and documented to reflect the reason for and the source of the variance.**

**C0** – No IT budget exists.

**C1** – IT budget variances are not reviewed.

**C2** – IT budget variances are reviewed on an ad hoc basis, typically when a significant and unexpected variance occurs.

**C3** – IT budget variances are reviewed on an ad hoc basis, typically when a variance exceeds a pre-set threshold.

**C4** – IT budget variances are reviewed in a formal, documented manner. Variance thresholds are established in order to focus on the most important changes.

**C5** – IT budget variances are reviewed in a formal, documented manner. Changes to the IT budget are allowed and documented throughout the year as business requirements evolve. Data is analyzed to understand the financial trends in the IT budget.

## Chart Current State

Based on the assessment and documentation of your IT finance's current state, your capabilities might look like those shown in Table 19.3 and Figure 19.3. Since much of the finance process resides outside the IT department, you may not be able to modify organizational

**Table 19.3   IT Finance Capabilities Ratings**

| Dimension | Rating | Definition |
|---|---|---|
| **Strategic** | 3 | IT budgets are driven by strategic objectives. |
| **Value** | 4 | IT value assessments are presented to the organization. |
| **Budget** | 4.5 | An operational budget is prepared and reviewed periodically. |
| **Change** | 3.5 | Operational budget changes are documented. |
| **Capital** | 3 | Capital budget requests are strategically aligned and documented. |
| **Variance** | 2 | Variances are reviewed and documented, including the reason/source. |

**Figure 19.3  IT finance capabilities radar-style chart.**

approaches to finance, but there are certainly steps you can take in your renovation project to improve how you manage finance inside the IT department.

## Summary: Future State Notes

With increasing downward pressure on IT budgets and increasing demands on IT capabilities, HIT leaders need to be well-versed in the financial management processes of their organization. Being able to demonstrate sound financial management and tying IT expenditures to organizational strategies and value-added activities will yield the best results.

If any ideas for an improved future state for your organization have come up during your assessment, be sure to make a note of these. Later, you can pull these into your renovation plan or into your digital transformation plans.

## Chapter 20

# IT Technology Assessment

In Chapter 8, we discussed IT technologies from data centers to printers. In this chapter, we will assess your capabilities around these IT technologies. Your list of technologies will be your starting point for this assessment. As a reminder, this same list is an important foundational element for your BC plan's BIA as well as for any TBM initiative you may initiate, so the work can be leveraged in several ways.

## Define the Dimension

The most common elements used in assessing technology are the ones your team probably already uses. Elements such as the age of the asset, platform or operating system, useful life, and proximity to end of support (EOS)/end of life (EOL) are all key data points for your technology. Your first assessment point, then, is whether you have this data for each of these assets. You might think you have all of it or some of it, but how much is documented and tracked?

Next on the list of details is whether the asset is currently managed in IT and by whom. You should identify the team (and one or more individuals) responsible for the asset, its patch management cycle and status, and its backup status. For example, are backups stored OP, off-premise, in the cloud; are they full backups, incremental, etc.; are they tested and restored from time to time, etc.? Are your assets appropriately secured? For example, for servers, you might look at templates or images used for new servers to determine whether they are hardened by default, patched at the

DOI: 10.4324/9781003377023-23

time of provisioning, etc. How often are these settings reviewed? Are you leaving unused services turned on? Unused ports open? These are aspects of managing your IT technology that are sometimes handed over to the security team but should be fundamental to the team managing the asset.

In your assessment activities, you should look at unplanned downtimes. These include break-fix downtimes as well as planned downtimes that exceed the published window. For example, do you expect your EHR upgrades to take two hours, but they routinely take three or four hours due to unexpected issues? Are desktops and printers continuously breaking? These are rarely clocked as "downtimes," but these devices being broken, unusable, or offline has a tremendous cumulative impact on users

How many tickets do you have per day/per week for broken devices? What's your meantime to repair? While these metrics fall under service delivery and operations, they speak directly to the overall status of your IT technology program. If you are not replacing obsolete or failing equipment in a planful manner, you're causing daily productivity challenges and frustration for your users, which impacts patient care.

Through your cybersecurity function, you should have visibility to the security status of all your IT assets. This is another area that crosses into different functional areas, but can be included here. Do you have policies, procedures, or scripts that harden assets by default? Do you lock down servers, firewalls, and desktop devices via scripts or "golden image" deployment to enhance your cybersecurity stance, or is each device hand-built in an ad hoc manner?

Next, you might evaluate whether you have technology roadmaps in place. These take the data elements related to asset age and estimated useful life and map out your replacement plans. If you don't have your asset information, you can't create a detailed roadmap.

Transition plans are often associated with roadmaps, as they document how you plan to transition your technology from OP to cloud-based solutions, for example. Many healthcare organizations have moved some solutions to the cloud, but many are in a transitional state where they have a mixture of OP and cloud. Sometimes the transition has been planful, sometimes sudden, or sometimes chaotic. You may have a disorganized set of assets that need to be sorted out and addressed. This means determining what's OP, what's in the cloud, and what's currently in transition. It also means determining whether you have gaps or overlaps in these solutions. If things have been moved to the cloud in a disorganized manner, it's entirely possible you're paying for things you're not using, you have duplicate assets in two or more locations (or in two or more solutions), etc. This goes back to having a complete list of assets and their current state as your starting point.

As you look at your IT asset inventory, you'll want to review whether the organization is fully leveraging everything it has. The answer is most likely "no." Most organizations have assets that are underutilized or unused altogether. One of the easiest steps to take in your renovation project is to identify unused capabilities or underutilized systems and find ways to make better use of them or get rid of them.

In Chapter 15, we discussed IT value creation. As you are assessing your IT assets, you should keep value creation in mind. Some assets are required in order to provide basic functions such as network connectivity or user access. Other assets are intended to deliver a specific function that the organization relies on or has requested. In healthcare, that includes the EHR, associated applications like document management, faxing, and patient portals and systems like lab, pharmacy, surgical, or scheduling if you don't have an integrated EHR system. It also includes applications like finance, HR, supply chain, and business applications such as office productivity applications, messaging, secure chat, and videoconferencing.

Do you know what these assets cost the organization to acquire and maintain? Can you articulate the value each delivers? Or are these assets that seem to be on the periphery of the organization adding cost without value? If you haven't worked on articulating business value of IT in the past, this can be a great starting point. Remember, the objective in these assessments is to determine current state so you can decide which next step to take to advance the maturity of the capability. You don't have to move the dial on every capability, and certainly not all at once. When we develop the renovation plan later, we'll strategically select our first targets so we can make consistent and incremental progress.

Part of your IT technology assessment might include how IT technology is selected. Like other topics, this also crosses categories and touches on IT governance. However, sometimes IT governance focuses on software and applications and ignores IT hardware assets. For example, if you were like most healthcare organizations, you deployed a fleet of tablets or mobile devices during the early days of the COVID pandemic. Who selected the devices, who weighed in on the capabilities and capacity of the devices? Was it simply an IT decision based on what was available from your supplier at the time? That's a fine reason, but it should be documented. Was it a joint discussion with clinical leaders? How technology is selected and provisioned is both part of your IT governance function and part of your IT technology capability. Where are those assets today? Are they still being used, or are they shoved in a desk drawer or supply closet someplace? How the devices were selected and whether they are still in use and adding value are important to track. Sometimes decisions make sense in the moment, but years later, no one has reviewed the decision. Make sure you keep an eye on all your IT assets in this manner.

Finally, the management of assets and EOS and EOL status are important to know. EOL for a device typically is when the manufacturer will no longer market or sell a particular model. This often coincides with EOS, but in some cases, the manufacturer (or third parties) will provide support at a premium. Knowing when a product is EOL and EOS is critical. Obsolete equipment poses higher security risks, costs more to support and maintain, and is more likely to cause unexpected downtimes. Do you know when these EOL/EOS events are for your key assets? Does your roadmap reflect these? Does your capital or operational budget account for these refresh cycles? Does your transition plan address these end points and have clear decisions around remaining OPs or going to the cloud?

These are all part of lifecycle management, IT asset management, and technology management and are assessed here. It is not uncommon to find a few IT assets, such as servers, storage, or databases, sitting spinning someplace (OP, cloud) that are unmanaged and unknown. They create hidden costs and security risks, so ensuring you know all your assets and their end-of-life points is an important, but often overlooked, task.

For reference, below is the list of asset categories we defined in Chapter 8. Feel free to add or remove any IT elements you deem appropriate. If you want to do a thorough job of this, you should use each capability statement with each technology category (and subcategories you may define) to assess the maturity of that capability. This will give you the most detailed data possible as input for your renovation plan. In this assessment, we'll keep it at the top level for brevity, but do expand your assessment as needed.

- Data centers
- Servers, storage, and platforms
- Cloud solutions
- Network components
- Telcom and connectivity
- Enterprise data warehouse and database systems
- Enterprise applications and shadow IT

- IT Infrastructure applications
- End-user devices
- Cybersecurity

Since this can seem a bit daunting to undertake, so you might choose to assign segments to your various teams to work in parallel. You can break assessments down into smaller segments. If you approach this work in an agile manner, you can define two-week segments of work for each of the teams and set manageable goals and deliverables so that you make continuous progress. Don't let the perceived enormity of the task cause you to simply freeze in your tracks. Instead, break the work down into tasks small enough to be manageable for each team to accomplish in short timeframes.

## Write Capability Statements

The capability statements define the optimal future state. These are used to assess your current capabilities and define a path toward improvement and optimization.

*Note that in the list below, we assess utilization and value. Utilization and value are not the same thing. Something can be heavily used because it's the 'least worst option,' but the amount of effort it takes to use that solution might mean it's not really delivering value that another, more optimal solution, might deliver.*

1. **[INVENTORY]** All assets are inventoried, known, and managed.
2. **[STATUS]** Current status of all assets is known.
3. **[FUNCTION]** Assets function as expected with minimal unexpected downtimes.
4. **[SECURITY]** All assets are included in cybersecurity solutions.
5. **[ROADMAP]** All assets have a technology roadmap.
6. **[TRANSITION PLAN]** All assets have a transition plan defined.
7. **[UTILIZATION]** All assets are utilized fully.
8. **[VALUE]** All enterprise applications are delivering value.
9. **[SELECTION]** The organization is fully engaged with selecting technology solutions.
10. **[DECOMMISSION]** Unused assets are decommissioned in a timely and secure manner.

# Assess the Capability

Each capability is stated along with five levels of capability statements. You can modify the statements to suit your needs. These are provided to be used as-is or as a starting point for your own customized set of statements.

1. **[INVENTORY] All assets are inventoried, known, and managed.**
   **C0** – There is no current IT asset inventory or list.
   **C1** – There are some lists of IT assets, none are complete.
   **C2** – There is several IT asset inventory lists, these asset lists may not be complete.
   **C3** – There is a current IT asset inventory list, it may not be comprehensive.
   **C4** – There is a current IT asset inventory list, it is fairly comprehensive and detailed.
   **C5** – There is a current IT asset inventory list, it is comprehensive, detailed, and kept current.

2. **[STATUS] Current status of all assets is known.**
   **C0** – The current status of IT assets is unknown.
   **C1** – The current status of IT assets is partially known.
   **C2** – The current status of some IT assets is known.
   **C3** – The current status of most IT assets is known.
   **C4** – The current status of all IT assets is known, there is an ad hoc process for keeping data current.
   **C5** – The current status of all IT assets is known, there is a process in place for keeping data current.

3. **[FUNCTION] Assets function as expected with minimal unexpected downtimes.**
   **C0** – Assets do not function as expected, there are frequent unexpected downtimes.
   **C1** – Assets do not function as expected, there are multiple unexpected downtimes.
   **C2** – Assets do not function as expected, there are occasional unexpected downtimes.
   **C3** – Assets function somewhat as expected, unexpected downtimes do occur but less frequently than in the prior 24 months.
   **C4** – Assets function mostly as expected, unexpected downtimes are somewhat rare.
   **C5** – Assets function mostly as expected, unexpected downtimes are quite rare.

4. **[SECURITY] All assets are included in cybersecurity solutions.**

   **C0** – No IT assets are included in cybersecurity solutions.

   **C1** – A few IT assets are included in cybersecurity solutions.

   **C2** – Many IT assets are included in cybersecurity solutions, there is no process for verifying all assets are accounted for.

   **C3** – Most IT assets are included in cybersecurity solutions, there is no process for verifying all assets are accounted for.

   **C4** – All IT assets are included in cybersecurity solutions and this is verified through periodic audit.

   **C5** – All IT assets are included in cybersecurity solutions and this is verified through scheduled and validated audits. Monitoring and auditing data are analyzed regularly.

5. **[ROADMAP] All assets have a technology roadmap.**

   **C0** – No assets have a technology roadmap.

   **C1** – One or two asset categories have a roadmap outline.

   **C2** – Some asset categories have roadmap outlines, very few have detailed roadmaps.

   **C3** – Some asset categories have detailed roadmaps.

   **C4** – Most asset categories have detailed roadmaps.

   **C5** – All asset categories have detailed roadmaps using data as input for planning.

6. **[TRANSITION PLAN] All assets have a transition plan defined.**

   **C0** – No assets have transition plans defined.

   **C1** – A few asset categories have transition plans identified, none are well-defined.

   **C2** – Some asset categories have transition plans identified, a few are well-defined.

   **C3** – Many asset categories have well-defined transition plans.

   **C4** – Most asset categories have well-defined transition plans.

   **C5** – All asset categories have well-defined transition plans and have been reviewed with organizational leaders.

7. **[UTILIZATION] All assets are utilized fully.**

   **C0** – It is unknown if all IT assets are fully utilized.

   **C1** – It is unknown if all IT assets are fully utilized, a few are known to be well-utilized.

   **C2** – It is unknown if all IT assets are fully utilized, some are known to be well-utilized.

   **C3** – It is generally known if IT assets are fully utilized, some assets may still be unknown.

**C4** – Most IT assets are fully utilized, some assets are under-utilized.

**C5** – All IT assets are fully utilized, data is used to identify under-utilized assets, which are then reviewed by the organization (IT and operations), and decommissioned as appropriate.

8. **[VALUE] All enterprise applications are delivering value.**

**C0** – Value of enterprise applications has never been evaluated.

**C1** – Value of enterprise applications has been discussed, never evaluated.

**C2** – Value of enterprise applications has been discussed for major applications.

**C3** – Value of enterprise applications has been developed for major applications; value conversations have not yet occurred with operational leaders.

**C4** – Value of enterprise applications has been developed for most applications; value discussions happen occasionally with operational leaders.

**C5** – Value of enterprise applications has been developed for all applications; value discussions happen regularly with operational leaders.

9. **[SELECTION] The organization is fully engaged with selecting technology solutions.**

**C0** – The organization does not engage with selecting technology solutions.

**C1** – The organization rarely engages with selecting technology solutions and never in a planful manner.

**C2** – The organization occasionally engages with selecting technology solutions, usually in an ad hoc manner.

**C3** – The organization often engages with selecting technology solutions, usually through the documented (defined) process.

**C4** – The organization almost always engages with selecting technology solutions, primarily through the documented (defined) process.

**C5** – The organization always engages with selecting technology solutions through the documented (defined) process, which is continuously improving with operational input.

10. **[DECOMMISSION] Unused assets are decommissioned in a timely and secure manner.**

**C0** – There is no defined process for decommissioning IT assets.

**C1** – There is no defined process for decommissioning IT assets, older assets are sometimes removed in an ad hoc manner.

**C2** – There is no defined process for decommissioning IT assets, some older assets are removed and documented.

**C3** – There is an ad hoc process for decommissioning IT assets, most are removed and documented appropriately.

**C4** – There is a well-defined process for decommissioning IT assets, most are removed and documented appropriately.

**C5** – There is a well-defined process for decommissioning IT assets, all are consistently removed and documented appropriately.

## Chart Current State

We have ten dimensions defined, and of course, you can add or remove dimensions. You can also modify any of the capability statements to better reflect your environment. As a reminder, C0 generally means you don't have that capability at all, and C5 indicates you not only have that capability but you have mastered and improved it. Use this scale to modify the elements as you see fit. Table 20.1 shows an example of the matrix, and Figure 20.1 shows that data in a radar chart.

**Table 20.1   IT Technology CMMI Ratings Matrix**

| Dimension | Rating | Description |
| --- | --- | --- |
| **Inventory** | 3.5 | All assets are inventoried, known, and managed. |
| **Status** | 3 | Current status of all assets is known. |
| **Function** | 4 | Assets function as expected with minimal unexpected downtimes. |
| **Security** | 3.5 | All assets are included in cybersecurity solutions. |
| **Roadmap** | 2.5 | All assets have a technology roadmap. |
| **Transition plan** | 1 | All assets have a transition plan defined. |
| **Utilization** | 3.5 | All assets are fully utilized. |
| **Value** | 3 | All enterprise applications are delivering value. |
| **Selection** | 2.5 | The organization is fully engaged with selecting technology solutions. |
| **Decommission** | 4 | Unused assets are decommissioned in a timely and secure manner. |

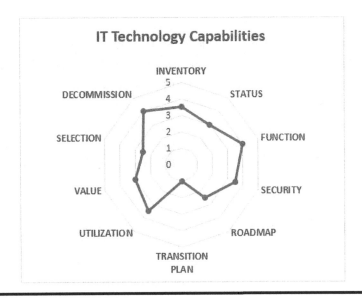

**Figure 20.1  IT technology capabilities radar-style chart.**

## Summary: Future State Notes

Documenting your current state of IT technology is a detailed process. Your IT technology assessment results will drive a large portion of your renovation plan. Your IT technologies will also be at the center of your subsequent digital transformation efforts, so this is a great investment of your time and focus.

As you work your way through this task, be sure to capture ideas and thoughts you have around technology, applications, and innovation as you go. You will no doubt think of some great improvements to make to your environment as you look at these details, and this is the time to capture those thoughts. When you develop your renovation plan, you can come back to these notes and make sure you are applying all your great ideas to your renovation work. The ideas that come from looking deeply at your environment and envisioning your future potential can be inspiring as you undertake your renovation project.

*Chapter 21*

# IT Service Management & IT Operations Assessment

In Chapter 9, we described many elements of IT service management (ITSM) and IT operations management (ITOM). This includes service requests to asset management (ITAM), user provisioning to vendor management, and more. We discussed the various frameworks that can be used to define these elements in an organization.

In this chapter, we will take these elements at a high level and develop capability statements for each. However, you are encouraged to take this as a starting point, not an ending point. The methods by which you manage your IT department's service delivery are complex and detailed. Every organization addresses these elements somewhat differently, so you'll need to customize this to meet your needs.

## Define the Dimension

We define the ideal state for each of these categories of ITSM. Some of these topics overlap with other chapters and other assessments, such as asset management and cybersecurity. You can assess them separately or as part of your ITSM and ITOM assessments.

### *Service Request Management Process*

The service request process relates to how users request services (break/fix, upgrades, replacements, new equipment, new accounts, etc.). It describes

DOI: 10.4324/9781003377023-24

how you manage these requests, from first call resolution statistics to managing service tickets to end-user communication and everything in between.

Service request management typically includes the use of KPIs and SLAs to define how service will be delivered (first call resolution, closed within SLA, end user quality survey data, etc.).

## Knowledge Management Process

The knowledge management process has to do with documenting IT knowledge. This includes information about how systems and applications are configured, common problems and their resolutions, and technical articles on how to perform certain functions, as well as common end-user questions. This describes whether you have formal, written processes in place to capture IT knowledge and whether you have systems/tools in place to manage that knowledge. It also describes how well you advance this capability within your department.

## IT Asset Management Process

We talked at length about ITAM in Chapter 8. You can include it here as part of your IT operations, or you can include it in your IT technology assessment. We'll review high-level ITAM capabilities here. You can also refer to Chapter 20 for the IT Technology Assessment tasks.

## Incident Management Process

Incident and problem management processes are part of a standard ITIL and ITSM frameworks. Incidents track items that are broken; problems are collections of related incidents. How well you manage incidents and problems is often a function of both your procedures and your ticket management system. If you have a modern system in place, you likely handle incidents and problems in a manner well-aligned with ITIL and ITSM. If you are working with an old system that does not align to current methodologies, you may find opportunities to improve these processes either through developing better processes/workflows or by upgrading your service management system.

## Problem Management Process

Problems are typically defined as a collection of incidents. For example, if you have multiple desktop systems with the same symptoms, each desktop ticket is an incident, and the collection of related desktop tickets would be associated with a problem ticket. This may or may not be how you manage incidents and problems in your organization, so feel free to define and assess these in whatever method is aligned with your current practices. Just be sure your current practices aligned with current industry methods and frameworks and aren't leftover artifacts of broken processes from the past.

## Change Management Process

Change management for the purposes of this chapter and its associated assessments has to do with managing change to IT systems. Having a strong change management process in place ensures that substantial changes to both hardware and software systems are brought to a team that reviews and approves all such changes. A well-defined change management process also ensures that each change is well-documented, is tested (to the degree possible), and that viable back-out plans are identified. All changes should be documented so that it is clear who is making system changes and when they are made. This drives both accountability and transparency. In the event the change breaks something, strong change control ensures the change can be tracked down and reversed (not always possible) or mitigated in a timely manner.

## Information Security Management

This is related to cybersecurity so you may cover this element the cybersecurity assessment discussed in Chapter 24. As part of service management and operations, you should have information security fundamentals incorporated into your daily and weekly operations. For example, what is the policy, procedure, and process for managing patches, especially operating system patches that are released on a published schedule? Do you have a "patch Tuesday" or some other defined schedule for downloading, evaluating, testing, and then deploying operating system patches? These are operational items that are part of your information security stance. Whether you assess them here as part of operations or in your cybersecurity assessment is less important than that you include these items in your operations so they are not seen as solely in the domain of your cybersecurity team. Your assessment in this chapter would include whether you have basic system patching, hardening, and monitoring set up as part of IT operations.

## IT Project Management

Every HIT department runs projects that vary widely in size and complexity. In any given week, most HIT departments are running a wide variety of IT projects. Most teams identify projects by size and complexity, so a small project might be defined as involving one IT team and taking less than 40 hours; a medium project might involve two to four teams (IT or stakeholders) and taking between 40 and 120 hours, and a large project might be defined as taking multiple teams across the enterprise and requiring more than 120 hours of work. Your definitions will be unique to your organization, but you should have a strong project management function that oversees IT projects of all sizes. Through your IT governance function, you should also have a strong intake process for projects. Project fundamentals such as charter, scope, timeline, budget, and more should be clearly defined. Managing tasks, deliverables, and timelines should be a core competency of your IT team, whether through managers or dedicated project managers.

## IT Automation Management

Increasingly, IT departments are turning to automation to improve service delivery. From end-user provisioning to approvals requiring multiple levels of review and signature and everything in between, IT departments are leveraging business process automation (BPA) and robotic process automation (RPA) to perform the rote, repetitive tasks required of the IT function. This frees up human staff to perform work they are uniquely qualified to do and relieves them of the often boring, repetitive work. These automations reduce human error, often improve turnaround time, and generally improve security. Any HIT department not actively using automation should include this as part of the renovation project.

Alternatively, you could make this a digital improvement effort preceding larger digital transformation projects.

## IT Communication Management

IT communication capabilities have to do with the various mechanisms you use internal and external to IT to communicate. This includes communication from emergency situations, such as a potential cyberattack or a major system outage, as well as routine communication like team status, project status, or even ticket status. It also includes how you, as an IT leader, communicate with your direct reports, your teams, and the IT staff overall. Finally, it covers how IT communicates with the organization. Do you have a defined communication method, or is it ad hoc? Is it just to announce downtimes or system changes, or do you regularly tout the value IT is providing to the organization? These are your communication capabilities.

## Cloud Management

Since most HIT departments have at least some IT assets in the cloud, you will need to assess how well you manage these assets. Managing cloud assets has to do with ensuring the confidentiality, integrity, and availability of cloud systems/data; securing those assets so that only those users with a business need have access; backing up and restoring those assets; and managing upgrades, updates, patches, and other changes to the cloud-based system. It also entails managing and containing costs as organizational demand drives utilization. Many HIT organizations still perform these duties in an ad hoc manner, so there may be an opportunity for you to improve your capabilities in this regard.

## DevOps/Agile

As we discussed previously, when we use the term DevOps/Agile here, we are largely referring to it as the process of delivering IT value more quickly, in smaller increments. When work is broken down into short time frames, often referred to as sprints, staff focus on delivering complete units of work in the specified time. This leads to clarity around the deliverables, more frequent delivery of functionality for the organization, and more insight into progress and productivity. While other methods of project and IT work delivery are still used, adopting a more agile approach to IT delivery not only can reduce some of the chaos in the department, it also can show continuous progress to the organization. Rather than waiting eight months for a project to be completed, incremental units of work delivered every two to four weeks can help the organization see progress and perhaps receive interim value from project deliverables.

## *Vendor Management*

IT vendor management is an increasingly important skill for IT departments. The value IT brings to the organization hinges largely on how well vendor relationships are managed. Are contracts well-written and clear? Do they reflect the operational requirements of the organization? Are there concrete remedies for failure to deliver? Is pricing clear, fair, and sized to meet your needs? Beyond contract management, are vendors held accountable for deliverables? Do they communicate in a clear and effective manner? Are they partners in your business, or do they view your organization as just another business transaction? Your ability to manage vendors across the IT spectrum (hardware, software, contract labor, service delivery, consulting, etc.) will have a large impact on your IT department's overall success.

# Write Capability Statements

The capability statements define the optimal future state. These are used to assess your current capabilities and define a path toward improvement and optimization. We're using abbreviations here so that when we chart the assessment results, the chart is easier to read.

1. **[IT SERVICE MANAGEMENT – ITSM]** IT has a well-defined service request management system to ensure excellent end user service to the organization. KPIs and SLAs are defined and used to improve IT service delivery.
2. **[KNOWLEDGE MANAGEMENT – KM]** IT has a well-defined knowledge management system to capture IT knowledge for internal and external users.

3. **[IT ASSET MANAGEMENT – ITAM]** IT has a well-defined and implemented asset management program to ensure all assets are accounted for, managed, and decommissioned, as appropriate.

4. **[INCIDENT MANAGEMENT – IM]** IT has a well-defined incident management process and responds to IT incidents according to policy, procedure, and defined metrics. The process includes root cause analysis and development of countermeasures.

5. **[PROBLEM MANAGEMENT – PBM]** IT has a well-defined problem management process and responds to IT problems according to policy, procedure, and defined metrics. The process includes root cause analysis and development of countermeasures.

6. **[CHANGE MANAGEMENT – CM]** IT has a well-defined change management process so that all system and application changes are documented, reviewed, tested, and approved via a change oversight function.

7. **[SECURITY MANAGEMENT – SEC]** IT has well-defined information security program, policies, and procedures that are incorporated into IT daily operations.

8. **[PROJECT MANAGEMENT – PM]** IT has a well-defined project management function, ideally functioning through a Project Management Office framework, to ensure IT projects are approved via governance and managed according to PM best practices. Project results are reviewed with operational owners on a periodic basis.

9. **[AUTOMATION – AUTO]** IT has automated many basic, repetitive tasks within IT to reduce cost, reduce error, improve turnaround time, improve security, improve end user experience, and better utilize IT staff capabilities for more advanced work.

10. **[COMMUNICATION MANAGEMENT – COM]** IT has a communication management plan or approaches organizational communication in an organized and transparent manner. Internal and external stakeholders see value in the IT communication channels.

11. **[CLOUD MANAGEMENT – CLOUD]** IT has a well-defined cloud management strategy and cloud processes to ensure all cloud solutions are actively managed within IT. There is no shadow IT.

12. **[AGILE PROCESSES – AGILE]** IT utilizes agile concepts and methods to deliver IT results in smaller increments more frequently, adding

value to end users consistently, and improving turnaround time on key deliverables.

13. **[VENDOR MANAGEMENT – VEND]** IT has a well-define vendor management process that includes strong vendor contract management, negotiation skills, and vendor management skills so that vendor relationships are positive, productive, and in line with contract and organizational expectations.

## Assess the Capability

Each capability is stated along with five levels of capability statements. You can modify the statements to suit your needs. These are provided to be used as-is or as a starting point for your own customized set of statements.

1. **[IT SERVICE MANAGEMENT – ITSM] IT has a well-defined service management process.**
   C0 – There is no service management process.
   C1 – There is an ad hoc service management process in place.
   C2 – There is a service management process in place, it is sometimes used. No KPIs or SLAs are defined.
   C3 – There is a service management process in place, it is frequently used. Some KPIs or SLAs are defined.
   C4 – There is a formal service management process in place, it is consistently used. KPIs and SLAs are defined and frequently reviewed.
   C5 – There is a formal service management process in place. KPIs and SLAs are regularly reviewed and opportunities for improvement are identified through analyzing service management data.

2. **[KNOWLEDGE MANAGEMENT – KM] IT has a well-defined knowledge management process.**
   C0 – There is no knowledge management process.
   C1 – There is ad hoc knowledge management, information is not standardized or centralized.
   C2 – There is ad hoc knowledge management, information is somewhat standardized, it is not centralized.
   C3 – There is formal knowledge management in place, information is standardized and centralized.

**C4** – There is formal knowledge management in place, creating and updating information is part of staff job descriptions.

**C5** – There is formal knowledge management in place, staff are required to create and update content, an editorial group oversees the continuous improvement of this function. Utilization data is regularly reviewed and drives decisions.

3. **[IT ASSET MANAGEMENT – ITAM] A well-defined ITAM process is in place.**

   **C0** – There is no asset management process in place.

   **C1** – There is no asset management process in place, a few assets are documented in an ad hoc manner.

   **C2** – There is no asset management process in place, some assets are documented in an ad hoc manner.

   **C3** – There is an asset management process in place, many assets are documented in an ad hoc or informal manner. Data may not be complete.

   **C4** – There is an asset management process in place, it is formalized and substantially complete.

   **C5** – There is an asset management process in place, it is formalized and complete. Data is used to help articulate the value of the IT investments the organization makes.

4. **[INCIDENT MANAGEMENT – IM] A well-defined incident management process is in place.**

   **C0** – There is no incident management process in place.

   **C1** – There is no incident management process in place, incidents are handled on an ad hoc basis.

   **C2** – There is an ad hoc incident management process in place, it is used intermittently.

   **C3** – There is an incident management process in place, it is used frequently but not consistently.

   **C4** – There is an incident management process in place, it is used consistently.

   **C5** – There is an incident management process in place, it is used very consistently and has been continuously improved over time. Data is collected and analyzed on a periodic basis.

5. **[PROBLEM MANAGEMENT – PBM] A well-defined problem management process is in place.**

   **C0** – There is no problem management process in place.

   **C1** – There is no problem management process in place, problems are handled differently by everyone in the department.

**C2** – There is a loosely defined problem management process in place, it is used intermittently.

**C3** – There is a problem management process in place, it is used frequently but not consistently.

**C4** – There is a problem management process in place, it is used consistently.

**C5** - There is a problem management process in place, it is used very consistently and has been continuously improved over time. Data is collected and analyzed on a periodic basis.

6. **[CHANGE MANAGEMENT – CM] A well-defined change management process is in place.**

    **C0** – There is no change management process in place.

    **C1** – There is no change management process in place, changes are occasionally reviewed in advance.

    **C2** – There is an ad hoc change management process in place, changes are sometimes reviewed in advance.

    **C3** – There is a change management process in place, changes are typically reviewed in advance, sometimes documented appropriately.

    **C4** – There is a change management process in place, changes are always reviewed in advance and always documented appropriately.

    **C5** - There is a change management process in place, changes are always reviewed in advance and documented appropriately. Using data, the function has improved over time and is optimized.

7. **[INFORMATION SECURITY – SEC] A well-defined information security management program is in place.**

    **C0** – There is no information security process in place.

    **C1** – There is no information security process in place, each team manages infosec in an ad hoc manner.

    **C2** – There is an ad hoc information security process in place, the infosec team works in a piecemeal fashion.

    **C3** – There is a formal information security function in place, infosec is still less structured than desired.

    **C4** – There is a formal information security function in place, infosec is typically consistent and structured.

    **C5** – There is a formal information security function in place, infosec is very well developed and leverages best practices to evolve the function. Data is used to analyze current program effectiveness.

8. **[PROJECT MANAGEMENT – PM] A well-defined IT project management process is in place.**

   **C0** – There is no project management function in place.

   **C1** – There is no project management function in place, projects are sometimes documented.

   **C2** – There is an ad hoc project management function in place, documentation and processes are inconsistent.

   **C3** – There is an informal project management function in place, projects sometimes follow project management best practices.

   **C4** – There is a formal project management function in place, projects usually follow project management best practices.

   **C5** - There is a formal project management function in place, projects always follow project management best practices and a project management office function has been established. Data is used to optimize the process.

9. **[AUTOMATION – AUTO] Many IT automation processes have been implemented.**

   **C0** – There is no IT automation in place.

   **C1** – There are one-off cases of scripts or basic automation of few functions.

   **C2** – There are ad hoc scripts or basic automation of some functions.

   **C3** – There are ad hoc scripts for defined categories of work.

   **C4** – There is formal automation for defined categories of work using standard automation tools.

   **C5** – There is formal automation for many categories of work using standard automation tools. Automation has reduced cost, optimized IT operations, and/or been widely leveraged operationally for tasks outside of IT.

10. **[COMMUNICATION MANAGEMENT – COM] IT communication management has been defined and implemented.**

   **C0** – There is no communication management in place.

   **C1** – There is occasional IT communication.

   **C2** – There is ad hoc IT communication.

   **C3** – There are IT communication methods that are frequently used.

**C4** – There is an IT communication management plan in place.

**C5** – There is an IT communication management plan in place that operational leaders find informative.

11. **[CLOUD MANAGEMENT – CLOUD] A well-defined cloud management process is in place.**

   **C0** – There is no cloud management in place.

   **C1** – There is ad hoc cloud management of some resources.

   **C2** – There is ad hoc cloud management for most resources.

   **C3** – There is formal cloud management for most resources.

   **C4** – There is formal cloud management for all resources.

   **C5** – There is an optimized cloud management program in place that has yield significant savings, risk reduction, or optimization. Data is collected and analyzed for continuous improvement.

12. **[AGILE PROCESSES – AGILE] A well-defined DevOps/Agile process has been implemented.**

   **C0** – There are no agile methods in use.

   **C1** – There are sporadic attempts at agile methods, with mixed results.

   **C2** – There are ad hoc attempts at agile methods, with mixed results.

   **C3** – There are basic agile methods in place, with mixed results.

   **C4** – There are intermediate agile methods in place, with generally positive results.

   **C5** – There are advanced agile methods in place, with very positive results. Data are analyzed to improve the process.

13. **[VENDOR MANAGEMENT – VEND] A well-defined vendor management process is in place.**

   **C0** – There is no vendor management in place.

   **C1** – There is no formal vendor management in place, some IT managers perform this function. Contracts are not managed well or at all. Issues with vendors are almost constant.

   **C2** – There is ad hoc vendor management in place, most IT managers perform this function. Contracts are managed intermittently or poorly. Issues with vendors are frequent.

   **C3** – There is informal vendor management in place, all IT managers perform this function. Contracts are managed frequently and with mixed results. Issues with vendors are occasional.

   **C4** – There is formal vendor management in place, all IT managers perform this function. Contracts are consistently managed with generally good results. Issues with vendors are infrequent.

**C5** – There is formal vendor management in place, all IT managers are trained in vendor and contract management with very good results. Issues with vendors are minimal.

# Chart Current State

Based on your assessment of your current state, you might end up with a matrix and chart that look like those shown in Table 21.1 and Figure 21.1, respectively.

**Table 21.1   IT Service Management CMMI Ratings Matrix**

| Dimension | Rating | Description |
| --- | --- | --- |
| **Service Request (ITSM)** | 4 | IT has a well-defined service request management system. |
| **Knowledge Management (KM)** | 3 | IT has a useful knowledge management system. |
| **IT Asset Management (ITAM)** | 2.5 | IT has a well-defined asset management program. |
| **Incident Management (IM)** | 3 | IT has a well-defined incident management program. |
| **Problem Management (PBM)** | 3 | IT has a well-defined problem management process. |
| **Change Management (CM)** | 3.5 | IT has a well-defined change management process. |
| **Information Security Mgt (SEC)** | 2.5 | IT has a well-defined information security program. |
| **Project Management (PM)** | 4 | IT has a well-defined project management function. |
| **Process Automation (AUTO)** | 2.5 | IT has automated many basic, repetitive tasks within IT. |
| **Communication Mgt (COM)** | 2 | IT has a communication management plan. |
| **Cloud Management** | 2 | IT has a well-defined cloud management strategy. |
| **Agile (AGILE)** | 2 | IT utilizes agile concepts and methods to deliver IT results. |
| **Vendor Management (VEND)** | 4 | IT has a well-defined vendor management process. |

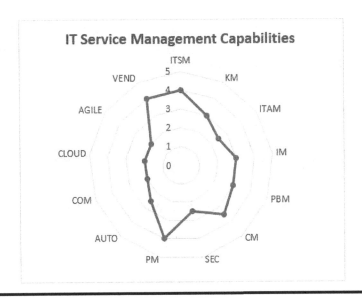

**Figure 21.1  IT service management capabilities radar-style chart.**

# Summary: Future State Notes

ITSM and ITOM are the heart of the work you do in IT. Ensuring these capabilities are at mid-level or better in terms of capabilities should be a priority. As you look at your renovation plan, other improvements may be dependent upon strong ITSM/ITOM capabilities, so you will need to sequence your renovation work accordingly.

We have defined 13 dimensions of service delivery and IT operations; you may have defined more or fewer. In your future state notes, you may want to jot down ideas about capabilities you have yet to develop at all or capabilities that you need to improve during or after your renovation project. IT operations are continually evolving process, and as the HIT environment continues to change in the years ahead, your IT operations will need to continue to improve. These are foundational to future success, so you may want to front-load your renovation project with initiatives that will improve ITSM and IT operations first.

*Chapter 22*

# IT Business Intelligence & Data Analytics Assessment

In Chapter 10, we discussed high-level business intelligence (BI) and data analytics (DA) capabilities. Since this is a rapidly evolving area of competence for most healthcare organizations, our assessment will cover only these high-level items. You can develop a more detailed assessment based on these elements and your unique BI/DA environment. You can also review the references and resources listed at the end of Chapter 10 for more information on advancing your BI/DA capability.

## Define the Dimension

Perhaps one of the most important foundational elements to any BI/DA function is to ensure there is a well-defined governance process, both for BI/reporting intake and projects as well as for the data itself. As we discussed in Chapter 10, data governance and data management are not the same, but they are closely related. Data governance refers to managing the reporting and analytics functions, whereas data management has to do with the processes around managing the data itself. BI governance is often the process by which reporting requests are reviewed and prioritized, so we've included BI governance along with data governance in this assessment. Sound data governance is required in order to have a reliable and trusted BI/DA function. Assessing these capabilities in your organization is a good first step.

DOI: 10.4324/9781003377023-25

The BI/DA function typically evolves from the informal or ad hoc use of spreadsheets to enterprise data warehouses (EDW), data cubes, and online analytical processing (OLAP), among others. Therefore, assessing the technological capabilities of this function is a critical element. It's important to assess where your organization really is in this respect. Do you have a wild environment of ad hoc spreadsheets or a more orderly BI function where data is managed in an EDW and users can access segments of that data for specific needs? Understanding how data is used, by whom, and how it is stored and managed is vital. This enables the organization to move from descriptive to predictive to prescriptive analytical capabilities.

Current thinking in data management is that IT should be the source of centralized data management so data integrity can be maintained (deduplicated, secured, validated, etc.). However, enterprise user access to data should be decentralized to facilitate the easy, secure, and accurate use of data across the organization.

Finally, having operational leaders engaged in these conversations around data governance, data management, and user access methods is crucial to ensure the BI/DA function is not only aligned with the organization's objectives but so that it can facilitate the strategic objectives of the organization through providing fast, reliable access to the massive data sets that are now part of the healthcare landscape.

## Write Capability Statements

The capability statements define the optimal future state. These are used to assess your current capabilities and define a path toward improvement and optimization.

1. [**BI GOVERNANCE**] Business intelligence work is driven through a formal BI governance function.
2. [**DATA GOVERNANCE**] Data is governed through a formal data governance function.
3. [**DATA MANAGEMENT**] Data is managed using a framework such as DAMA, with well-defined dimensions and capabilities.
4. [**EDW**] Data is presented to end users through a variety of sophisticated tools such as EDW, data cubes, and OLAP.

5. [**ADVANCED DATA**] BI/DA provides descriptive, diagnostic, predictive, or prescriptive capabilities to the organization.
6. [**DECENTRALIZED**] Data management is centralized, but user access is decentralized.
7. [**OPS ENGAGEMENT**] Operational leaders are actively engaged in ensuring BI and DA functions are aligned with organizational needs.

## Assess the Capability

Each capability is stated along with five levels of capability statements. You can modify the statements to suit your needs. These are provided to be used as-is or as a starting point for your own customized set of statements.

1. [**BI GOVERNANCE**] Business intelligence work is driven through a formal BI governance function.
   **C0** – There is no BI governance function.
   **C1** – There is no BI governance function, few BI requests are formalized.
   **C2** – There is an ad hoc BI governance function, some BI requests are formalized.
   **C3** – There is an informal BI governance function, many BI requests are formalized.
   **C4** – There is a formal BI governance function, almost all BI requests are formalized and follow the established framework.
   **C5** – There is a formal BI governance function, all BI requests are formalized, the function is optimized. Data is used to assess the effectiveness of the governance function.
2. [**DATA GOVERNANCE**] Data is managed through a formal data governance function.
   **C0** – There is no data governance function.
   **C1** – There are foundational elements in place, few data elements are reviewed or managed.
   **C2** – There is an ad hoc data governance function, some data elements are reviewed or managed.
   **C3** – There is an informal data governance function, many data elements are reviewed or managed.

**C4** – There is a formal data governance function, almost all data elements are managed, a data framework (e.g., DAMA) has been selected or initially implemented.

**C5** – There is a formal data governance function, all data elements are managed using an established framework. The process is optimized. Data is used to assess the effectiveness of the function.

3. **[DATA MANAGEMENT]** Data is managed using a framework such as DAMA, with well-defined dimensions and capabilities.

**C0** – No data framework is used.

**C1** – No data framework is used; several have been reviewed.

**C2** – No data framework is used; one has been selected and will be implemented (future state).

**C3** – A data framework has been selected; initial implementation is in progress.

**C4** – A data framework has been implemented; initial stages of operationalizing this function are underway.

**C5** – A data framework has been implemented; process has been operationalized and optimized.

4. **[EDW]** Data is presented to end users through a variety of sophisticated tools such as EDW, data cubes, and OLAP.

**C0** – Users work with data in spreadsheets.

**C1** – Users work with data from reports that are published and distributed.

**C2** – Users work with data via ad hoc data queries using databases (SQL, etc.)

**C3** – Users work with data via pre-built charts, graphs, and dashboards.

**C4** – Users work with data via advanced tools such as OLAP, data cubes, etc.

**C5** – Users work with data performing data mining and predictive analytics.

5. **[ADVANCED DATA]** BI/DA provides *descriptive, diagnostic, predictive,* or *prescriptive* capabilities to the organization.

**C0** – There is no BI/DA function.

**C1** – There is a very preliminary BI/DA function that is solely descriptive and reactive.

**C2** – There is a basic BI/DA function that is primarily descriptive in nature. There is organizational awareness of the need to mature the capability.

**C3** – There is intermediate BI/DA function that is descriptive/diagnostic and at times predictive. There is organizational interest in maturing this capability.

**C4** – There is intermediate to advanced BI/DA function that is descriptive, diagnostic, predictive, and at times prescriptive. There is organizational participation in maturing this capability.

**C5** – There is advanced BI/DA function that is descriptive, diagnostic, predictive, and prescriptive, as needed. There is strong organizational participation in maturing this capability.

6. **[DECENTRALIZED]** Data management is centralized, but user access is decentralized.

**C0** – There is no formal data access management.

**C1** – There is no formal data access management, but all access is maintained in IT.

**C2** – There is ad hoc data access management, but all access is maintained in IT.

**C3** – There is informal data access management, but some user access is decentralized.

**C4** – There is formal data access management, most user access is decentralized.

**C5** – There is formal data access management that is centralized in IT, almost all user access is decentralized. This process has been operationalized and optimized.

7. **[OPS ENGAGEMENT]** Operational leaders are actively engaged in ensuring BI and DA functions are aligned with organizational needs.

**C0** – Operational leaders are not engaged in the BI/DA function at all.

**C1** – Operational leaders are occasionally engaged in the BI/DA function.

**C2** – Operational leaders are frequently engaged in the BI/DA function.

**C3** – Operational leaders are regularly engaged in the BI/DA function.

**C4** – Operational leaders are always engaged in the BI/DA function and work to align BI/DA efforts with organizational objectives.

**C5** – Operational leaders are always engaged in the BI/DA function, the BI/DA efforts are well-aligned with organizational objectives through continuous stakeholder engagement.

## Chart Current State

Table 22.1 and Figure 22.1 show examples of a matrix and radar chart for a BI/DA function that are in place, but still in its early stages.

**Table 22.1   BI/DA CMMI Ratings Matrix**

| Dimension | Rating | Description |
|---|---|---|
| **BI Governance** | 4 | Business intelligence work is driven through a formal BI governance function. |
| **Data Governance** | 3.5 | Data is managed through a formal data governance function. |
| **Data Management** | 2 | Data is managed using a framework such as DAMA, with well-defined dimensions and capabilities. |
| **EDW** | 3 | Data is presented to end users through a variety of sophisticated tools such as enterprise data warehouses, data cubes, OLAP, and more. |
| **Advanced Data** | 3 | BI/DA provides descriptive, diagnostic, predictive, or prescriptive capabilities to the organization. |
| **Decentralized** | 3 | Data management is centralized but user access is decentralized. |
| **OPS Engagement** | 2.5 | Operational leaders are actively engaged in ensuring BI and DA functions are aligned with organizational needs. |

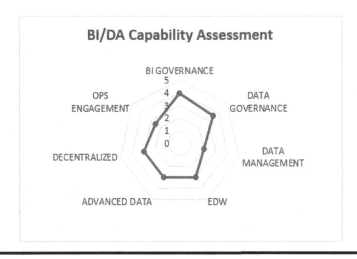

**Figure 22.1   BI/DA ratings radar-style chart.**

# Summary: Future State Notes

Many healthcare organizations are focusing heavily on the BI/DA function now, so this may be an area of rapid acceleration, both in demand and capability. This will put pressure on your current state and your renovation plans. Demand is high, pressure is increasing, and yet developing these capabilities is not something that happens quickly. Having a clear assessment of where you are in your capabilities related to data will help you manage the organization's requests and requirements. Even with enthusiastic business partners, you will need to instill process and discipline to manage demand that will undoubtedly outstrip capacity. If your organization lacks the data governance, management, and frameworks needed to be successful long-term, the near-term results could turn into chaotic churn.

Jot down your thoughts about where you are, where your organization needs you to be, and how you might get there. Your IT renovation project may include this capability as an item on the larger plan, or you may choose to create a separate renovation plan for the BI function. This may give you the ability to hire outside experts and resources to help you mature this capability because the organization may have the willingness to pay for this improvement (vs. basic IT renovation). If you find yourself with the opportunity to light this up quickly or with help from outside resources, be sure to build into your contracts, Statements of Work, project plans, and expectations (internal and external) that you intend to build the whole capability, not just address an immediate pain point. In other words, never let a good crisis go to waste – use the strong demand to develop a *mature* capability and deliver what the organization needs for the long-term.

*Chapter 23*

# IT Business Continuity & Disaster Recovery Assessment

In Chapter 11, we discussed the high-level elements found in any business continuity/disaster recovery (BC/DR) plan. We will use those elements here to review the maturity of your BC/DR capability. Since plans vary so widely across organizations, it is important you incorporate your specific environmental factors in this assessment by modifying (add/change/delete) elements to reflect your capabilities.

## Define the Dimension

A well-crafted HIT BC/DR plan will not only meet regulatory and financial requirements (such as Joint Commission, HIPAA, or insurance requirements), but it will minimize risk for the organization. These plans typically are referred to as BC plans or BC/DR plans. The plan assesses the IT risk the organization is exposed to, articulates the potential impact, and defines strategies to address those risks. A good plan should also include emergency response and recovery plans, which should be tested, trained, and audited on a periodic basis.

Most healthcare organizations have some sort of BC/DR plan, but many have plans that were written five or ten years ago and have not been maintained, updated, or modified to reflect the current state. How has your network topology changed? What applications have been added to (and removed from) the environment? Which applications are in the cloud and

DOI: 10.4324/9781003377023-26

which are still on-premise? Who's auditing your backups, and has anyone tested the ability to recover from backups recently? Who oversees managing a cybersecurity event? How often do you practice incident response?

The list of questions goes on, but the point is that if you have an old plan, you essentially have no plan. Creating and maintaining a BC/DR plan is never at the top of anyone's list of IT tasks they look forward to, but it is a necessary component of IT and one that is foundational to the security of healthcare systems today.

One final note before we begin the assessment. Cloud technologies have made their way into all aspects of HIT. Sometimes they are the backbone of an organization's BC/DR plans; sometimes they need to be included in the BC/DR planning process. Regardless of how cloud technologies are used in your organization today, be sure to include all aspects in your assessment of your BC/DR plan capabilities.

## Write Capability Statements

The capability statements define the optimal future state. These are used to assess your current capabilities and define a path toward improvement and optimization.

1. **[RISK ASSESSMENT]** A formal risk assessment has been conducted and results documented.
2. **[BUSINESS IMPACT ANALYSIS]** A formal business impact analysis (BIA) has been conducted and results documented.
3. **[RISK MANAGEMENT]** Risk management and mitigation strategies have been developed for each identified risk.
4. **[BC/DR PLAN]** A formal BC/DR plan has been developed, reviewed by appropriate stakeholders, and approved by leadership.
5. **[EMERGENCY RESPONSE]** Emergency response and recovery plans are clearly articulated for key emergency responses.
6. **[TESTING, TRAINING, AUDITING]** Testing, training, and auditing of the BC/DR and emergency response plans occur on a periodic basis, no less than annually.
7. **[MAINTENANCE]** The BC/DR plan is maintained and reviewed annually. It is updated whenever substantial organizational or IT changes occur.

## Assess the Capability

Each capability is stated along with five levels of capability statements. You can modify the statements to suit your needs. These are provided to be used as-is or as a starting point for your own customized set of statements.

1. **[RISK ASSESSMENT] A formal risk assessment has been conducted.**

    **C0** – No risk assessment has been conducted.

    **C1** – No risk assessment has been conducted; some risks have been identified.

    **C2** – No risk assessment has been conducted; numerous risks have been identified and some risk mitigation plans may be known or in place.

    **C3** – An ad hoc risk assessment has been conducted; numerous risks have been identified; some have been mitigated.

    **C4** – A formal risk assessment has been conducted; risks have been identified and mitigation plans are in place or being created to address all identified risks.

    **C5** – A formal risk assessment has been conducted; risks have been identified, mitigation plans are in place and well-documented.

2. **[BUSINESS IMPACT ANALYSIS] A formal BIA has been conducted and results documented.**

    **C0** – No BIA has been conducted.

    **C1** – No BIA has been conducted; some elements of a BIA are known.

    **C2** – No BIA has been conducted; many elements of a BIA are known or the process is just underway.

    **C3** – An ad hoc BIA has been conducted; many elements are known; data needs to be incorporated into the BC/DR plan.

    **C4** – A formal BIA has been conducted; the BC/DR plan incorporates most of this data effectively.

    **C5** – A formal BIA has been conducted; the BC/DR plan incorporates this data very effectively and the BIA is reviewed periodically to ensure currency.

3. **[RISK MANAGEMENT] Risk mitigation strategies have been developed for each identified risk.**

    **C0** – No risk mitigation strategies have been developed.

**C1** – No risk mitigation strategies have been developed; some risks have been addressed individually.

**C2** – No risk mitigation strategies have been developed; numerous risks have been addressed individually.

**C3** – An ad hoc risk mitigation plan has been developed; some risks are addressed in this plan.

**C4** – A formal risk mitigation plan has been developed; all or most risks are addressed in this plan.

**C5** – A formal risk mitigation plan has been developed, all identified risks are addressed in this plan. The plan is reviewed and updated on a periodic basis including after major IT changes.

4. **[BC/DR PLAN] A formal BC/DR plan has been developed, reviewed by appropriate stakeholders, and approved by leadership.**

   **C0** – No formal BC/DR plan has been developed.

   **C1** – No formal BC/DR plan has been developed; some BC elements are known or a BC plan more than four years old exists and has not been updated.

   **C2** – No formal BC/DR plan has been developed; numerous BC elements are known or a BC that is three to four years old exists and has not been updated.

   **C3** – An ad hoc or informal BC/DR plan has been outlined or a BC plan that is two to three years old exists and has not been updated.

   **C4** – A formal BC/DR plan has been developed based on the risk assessment and BIA data. Mitigation plans are in initial phases. A policy identifying requirements for a BC/DR plan exists.

   **C5** – A formal BC/DR plan has been developed based on the risk assessment and BIA data. It has been optimized and is reviewed, updated, and tested on a periodic basis. A policy identifying requirements for a BC/DR plan exists and is reviewed/updated periodically to reflect changes to the BC/DR approach.

5. **[EMERGENCY RESPONSE] Emergency response and recovery plans are clearly articulated for key emergency responses.**

   **C0** – There is no emergency response and recovery plan.

   **C1** – There is no emergency response and recovery plan; some emergency response information is known.

**C2** – There is no emergency response and recovery plan; emergency response activities have been identified.

**C3** – There is an ad hoc emergency response plan; it has not been reviewed or well-documented.

**C4** – There is a formal emergency response and recovery plan; it has been documented, reviewed, and staff have been trained. A policy regarding IT emergency response and recovery exists.

**C5** – There is a formal emergency response and recovery plan, it has been documented, reviewed, updated, and optimized. Staff have been trained and lessons learned incorporated into the plan. A policy regarding IT emergency response and recovery exists and is reviewed/updated periodically.

6. **[TESTING, TRAINING, AUDITING] Testing, training, and auditing of the BC/DR and emergency response plans occur on a periodic basis, no less than annually.**

    **C0** – There is no testing, training, or auditing of the BC/DR plan or no plan exists.

    **C1** – The BC/DR plan has not been tested in the past two years; there is no training or auditing of the BC/DR plan.

    **C2** – The BC/DR plan has not been tested in the past year; training occurred once or twice; there is no auditing of the plan.

    **C3** – The BC/DR plan has been tested in the past year; training has been sporadic or incomplete; there is minimal auditing of the plan.

    **C4** – The BC/DR plan has been tested in the past year; training occurs periodically; auditing occurs after training.

    **C5** – The BC/DR plan has been tested and updated in the past year; training occurs on a scheduled basis; the plan is audited annually.

7. **[MAINTENANCE] The BC/DR plan is maintained and reviewed annually. It is updated whenever substantial organizational or IT changes occur.**

    **C0** – There is no maintenance or review of the BC/DR plan or there is no BC/DR plan.

    **C1** – There is no maintenance and only sporadic review of the BC/DR plan or a plan is in development.

    **C2** – There is minimal maintenance and infrequent review of the BC/DR plan.

    **C3** – There is infrequent maintenance and review (less than annually) of the BC/DR plan.

**C4** – There is periodic maintenance and review (at least annually) of the BC/DR plan.

**C5** – There is scheduled maintenance and review of the BC/DR plan and it is updated whenever substantial changes to the IT environment or the overall organization occur.

# Chart Current State

Since most HIT organizations have a BC/DR plan of some sort in place, our example current state matrix and chart reflect having these elements in place, but not having policies, processes, and procedures in place for maintaining the plan. You may have a separate BC and DR plan; you may have an emergency response plan or an incident response plan. Regardless of the terminology used, you should have formal plans around maintaining business operations when disruptive events occur and assess the maturity of those capabilities in this activity. These are shown in the matrix and radar charts in Table 23.1 and Figure 23.1 respectively.

**Table 23.1   BC/DR Plan Ratings Matrix**

| Dimension | Rating | Description |
| --- | --- | --- |
| **Risk assessment** | 3 | A formal risk assessment has been conducted and results documented. |
| **Business impact analysis** | 2.5 | A formal BIA has been conducted and results documents. |
| **Risk management** | 3.5 | Risk management strategies have been developed for each identified risk. |
| **BC/DR plan** | 3 | A formal BC/DR plan has been developed, reviewed by appropriate stakeholders, and approved by leadership. |
| **Emergency response** | 3.5 | Emergency response and recovery plans are clearly articulated for key emergency responses. |
| **Testing, training, and auditing** | 2 | Testing, training, and auditing of the BC/DR and emergency response plans occur on a periodic basis, no less than annually. |
| **Maintenance** | 1 | The BC/DR plan is maintained and reviewed annually. It is updated whenever substantial organizational or IT changes occur. |

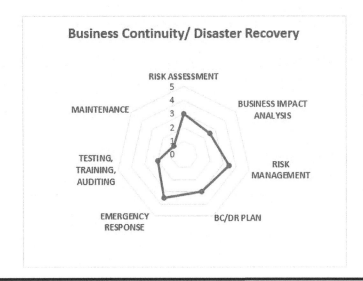

**Figure 23.1    BC/DR plan capabilities radar-style chart.**

## Summary: Future State Notes

As with other topics, you should capture any notes you have about your BC/DR capabilities and ideas you have about how you can advance your capabilities through your renovation efforts. Many elements tie together, so as you improve your technology and asset management capabilities, you will likely to see improvements in your BC/DR capabilities as well. Jot down these ideas so you can incorporate them into your renovation plan.

Remember, your lowest rating may not be your highest priority when developing your renovation plan. You will need to take a holistic look at your capabilities and determine which elements across all your IT functions should be your highest priorities based on all the factors.

# Chapter 24

# IT Cybersecurity Assessment

In Chapter 12, we briefly touched on cybersecurity elements. In this chapter, we will pull in those elements and develop an assessment. This will not lead to a detailed cybersecurity assessment, and you should not expect that the results of this assessment will fulfill regulatory requirements regarding assessing or auditing your cybersecurity functions. Instead, this will tell you about the overall capabilities of your program and identify opportunities to mature the function.

## Define the Dimension

The cybersecurity function within the IT department describes both strategic and tactical elements. Fundamentally, the requirement is that IT maintain the *confidentiality*, *integrity*, and *availability* of organizational data. Securing confidential data, both patient data and sensitive organizational data such as employee social security numbers, salaries, or home addresses, is the primary goal of cybersecurity activities. The broader picture is having a comprehensive program in place that ensures systems remain secure against all inappropriate and unauthorized access. These capability statements represent the key program elements.

As we discussed in Chapter 12, the deployment of and reliance on cloud-based solutions significantly impacts your cybersecurity stance. Securing cloud solutions can be complex, especially in multi-cloud or hybrid cloud environments. IAM, along with PAM, can be particularly challenging. Ensure that all your cloud solutions are included in your cybersecurity assessments

DOI: 10.4324/9781003377023-27

so you do not have any gaps in your readiness. Software such as CASB solutions can assist in these efforts. Note also that your BC/DR plan may or may not encompass your cybersecurity response or incident response plan. These can be tied together or remain separate as long as you have formal plans that cover all aspects.

## Write Capability Statements

The capability statements define the optimal future state. These are used to assess your current capabilities and define a path toward improvement and optimization.

1. [**FRAMEWORK**] A cybersecurity framework suitable for healthcare IT has been implemented.
2. [**FUNDAMENTALS**] Fundamental cybersecurity processes are fully in place.
3. [**IMPROVE**] There is a formal process to continually improve cybersecurity practices.
4. [**USER TRAINING**] Effective, formal end user cybersecurity training is delivered to the organization.
5. [**INCIDENT**] A thorough incident response plan has been developed and is practiced regularly.
6. [**ROADMAP**] A roadmap for further developing cybersecurity capabilities has been implemented.

## Assess the Capability

Each capability is stated along with five levels of capability statements. You can modify the statements to suit your needs. These are provided to be used as-is or as a starting point for your own customized set of statements.

Cybersecurity assessments require far more detail than discussed here. This section is intended to make visible high-level capabilities and potential gaps for investigation. Your cybersecurity assessment could certainly follow a similar structure (assess the capabilities of each element) and you could use your framework for the guide. For example, if using NIST CSF, you could assess your capabilities across the dimensions of each of the five areas defined in NIST CFS: Identify, Protect, Detect, Respond, Recover, and optionally, Core, Tiers, Profile. If you download the workbook from NIST [24.1], you will see there are 131 separate items called out. This is a very helpful guide for your cybersecurity assessment, but outside the scope of this chapter.

1. **[FRAMEWORK] A cybersecurity framework suitable for healthcare IT has been implemented.**
   **C0** – There is no cybersecurity framework selected.
   **C1** – A framework has been selected but is not used.
   **C2** – A framework has been selected and is occasionally used.
   **C3** – A framework has been selected and is used in an ad hoc manner.
   **C4** – A framework has been selected and is always used.
   **C5** – A framework has been selected, always used, and use is continually enhanced.

2. **[BASICS] Fundamental cybersecurity processes are fully in place.**
   **C0** – There is no focus on basic security hygiene.
   **C1** – There are some security hygiene activities.
   **C2** – There are numerous security hygiene activities, but no formal tracking.
   **C3** – There is a formal security hygiene program with ad hoc tracking.
   **C4** – There is a formal security hygiene program with very consistent tracking.
   **C5** – There is a formal security hygiene program that is always tracked and used to enhance capabilities. Data is used to improve the program.

3. **[SOLUTIONS] Evolve your cybersecurity solutions.**
   **C0** – There are no efforts to evolve cybersecurity solutions.
   **C1** – There are occasional efforts to evolve cybersecurity solutions.
   **C2** – There are ad hoc efforts to evolve cybersecurity solutions.
   **C3** – There are frequent efforts to evolve cyber security solutions.
   **C4** – There are consistent efforts to evolve cyber security solutions.
   **C5** – There are sophisticated and innovative efforts to evolve the cyber security solutions. Data is used to identify opportunities for improvement.

4. **[TRAINING] Educate your end users.**

   **C0** – There is no end user education program.

   **C1** – There is no formal end user education program.

   **C2** – There are some end user education initiatives, but nothing programmatic.

   **C3** – There is a basic end user education program or it is just being implemented.

   **C4** – There is an end user education program that is consistently delivered.

   **C5** – There is an excellent end user education program that is consistently delivered. Data is used to evaluate and improve the program.

5. **[INCIDENT RESPONSE] Develop and practice incident response.**

   **C0** – There is no incident response plan.

   **C1** – There is an incident response plan that is out of date or never reviewed.

   **C2** – There is an incident response plan that may be updated occasionally.

   **C3** – There is an incident response plan that is updated every couple of years and practiced periodically.

   **C4** – There is an incident response plan that is updated annually and practiced at least annually.

   **C5** – There is an incident response plan that is updated annually and practiced quarterly. Data from lessons learned is incorporated into the plan.

6. **[GROW] Grow your cybersecurity capabilities.**

   **C0** – There is no plan to grow or enhance cybersecurity capabilities.

   **C1** – There is no formal plan to grow or enhance cybersecurity capabilities.

   **C2** – There is no formal plan to grow cybersecurity capabilities, but there are some largely reactive, ad hoc initiatives.

   **C3** – There is no formal plan to grow cybersecurity capabilities, but there are numerous ad hoc initiatives.

   **C4** – There is a formal plan to grow cybersecurity capabilities, it progresses unevenly at times.

   **C5** – There is a formal plan to grow cybersecurity capabilities, it progresses consistently and the maturity of the capability continues to grow. Data is used to guide decisions on where to enhance capabilities.

# Chart Current State

Once you have assessed and charted your current state, you might have a chart that looks something like that shown in Table 24.1 and Figure 24.1. It's not uncommon to see healthcare organizations with a framework selected and in active use, with basic cybersecurity hygiene pretty well dialed in, and some efforts to educate end users. Your incident response plan may need a bit of work and chances are really good that you need to spend a bit more time practicing incident response with your IT team, but overall, you have the fundamentals covered.

**Table 24.1   Cybersecurity CMMI Ratings Matrix**

| Dimension | Rating | Definition |
|---|---|---|
| **Framework** | 4 | Select a cybersecurity framework. |
| **Basics** | 5 | Focus on basic security hygiene. |
| **Solutions** | 3 | Evolve your cybersecurity solutions. |
| **Training** | 2.5 | Educate your end users. |
| **Incident response** | 3 | Develop and practice incident response. |
| **Grow** | 2.5 | Grow your cybersecurity capabilities. |

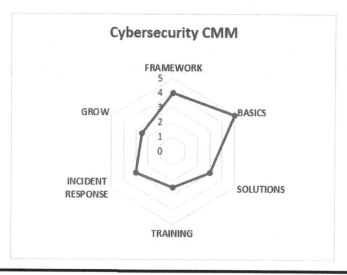

**Figure 24.1   Cybersecurity capability radar-style chart.**

## Summary: Future State Notes

Cybersecurity has been an area of focus for many years, yet some healthcare organizations still have ad hoc processes in place. Breaches are becoming increasingly common; insurance coverage is dropping while rates are climbing. It is imperative to have a strong, mature cybersecurity function in your organization. If you do not have this capability as dialed in as you'd like, this should be one of your top priorities. That said, many of the other IT capabilities assessed throughout this section contribute to (or detract from) your cyber readiness, so you may need to focus on IT operations or technology management in order to get to a more secure stance.

As you look at your opportunities for maturing your cyber capabilities, think about where your IT department is with respect to other capabilities. When we complete our assessments, we will summarize by looking at all the charts in one place, which will give us a great visual sense of where priorities should be. You may know right now what those should be and where, how, and when you will incorporate them into your renovation plan. If so, make a few notes here for future reference.

## Reference

[24.1] Computer Security Resource Center (CSRC), National Institute of Standards (NIST), Information Technology Laboratory (ITL), National Online Information Resources (OLIR), OLIR Focal Document Templates, "Cybersecurity Framework v1.1," no date, https://csrc.nist.gov/Projects/olir/focal-document-templates, accessed February 7, 2023. *Note: There are numerous other useful templates found here that can help guide your cybersecurity efforts.*

# Chapter 25

# IT Staffing Assessment

Your staffing assessment will cover several dimensions. As you prepare for your renovation project, you will need the right staff in the right roles. Additionally, you will need to update your methods of managing staff who are working fully remote, partially remote (hybrid), working from home on an ad hoc basis, or fully on-site. Most HIT organizations today have a mixture of all of these. How do you lead these types of teams, and are you prepared to make the most of this evolving configuration? Are your managers properly skilled at managing this new hybrid environment? While we will assess management and leadership skills separately, it becomes part of your overall staffing assessment. Let's begin by defining the dimension.

## Define the Dimension

IT staffing encompasses all the aspects of ensuring your IT department has the skills, resources, and capabilities it needs to provide fast, effective, reliable support to the organization. This includes not only maintaining day-to-day operations, but managing break/fix, cybersecurity, upgrades, and projects.

Your technology footprint has changed over the past five to ten years, so your staffing model should have changed along with it. However, if you are like vast majority of HIT departments, you have staffing models and job descriptions left from a decade ago. Your job descriptions should

DOI: 10.4324/9781003377023-28

encompass everything you support now and what you need to support your organization in the foreseeable future.

Your staffing models may also have been hardware heavy in the past – having IT staff who could "rack and stack" servers in a data center was an important skill in the past, but unless you're providing hosting services in a data center, you probably have less need for that skill and more need for the capabilities of managing virtual environments. It was once common to find systems engineers camped out in the data center with a terminal connected directly to a server. Now, you find a systems engineer sitting at a desk with three or four computer monitors, accessing virtual systems – some on-site, some located across town or thousands of miles away. Do your job descriptions reflect these changes?

Your IT staff need all the basic infrastructure skills they have always needed, but they also need to be proficient in whichever cloud platforms you're using. They need to understand cloud architecture, management systems, applications, connectivity, data management, identity and privileged account management, and security, among other things. Wherever your organization is headed, you will need to upskill and retool your team as part of your renovation project.

Technical skills are not the only types of skills needed by tomorrow's IT staff in healthcare. Having the ability to understand the business, how it operates, and what end users really need from IT systems is key to success. Having sound business skills like communication, collaboration, and project management, among others, will be even more important to HIT success going forward.

Reviewing and adjusting environmental issues such as workspace, requirements to be on-site or remote, work days and hours, on-call schedules, and managing productivity are all functions of management, but are all staffing related functions you should review as you develop your renovation plan.

Finally, looking at whether you have optimized your IT processes and whether you have automated them should be part of your staffing review. If you can offload repetitive, necessary, but non-value-added work through automation, you can better leverage the staff you have. This is one way of creating more capacity without increasing headcount. In environments where headcount (FTEs) is more heavily scrutinized (or restricted) than operational expenses, automation might be a way of expanding your capacity. Certainly, you should examine these dimensions as part of your overall renovation plan.

# Write Capability Statements

The capability statements define the optimal future state. These are used to assess your current capabilities and define a path toward improvement and optimization.

1. **[ROLES]** IT has defined the roles and updated job descriptions needed for the future.
2. **[FIT]** IT has the right staff in the right roles and teams are diverse.
3. **[DEMAND]** IT can meet or manage the IT demand of the organization.
4. **[TECH SKILLS]** IT staff have the technical skills needed for the future.
5. **[BUS SKILLS]** IT staff have the business skills needed for the future.
6. **[SCHEDULES]** IT staff schedules flex to meet the needs of the department and the organization.
7. **[PRODUCTIVITY]** IT staff are fully engaged and productive.
8. **[AUTOMATION]** IT leverages automation of routine IT tasks to free up IT staff for value-added work.

# Assess the Capability

Each capability is stated along with five levels of capability statements. You can modify the statements to suit your needs. These are provided to be used as-is or as a starting point for your own customized set of statements.

1. **[ROLES] IT has defined the roles needed for the future.**
   **C0** – IT has not defined the IT roles or updated job descriptions needed for the future.
   **C1** – IT has not defined the IT roles or updated job descriptions needed for the future, but some planning has occurred.
   **C2** – IT has not defined the IT roles needed for the future, but some advanced roles have been defined.
   **C3** – IT has begun to define the IT roles needed for the future, some advanced roles have been defined, job descriptions updated, and a few positions hired.

**C4** – IT has defined the IT roles needed for the future; a matrix of skills mix needs has been developed. Many job descriptions have been updated; some positions have been hired.

**C5** – IT has defined the IT roles needed for the future; a matrix of skills mix needs has been developed. All job descriptions have been updated; all needed positions are posted or hired.

2. **[FIT] IT has the right staff in the right roles and teams are diverse.**

   **C0** – IT does not have the right staff in the right roles, or the teams lack diversity.

   **C1** – IT does not have the right staff, some of the roles needed have been identified, or the teams lack diversity.

   **C2** – IT does not have the right staff, many of the roles needed have been identified, some have been defined via updated job descriptions. Teams have some diversity.

   **C3** – IT has some of the right staff, many of the needed roles have been identified, many have been defined via updated job descriptions, few have been hired. Teams have some diversity.

   **C4** – IT has many of the right staff, most of the roles needed have been identified, most have been defined via updated job descriptions, many have been hired. Teams are diverse and reflect the local demographic trends.

   **C5** – IT has all the right staff in the right roles, all roles have been identified, defined via updated job descriptions, and hired. Teams are diverse and reflect the local demographic trends.

3. **[DEMAND] IT can meet the IT demand of the organization.**

   **C0** – IT cannot meet the IT demand of the organization. There is a critical backlog of demand.

   **C1** – IT cannot meet the IT demand of the organization. There is a major backlog of demand.

   **C2** – IT cannot meet the IT demand of the organization. There is a significant backlog of demand.

   **C3** – IT sometimes can meet the IT demand of the organization. There is a backlog of demand.

   **C4** – IT generally can meet the IT demand of the organization. There is a manageable backlog of demand.

**C5** – IT can meet the IT demand of the organization. There is an acceptable backlog of demand and capacity for optimization within the department. Data is used to drive resource decisions.

4. **[TECH SKILLS] IT staff have the technical skills needed for the future.**

   **C0** – IT staff do not have the technical skills needed for the future.

   **C1** – IT staff do not have the technical skills needed for the future; technical requirements are in development.

   **C2** – Most IT staff do not have the technical skills needed for the future; technical requirements are in development.

   **C3** – Some IT staff do not have the technical skills needed for the future; technical requirements are largely complete and are being incorporated into new job descriptions.

   **C4** – Many IT staff have the technical skills needed for the future; technical requirements are complete and are incorporated into new job descriptions.

   **C5** – All or almost all IT staff have the technical skills needed for the future; technical requirements are complete and are incorporated into new job descriptions.

5. **[BUS SKILLS] IT staff have the business skills needed for the future.**

   **C0** – IT staff do not have the business skills needed for the future.

   **C1** – IT staff do not have the business skills needed for the future; these skills are being defined.

   **C2** – IT staff do not have the business skills needed for the future; these skills have been defined.

   **C3** – IT staff have some of the business skills needed for the future; skills have been defined and training plans are in development.

   **C4** – IT staff have some or many of the business skills needed for the future; skills have been defined and training plans are complete or training is underway.

   **C5** – IT staff have most or all of the business skills needed for the future; skills have been defined and training is underway or has been completed. Periodic skills assessments are performed.

6. **[SCHEDULES] IT staff schedules flex to meet the needs of the department and the organization.**

   **C0** – Staff scheduling has not changed.

**C1** – Staff scheduling is being evaluated, but it primarily reflects the same model as prior.

**C2** – Staff scheduling has been evaluated and discussed; some changes are being evaluated.

**C3** – Staff scheduling has changed slightly; long-term or permanent solutions are still undecided.

**C4** – Staff scheduling has changed and is more flexible to meet both staff and organizational needs.

**C5** – Staff scheduling has been completely revamped to effectively meet today's staff and organizational needs. Using data, the process continues to be optimized.

7. **[PRODUCTIVITY] IT staff are fully engaged and productive.**

   **C0** – There is no process in place to evaluate engagement or productivity.

   **C1** – There is no process in place to evaluate engagement, basic productivity metrics are being developed.

   **C2** – There is no process in place to evaluate engagement, basic productivity metrics are defined and sometimes used.

   **C3** – There is no process in place to evaluate engagement, productivity metrics are defined and frequently used.

   **C4** – There is an ad hoc or informal process in place to evaluate engagement, productivity metrics are defined and always used.

   **C5** – There is a strong process in place to evaluate engagement, productivity metrics are well-defined and continue to evolve to meet the changing needs of the organization.

8. **[AUTOMATION] IT leverages automation of routine IT tasks to free up IT staff for value-added work.**

   **C0** – No IT processes have been improved or automated.

   **C1** – Few IT processes have been improved or automated.

   **C2** – Some IT processes have been improved or automated, not both.

   **C3** – Some IT processes have been improved and automated.

   **C4** – Many IT processes have been improved and automated.

   **C5** – Most IT processes have been improved and automated. Data is used to drive these automation efforts, monitor results, and identify automation opportunities.

# Chart Current State

Assuming your IT department is having the same challenges as your peers, your capabilities in this area might be lower than you would like. The examples shown in Table 25.1 and Figure 25.1 show the matrix and capabilities chart, respectively. They reflect likely challenges in several areas.

**Table 25.1    IT Staffing CMMI Ratings Matrix**

| Dimension | Rating | Definition |
|---|---|---|
| **Roles** | 3 | IT has defined the roles and updated job descriptions needed for the future. |
| **Fit** | 2 | IT has the right staff in the right roles and teams are diverse. |
| **Demand** | 2 | IT can meet the IT demand of the organization. |
| **Tech skills** | 3 | IT staff have the technical skills needed for the future. |
| **Bus skills** | 2 | IT staff have the business skills needed for the future. |
| **Schedules** | 3.5 | IT staff schedules flex to meet the needs of staff, the department and the organization. |
| **Productivity** | 3 | IT staff are fully engaged and productive. |
| **Automation** | 2 | IT leverages automation of routine IT tasks to free up IT staff for value-added work. |

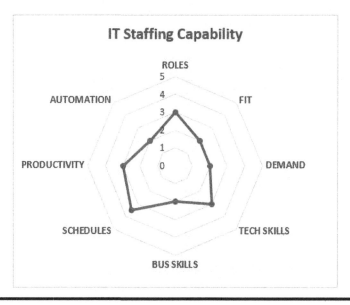

**Figure 25.1    IT staffing capabilities radar-style chart.**

## Summary: Future State Notes

IT staffing is increasingly part of your foundational success. Evaluating this capability and increasing your abilities in this area will pay dividends in the future. If you lack the staff capabilities for your digital transformation, efforts will fall short of expectations or fail altogether.

As you develop your renovation plan, you can look to improve capabilities regarding staffing through several different methods. For example, you might choose to look at a few process improvement projects to review and improve internal IT processes and automate those. From there, you could re-vamp some existing jobs to make better use of your human capital – things that require human intervention, human decision-making, or human management. IT staffing in healthcare is always a challenge, so be sure to make note here of any insights or innovative solutions that have come to mind while working through this assessment.

# Chapter 26

## IT Management & Leadership Assessment

In Chapter 14, we discussed the primary difference between management and leadership as one of managing complexity or change. We also discussed the importance of having both kinds of leaders in your IT department. Sometimes these traits are found in one person, but often people will have greater strength in one dimension or the other. In this chapter, we will look at assessing the strengths of your IT leadership team to ensure you have the skills and traits you'll need not only to undertake a successful renovation project, but to lead your IT function in the future as healthcare and healthcare technology continue to evolve rapidly.

### Define the Dimension

For the sake of simplicity, we will refer to all your IT leaders as IT managers, whether they are leads, supervisors, managers, directors, or executives (Chief Technology Officer, Chief Information Security Officer, Chief Innovation Officer, etc.).

As we discussed in Chapter 14, you need managers who can oversee and improve daily operations to ensure the day-to-day needs of the organization are met. At the same time, you need IT managers who can see the future vision and facilitate moving both IT and the organization in that direction. These leaders need to have high emotional intelligence to work with a

DOI: 10.4324/9781003377023-29

variety of stakeholders. Additionally, they need to be strong communicators and not the stereotypical IT geek who speaks in technical jargon and acronyms.

Though it seems obvious, not all IT managers are hired with an eye toward "softer" traits like accountability, honesty, and transparency, though these are often the skills that cause leaders to really stand out from the crowd.

IT managers must have excellent staff management skills, including hiring (for attitude, aptitude, and diversity) the right staff for the right roles. These days, finding someone who's done the exact set of tasks you need may be difficult or impossible; hiring someone with the desire and ability to learn and grow is where success will be found in the future. Managers also need to be able to have difficult conversations with staff, to manage performance, and to terminate staff who are unwilling or unable to succeed in today's HIT environment. These are basic managerial traits but are often underdeveloped skills in IT management, as we tend to hire for the ability to understand and manage complex technical environments.

IT managers must be able to understand and manage effectively within the financial realm by developing proposals and budgets, managing operational and capital expenditures, and managing project costs, to name a few. Ideally, IT managers have a basic understanding of how the healthcare organization in which they operate generates revenue, what its expenses are, what financial challenges it faces, and how regulatory changes impact the financial health of the organization.

Related to financial management is vendor management. Being able to effectively negotiate and manage contracts, manage vendor deliverables and relationships are vital skills, especially as more and more services move to the cloud. In some cases, an IT manager may not have any staff they manage directly and instead, they manage vendors and those relationships on behalf of the HIT function.

Finally, you can't assess all your IT managers with one stroke. So, you may break out your assessment into an overall assessment of all your IT managers' skills and then assess each of them individually. By doing this, you will be able to see who your most capable managers are and who your most capable leaders are. This will give you data for individualized development plans for each. As you improve the capabilities of each of the individuals, you will increase the capability of IT management function overall.

# Write Capability Statements

The capability statements define the optimal future state. These are used to assess your current capabilities and define a path toward improvement and optimization.

1. **[OPERATIONS]** IT managers excel at managing and improving daily operations.
2. **[INNOVATION]** IT managers excel at leading innovation and transformation.
3. **[EMOTIONAL INTEL]** IT managers have high emotional intelligence, excel at communication and collaboration.
4. **[ACCOUNTABLE]** IT managers demonstrate high degrees of accountability, honesty, and transparency.
5. **[STAFF DEV]** IT managers excel at staff development (including diversity, equity, inclusion) and engagement (building trust, engaging the team).
6. **[CRITICAL THINKING]** IT managers have excellent decision-making and critical thinking skills.
7. **[POSITIVE OUTCOMES]** IT managers consistently negotiate and achieve positive outcomes (internal and external to IT).
8. **[CHANGE MGMT]** IT managers support, adhere to, and demonstrate strong change management.
9. **[FINANCE]** IT managers have strong financial management skills and understand both healthcare finances and HIT finances.
10. **[VENDOR MGMT]** IT managers have strong vendor management skills.

# Assess the Capability

Each capability is stated along with five levels of capability statements. You can modify the statements to suit your needs. These are provided to be used as-is or as a starting point for your own customized set of statements.

1. **[OPERATIONS] IT managers excel at managing and improving daily operations.**
   **C0** – IT managers do not manage or improve daily operations at all.
   **C1** – IT managers do not manage or improve daily operations very well.

**C2** – IT managers manage or improve daily operations at a very basic level.

**C3** – IT managers manage or improve daily operations in an ad hoc manner with limited success.

**C4** – IT managers manage or improve daily operations in an informal manner with moderate success.

**C5** – IT managers manage or improve daily operation in a consistent and formal manner with strong success. Data is used to guide these activities.

2. **[INNOVATION] IT managers excel at leading change, innovation, and transformation.**

**C0** – IT managers do not lead innovation or transformation.

**C1** – IT managers do not lead innovation or transformation except on rare occasions.

**C2** – IT managers do not lead innovation or transformation on a regular basis.

**C3** – IT managers lead innovation or transformation on an ad hoc basis with limited success.

**C4** – IT managers lead innovation or transformation on an informal basis with moderate success.

**C5** – IT managers lead innovation or transformation in a formal manner with strong success. Data is used to track and improve change management efforts.

3. **[EMOTIONAL INTEL] IT managers have high emotional intelligence, excel at communication and collaboration.**

**C0** – IT managers do not have high emotional intelligence and do not communicate/collaborate well.

**C1** – IT managers do not have high emotional intelligence and/or do not communicate or collaborate well. (i.e., managers have some of one of these traits).

**C2** – IT managers have low to moderate emotional intelligence; they communicate or collaborate with minimal effectiveness.

**C3** – IT managers have moderate emotional intelligence; they communicate or collaborate with moderate effectiveness.

**C4** – IT managers have moderate to high emotional intelligence; they communicate or collaborate with moderate or strong effectiveness.

**C5** – IT managers have high emotional intelligence; they communicate and collaborate with strong effectiveness and consistently model this behavior for staff.

4. **[ACCOUNTABLE] IT managers demonstrate high degrees of accountability, honesty, and transparency.**

   **C0** – IT managers do not demonstrate accountability, honesty, and transparency.

   **C1** – IT managers demonstrate accountability, honesty, and transparency on rare occasions.

   **C2** – IT managers demonstrate accountability, honesty, and transparency on occasion.

   **C3** – IT managers demonstrate accountability, honesty, and transparency on a frequent basis.

   **C4** – IT managers demonstrate accountability, honesty, and transparency on a consistent basis.

   **C5** – IT managers always demonstrate accountability, honesty, and transparency and model this behavior for staff.

5. **[STAFF DEV] IT managers excel at staff development (including diversity, equity, inclusion) and engagement (building trust, engaging the team).**

   **C0** – IT managers do not excel at staff development and engagement.

   **C1** – IT managers do a very basic job of staff development and engagement with generally weak results.

   **C2** – IT managers do a basic job of staff development and engagement with inconsistent results.

   **C3** – IT managers do a basic to intermediate job of staff development with occasionally good results.

   **C4** – IT managers do an intermediate job of staff development with frequent good results.

   **C5** – IT managers do a very good to excellent job of staff development with consistently strong results.

6. **[CRITICAL THINKING] IT managers have excellent decision-making and critical thinking skills.**

   **C0** – IT managers have poor decision-making and critical thinking skills.

   **C1** – IT managers have basic decision-making or basic critical thinking skills (but not both).

   **C2** – IT managers have basic to intermediate decision-making or critical thinking skills (but not both).

   **C3** – IT managers have basic to intermediate decision-making and critical thinking skills.

**C4** – IT managers have intermediate to expert decision-making and critical thinking skills.

**C5** – IT managers have expert decision-making and critical thinking skills and model these skills for staff.

7. **[POSITIVE OUTCOMES] IT managers consistently negotiate and achieve positive outcomes (internal and external to IT).**

**C0** – IT managers do not negotiate or achieve positive outcomes.

**C1** – IT managers do not often negotiate or achieve positive outcomes.

**C2** – IT managers occasionally negotiate or achieve positive outcomes.

**C3** – IT managers frequently negotiate and achieve positive outcomes.

**C4** – IT managers regularly negotiate and achieve positive outcomes.

**C5** – IT managers always or almost always negotiate and achieve positive outcomes.

8. **[CHANGE MGMT] IT managers support, adhere to, and demonstrate strong change management.**

**C0** – IT managers do not adhere to or support strong change management.

**C1** – IT managers very infrequently adhere to or support strong change management.

**C2** – IT managers infrequently adhere to or support strong change management.

**C3** – IT managers frequently adhere to and support strong change management.

**C4** – IT managers almost always adhere to and support strong change management and encourage strong change management with staff.

**C5** – IT managers always adhere to strong change management and require strong change management with staff.

9. **[FINANCE] IT managers have outstanding financial management skills and understand both healthcare finances and HIT finances.**

**C0** – IT managers have poor financial management skills and no understanding of healthcare finances.

**C1** – IT managers have limited financial management skills and limited understanding of healthcare finances.

**C2** – IT managers have basic financial management skills and a basic understanding of healthcare and IT finances.

**C3** – IT managers have intermediate financial management skills and a basic to intermediate understanding of healthcare and IT finances.

**C4** – IT managers have advanced financial management skills and an intermediate to advanced understanding of healthcare and IT finances.

**C5** – IT managers have expert financial management skills and an advanced or expert understanding of healthcare and IT finances.

10. **[VENDOR MGMT] IT managers have strong vendor management skills.**

**C0** – IT managers have no vendor management skills.

**C1** – IT managers have very basic vendor management skills. There are constant issues with vendors.

**C2** – IT managers have limited vendor management skills. There are frequent issues with vendors.

**C3** – IT managers have intermediate vendor management skills. There are occasional issues with vendors.

**C4** – IT managers have advanced vendor management skills. There seldom are issues with vendors.

**C5** – IT managers have expert vendor management skills. There are almost never issues with vendors.

## Chart Current State

By now, you are very familiar with this next step. The example ratings matrix is shown in Table 26.1 and the radar-style chart of the maturity of the capability is shown in Figure 26.1.

## Individual Assessments

You might choose to assess each of your leaders individually. An example of this method is shown in Figure 26.2. You can see that Anish, Bella, and Chase are compared side by side. In Figure 26.3, the composite of these three managers is depicted. The dimensions are abbreviated to make the charts a bit easier to read.

Based on the composite chart, you can target where each person could grow and how that growth could best complement the team's overall competencies. You can create development plans customized to each person and focused on the departments overall needs. As you perform periodic assessments, you can chart progress by using baseline data and the new assessment data to reflect where growth is occurring. Visualizing that on the

**Table 26.1   Management and Leadership CMMI Ratings Matrix**

| Dimension | Rating | Description |
|---|---|---|
| **Operations** | 4.5 | IT managers excel at managing and improving daily operations. |
| **Innovation** | 3 | IT managers excel at leading innovation and transformation. |
| **Emotional Intelligence** | 2.5 | IT managers have high emotional intelligence, excel at communication and collaboration. |
| **Accountable** | 3 | IT managers demonstrate high degrees of accountability, honesty, and transparency. |
| **Development** | 2 | IT managers excel at staff developing (including diversity, equity, inclusion) and engagement (building trust, engaging the team) |
| **Critical Thinking** | 3 | IT managers have excellent decision-making and critical thinking skills. |
| **Positive Outcomes** | 3 | IT managers consistently negotiate and achieve positive outcomes (internal and external to IT). |
| **Change Management** | 3.5 | IT managers support, adhere to, and demonstrate strong change management. |
| **Finance** | 4 | IT managers have outstanding financial management skills and understand both healthcare finances and HIT finances. |
| **Vendor Management** | 4 | IT managers have strong vendor and contract management skills. |

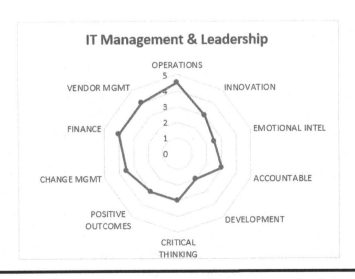

**Figure 26.1   Management and leadership capabilities radar-style chart.**

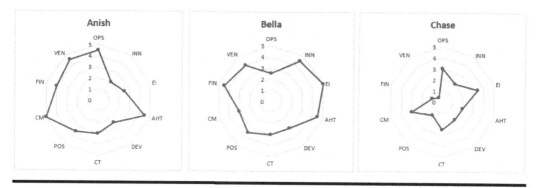

**Figure 26.2    IT manager comparison example (left to right: Anish, Bella, and Chase).**

manager's baseline radar chart can help you see where growth is occurring and what to focus on next. An example of how this might look is shown in Figure 26.4.

Clearly, this can be very sensitive information, so you want to perform this assessment as you would any sort of personnel or staff assessment. Maintain confidentiality, approach any discussion of shortfalls as a coaching session, and provide a path for development. If this assessment is discussed with the manager and a shared understanding of professional growth is developed, it can be a powerful process that sets the manager up for

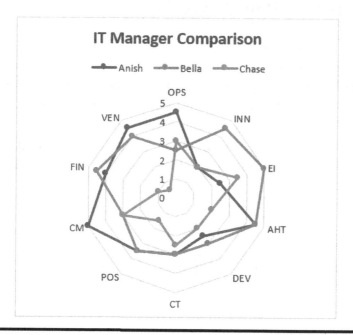

**Figure 26.3    IT manager composite example.**

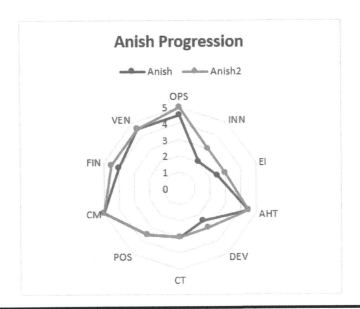

**Figure 26.4  IT manager Anish progress chart example.**

continued growth and success. This process can also be used internally during the interview process to visualize the strengths of various candidates so you can find the right fit for your team.

## Summary: Future State Notes

No doubt, as you have assessed your team and their current capabilities, you have thought about your upcoming renovation and your future state. Ideas about how each IT manager can be developed and how you can best leverage their innate skills, talents, and interests will help you create a well-balanced team. Having complementary skills and traits is what makes a team stronger, so any thoughts you have about how to accomplish this during (or after) your renovation planning should be captured while the thoughts are fresh in your mind.

# Chapter 27

# IT Value Creation Assessment

In Chapter 15, we discussed IT value creation and described the Technology Business Management (TBM) framework that is increasingly being used to quantify and articulate IT value. We discussed the framework and ways it could be implemented, starting from a very simple process to a more complex one.

In this chapter, we will take the same basic view of IT value creation and TBM and provide a process for assessing where you are with articulating the value of IT. We will not be assessing progress against the TBM framework specifically, though you're welcome to do so if you have TBM processes or tools in place. Most HIT organizations are not yet using TBM, even if they are aware of the framework, but many are working to articulate the value of HIT to their organizations. Be sure to modify this assessment to meet your specific needs and your situation so you can find ways to progress your capabilities in this area as part of your renovation project. You will need support for your renovation project, and part of that support will come from ensuring organizational leaders understand the current value of IT and the importance of renovating the IT function to enable future innovation as well.

## Define the Dimension

The IT Value Creation dimension captures the costs of IT and associates them with business functions to demonstrate the value of IT investments in delivering required functionality to operations. It makes IT costs visible and

DOI: 10.4324/9781003377023-30

transparent so that they are better understood by enterprise leaders and can be tied to specific lines of business, revenue streams, and outcomes. Many IT services are foundational in that they are required to be present and functional before higher-level IT can be provided. These include things like network, cybersecurity, connectivity (Internet and telephony), storage, and compute services. Higher level IT systems such as the EHR, HR systems, or financial systems all rely on these infrastructure services to perform reliably and securely. When IT costs are tied directly to business outcomes, the tone of the conversation typically shifts toward increasing value instead of reducing cost.

## Write Capability Statements

The capability statements define the optimal future state. These are used to assess your current capabilities and define a path toward improvement and optimization.

1. [**CURRENT STATE**] The current state of all IT systems is known and documented.
2. [**STAKEHOLDERS**] Organizational leaders are engaged in IT value conversations and decisions.
3. [**FRAMEWORK**] A framework for assessing, monitoring, and expressing IT value has been implemented.
4. [**COSTS**] IT costs are known, monitored, and optimized.
5. [**REPORT OUT**] IT value is communicated to the organization through defined methods.

## Assess the Capability

Each capability is stated along with five levels of capability statements. You can modify the statements to suit your needs. These are provided to be used as-is or as a starting point for your own customized set of statements.

1. **[CURRENT STATE] The current state of all IT systems is known and documented.**
   **C0** – No current state documentation exists.
   **C1** – Some current state documentation exists. It is not centralized, validated, or compiled.

C2 – Some current state documentation exists. It may be validated but may not be centrally stored or managed.

C3 – Current state documentation largely exists. Most is validated and centrally stored.

C4 – Current state documentation exists for all systems. Documentation is validated and centrally stored.

C5 – Current state documentation exists. A plan to improve and optimize the current state has been developed and implemented.

2. **[STAKEHOLDERS] Organizational leaders are engaged in IT value conversations and decisions.**

C0 – No organizational stakeholders are engaged.

C1 – Stakeholders are occasionally present in IT discussions, but value-based conversations do not occur.

C2 – Stakeholders are engaged on an ad hoc basis, some value-based conversations occur.

C3 – Stakeholders are engaged on a frequent basis, targeted value-based conversations occur periodically.

C4 – Stakeholders are actively engaged in a planned and productive manner. Value-based conversations occur regularly.

C5 – Stakeholders are actively engaged in IT discussions and a collaborative approach to planning for IT investments and projects occurs on a regularly scheduled basis. Data drives these discussions.

3. **[FRAMEWORK] A framework for assessing, monitoring, and expressing IT value has been implemented.**

C0 – No framework or process for classifying or organizing IT costs exists.

C1 – No framework or process for classifying IT costs exists, but most IT costs are known.

C2 – No framework or process for classifying IT costs exists, but most IT costs are known and categorized.

C3 – A basic framework and process exist for classifying and organizing IT costs. It is occasionally used in conversations with business leaders. The discussions about IT budgets have not yet changed substantially.

C4 – A basic or advanced framework and process exist for classifying and organizing IT costs. It is frequently used as a basis for enterprise discussions around IT. The discussions about IT budget have begun to change since initiating IT value-based discussions.

**C5** – An intermediate to advanced framework and process exist for classifying and organizing IT costs. The organization relies heavily on value-based data for IT decisions. The discussions about IT budgets have changed for the better since implementing a TBM framework.

4. **[COSTS] IT costs are known, monitored, and optimized.**

**C0** – No framework or process exists for capturing, evaluating, or reporting IT cost.

**C1** – No framework or process exists for capturing and evaluating IT costs, but costs are captured in an ad hoc manner.

**C2** – A framework exists, but it is used inconsistently or in an ad hoc manner.

**C3** – A framework exists, it is used frequently.

**C4** – A framework exists, it is used consistently. IT discussions around costs have improved.

**C5** – A framework exists, it is used consistently and has been rolled out to organizational leaders with success. It has been optimized as part of continuous process improvement efforts.

5. **[REPORT OUT] IT value is communicated to the organization through defined methods.**

**C0** – There is no process in place to discuss IT value with leaders.

**C1** – There is no process in place to discuss IT value with leaders, but there are occasional conversations with leaders on an ad hoc basis.

**C2** – There is an ad hoc process in place, there are more frequent conversations with leaders around IT value.

**C3** – There is a process for having value conversations with leaders and it is occasionally followed.

**C4** – There is a process for having value conversations with leaders and it is frequently followed.

**C5** – There is a process for having value conversations with leaders and it is always followed. It has been optimized using data as part of continuous improvement efforts.

## Chart Current State

Table 27.1 shows the dimensions and ratings, and Figure 27.1 depicts the results in graphical form. We used values that are somewhat representative of the current state in most healthcare organizations, so your ratings and

**Table 27.1   IT Value Creation CMMI Ratings Matrix**

| Dimension | Rating | Description |
| --- | --- | --- |
| **Current State** | 4 | The current state of IT systems, applications, and staffing has been assessed. |
| **Stakeholders** | 2.5 | Identify and engage with organizational leaders in IT value discussions. |
| **Framework** | 3 | Establish an IT value framework and process to classify and organize IT costs. |
| **Costs** | 1.5 | Establish an IT framework for capturing and reporting related IT cost data. |
| **Report Out** | 0 | Develop process for having value conversations with leaders on a periodic basis. |

chart might look similar. If you have been using a value-based approach to IT conversations, you may be much further along.

In this example, Figure 27.1, you can see that there is no process for having value conversations with leaders (report out). You might instinctively think you should start there, but you may choose to improve your cost accounting first. If you have data that reflects how, where, and for whom (in the organization) IT costs are expended, conversations with leaders will

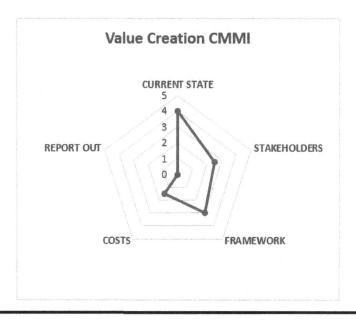

**Figure 27.1   IT value creation radar-style chart example.**

probably be more productive. The reminder here, as with all assessments we cover, is to start where it makes sense. That's not always with the lowest-rated capability. Critically analyze which next steps make the most sense for where you and your organization are today and where you need to be tomorrow.

## Summary: Future State Notes

Your first steps in value creation are to get a full inventory of your systems and then begin compiling your associated costs. From there, you can begin having value-based conversations with your organization. If, through this assessment process, you gained any insights into your IT organization related to value creation, make notes so you can incorporate them into your renovation project later.

# RENOVATION PLAN

*Chapter 28*

# Create Your Renovation Plan

At this point, you have reviewed the building blocks of IT and performed assessments of your current capabilities. You might be feeling a bit overwhelmed by the enormity of the task in front of you, you might not be sure where to direct your focus, or you might be energized and ready to race ahead. All of these are common responses, but the good news is you have all the information you need to create and implement your IT renovation plan. This chapter will help you organize the results of your assessment work and guide you through developing your renovation plan from end-to-end.

You probably will find that there are some areas where you'll need to perform additional work to yield a more detailed assessment. You might also find there are areas you choose to reassess now that you have a more comprehensive view of your overall state. It is fine to go back and revise prior work, just don't fall into the trap of never finishing your assessment. It will never be complete or perfect. It needs to be good enough to begin. Trust that what you have compiled through this process is what you'll need to create a comprehensive and actionable renovation plan.

At the end of each assessment chapter, you were encouraged to make note of your thoughts and observations pertaining to that dimension. This is a good time to review and compile those notes. As you create your renovation plan, having these observations visible will help you incorporate them into the plan.

## Summary of Assessment Findings

The first step in developing your renovation plan is reviewing all your assessment results together. You have likely performed your assessments over time in an ad hoc manner as time allowed, so this is the time to take

DOI: 10.4324/9781003377023-32

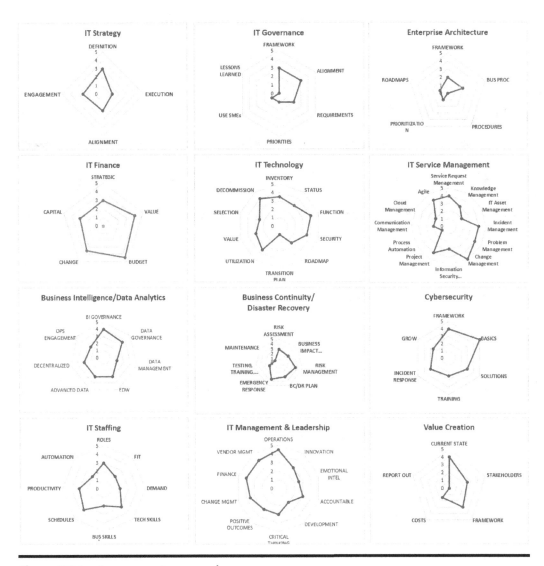

**Figure 28.1  Assessment summaries.**

the data and look at all your assessments as one. An example is shown in Figure 28.1. You can take all your assessment findings and lay them out in this manner.

Viewing your summaries in this way gives you an instant snapshot view of all your assessments, which can be very informative when seen in total. Additionally, you could average out the score for each dimension and generate a top-level chart of your capabilities, as shown in Figure 28.2. While it might not convey the underlying details with great accuracy, it certainly gives you an at-a-glance sense of where you are.

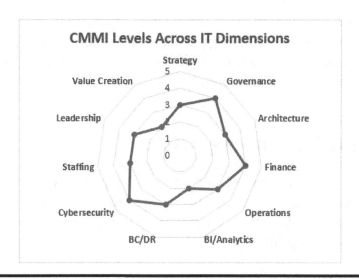

**Figure 28.2    Top-Level summary across all dimensions.**

This is a great visual showing where you are today. You can also keep these as your baseline assessments and compare your results as you work through a phased renovation plan. Since you will have to prioritize what to work on first and how far you want to take each capability, it's a good idea to take periodic snapshots along the way. Figure 28.3 shows an example of a baseline and a snapshot after Phase 1 of a renovation project. You can see where you are moving the capabilities and if your progress is tracking with

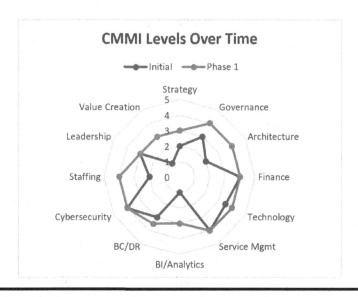

**Figure 28.3    Top-Level summary after renovation phase 1.**

your expectations. While these are qualitative assessments for the most part, the capability statements help keep results comparable from one iteration to the next. This process isn't meant to yield quantitative results; it's meant to help you mature capabilities over time.

## Analyzing IT Current State Results

With all these elements laid out, you can get a clear sense of your current state. It's worth taking a few minutes to write out your impressions and ideas when reviewing this data. For example, based on your summary chart, you might write something like this:

> The IT function here is in an uneven state. Some capabilities are robust and well-developed while other capabilities do not exist at all. This unevenness creates issues within the IT function and adds to cybersecurity risk. Our focus will be to improve all the capabilities related to frameworks and foundational processes, so we shore up basic IT functions. We have not yet begun to consider enterprise architecture in any formal manner, and we will not prioritize EA at this time. We will prioritize ramping up our governance processes (IT and data) so we have more control over the incoming IT work and can better manage our productivity. While that work is underway, we will operationalize many of the IT technology improvements needed such as ensuring all systems are patched, all drives are encrypted, all servers/storage are backed up, etc. This will improve our overall operational function and reduce our cybersecurity risk. This can be done in parallel with other improvement efforts without over-burdening the teams.

When you lay out your charts, you can scan across all of them and pinpoint areas for improvement. You might want to do this in two ways. On the first pass, simply highlight the lowest capability on each chart, as shown in Figure 28.4. On the second pass, read each chart and decide if the lowest capability is actually what you want to focus on. In some cases, it is not. Create a list of these items and adjust accordingly. Figure 28.4 shows an example of identifying the lowest capability in each chart indicated by the solid line circle.

Your list would then begin with:

1. Strategy | Execution
2. IT Governance | Lessons Learned
3. Enterprise Architecture | Policies and Procedures

You can look at any of the charts in Figure 28.1 and identify your biggest opportunities. As mentioned throughout the assessments, these items may not represent your best opportunities for improvement, especially in your initial renovation phase. For example, you might select IT Governance | Requirements instead of Lessons Learned. If you're not doing a great job gathering requirements, Lessons Learned will be less helpful. So, in this case, you might choose that element instead, as indicated by the dashed line in Figure 28.4.

Using these visuals, you can highlight either the areas that need the most improvement or the elements you want to focus on first due to the criticality of the need or other factors such as dependencies or regulatory requirements, for example.

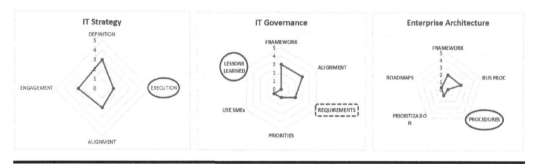

**Figure 28.4   Lowest capability example.**

# Identify Critical Outcomes

You have assessed the healthcare environment overall, the situation your organization is currently in, and the capabilities of your IT department. Given all those intersecting drivers, you should identify your critical outcomes for this project. In today's environment, you might be pressed to cut costs above all else; you might be required to drastically improve cybersecurity readiness; or you might be asked to drive digital transformation. So, before you develop your approach to renovation or your specific renovation plan, consider your critical outcomes first. These will identify the priorities in your project. This also gives you an opportunity to check in with your leadership team to validate your critical outcomes and objectives. If there is something going on in the organization that might alter your approach, you'll get insights from these conversations.

Ultimately, your renovation work will deliver a more functional HIT department. Once that exists, it will be much easier to respond to any number of drivers, including new requirements that emerge in the coming years.

Some examples of critical outcomes, in no specific order, are:

1. Reduce costs (or optimize IT spending).
2. Improve cybersecurity readiness.
3. Reduce complexity for end users.
4. Automate to reduce errors, improve quality, or augment staff.
5. Deliver better quality service.
6. Deliver innovation and/or digital transformation.
7. Position the organization as a leader in the HIT space.
8. Improve the health of the community through the intelligent use of technology.

Your critical outcomes will be unique to your organization, so start by defining two or three critical outcomes and building your plan around that. Review your assessment results with these priorities in mind so you have confidence that the priorities you set for renovation will improve your capabilities and deliver these required outcomes.

## Renovation Approach

We have listed five approaches to planning your renovation project here. There are certainly other ways to go about this work, and the best approach is the one that works well with your organization, your team, and your leadership style. With each, we'll mention the potential pitfalls you might encounter with the particular approach, so you can be on the lookout and develop countermeasures to avoid these problems.

Possible approaches to renovation:

1. Dimension by Dimension
2. Operational to Strategic

3. Easiest to Hardest
4. Shortest to Longest
5. Everything All at Once

## *Dimension by Dimension*

One approach is to work through each dimension at a time and connect them together in a serial manner until you've completed them all, as shown in Figure 28.5. Starting with Strategy and following the order of topics in this book is one approach. Strategy, governance, and architecture, for example, are more strategic in nature, so for some, this might be the best starting point.

**Figure 28.5    Dimension by dimension project.**

   The possible downside is that you don't get into the tactical work immediately, and this can lead to prolonging broken operational aspects of your IT function or a sense that this project won't make substantive changes to the IT function quickly. Sometimes your operational areas need remediation immediately, so starting in this manner might not be desirable.

## *Operational to Strategic*

Many people will opt to start with operational and tactical improvements and work their way to the more strategic items. Some logical starting points with this approach would be IT technology, service management, staffing, finance, BC, BI, and leadership, as shown in Figure 28.6. Each of these offers opportunities for quick wins and making noticeable improvements to IT operations. Working on these elements sometimes can be a bit easier because they are elements within IT's control. They are also elements that can be peeled out a process at a time and addressed.

**Figure 28.6    Operational to strategic.**

   The possible downside to this approach is that you may get bogged down and you spend too much time here, never making it to the more strategic end of the spectrum. Operational improvements are good, but without the more strategic improvements to provide the framework for sustained improvement, you might fall short of true renovation.

## Easiest to Hardest

You may have a sense that it would be easier to do X than Y. There may be a natural order of dimensions for you to tackle that gets increasingly more difficult. An example is shown in Figure 28.7. For example, you might feel governance is going to be difficult, and you want to save that work until after you've made some basic improvements in the department or in your project management processes.

**Figure 28.7   Easiest to hardest.**

The possible downside of this approach is that, like the operational to strategic approach, you might spend so much time and effort at the easy end of the spectrum that you lose steam before you hit the more difficult dimensions. Another possible downside is that by selecting easy items from various dimensions, you might have a renovation plan that lacks coherence and consistency. It might make it harder to see where the path is leading.

## Shortest to Longest

Achieving quick wins is sometimes a powerful force in making any sort of change. You may have some great ideas around quick wins that span various dimensions. Sometimes having a few key achievements makes it easier not only to rally the team around these changes but also to see actual improvements being made. Figure 28.8 depicts possible short-to-long efforts, though much depends on where you are in all your capabilities. As these initial elements take root, you can continue to tend those as you work on changes that will take longer to implement. For example, it might be quick work to improve your finance function because you just need to develop

**Figure 28.8   Shortest to longest.**

one key process to improve the capability. Leverage that momentum and mark one item as in progress or complete.

The possible downside to this approach is that you get bogged down in something that is supposed to be short but becomes lengthy for any number of reasons. Like the Easiest to Hardest approach, you might end up with a renovation plan that is hard to follow and understand if you're pulling elements from across all dimensions without a clear vision and rationale for your approach.

## *Everything All at Once*

This approach takes a parallel path through the renovation project, as shown in Figure 28.9. It assumes that you have different teams with different scopes. For example, you likely have an enterprise application team that is responsible for your EHR and other enterprise applications. You likely have server, network, infrastructure, and/or desktop teams that manage the various technologies along these lines. You may have a separate Service Desk function, you may have a project management office, or you may have a finance function within your IT department as well. If you are structured in this manner and it makes sense, you can launch projects within each team. The upside to this approach is that everyone will be engaged in some aspect of the renovation project right from the beginning, and that can be powerful.

The possible downside of this approach is that you will have a lot of renovation work underway at any given time, and that can lead to chaos, operational issues (i.e. one team unintentionally breaks or interferes with another team's work), or simply too many dependencies that require resolution. Very adept project management can mitigate some of the

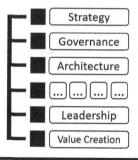

**Figure 28.9  Everything all at once.**

downside of this approach. Also, using Agile methods and only taking on small segments of work at a time can mitigate some of the risk of this approach.

Now, you should have a pretty good idea of where to start and how to approach creating your project plan.

## Create a Timebound Plan

The next step is to make this time-bound. It might be tempting to try to operationalize this and build it into your day-to-day operations, but that would be a mistake. If you don't set a start and finish date, this project may never achieve the results you require. You may get some early wins, but after that, it will become just another set of tasks that languish in some shadowy corner of IT. Set timelines for this work the way you would for any other project. You can specify the start and end dates for the total renovation project, or you can specify start and end for the first phase with a target or desired end date for the entire project.

The first approach will hold you accountable for completing the full project. The second approach will give you some flexibility to adjust as you go but brings with it the same risk of the project just slowly fading away without being completed. Figures 28.10 and 28.11 depict the two different approaches, both clearly timebound.

In Figure 28.10, the n + 12 signifies 12 months, but of course, you can measure your project in weeks or months and you can adjust as necessary. The longer you carry this out, the more likely this will be the project that never ends, so protect this vital work by elevating it to formal, mission-critical project status.

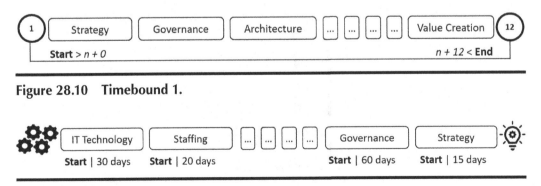

**Figure 28.10   Timebound 1.**

**Figure 28.11   Timebound 2.**

In Figure 28.11, you set a start date ("Start") and determine the acceptable duration for that segment. This gives you a more flexible start date but by defining the acceptable duration, each segment of work is clearly time-bound.

There are an almost infinite number of variations here. The key is to manage this like any other large, strategic project you've managed before. Since the topic is IT and is internal to a large degree, it can be difficult at times to maintain the project cadence and urgency that operational projects have. Commit to your project plan and include it in your IT Steering Committee meetings, your project report outs, and any other venues where project status is made visible. This is a foundational project for your future state, so it needs to be given the time, resources, and focus that all other large projects have.

## Setting Expectations around Results

As we've discussed, there's a risk that this project will be seen as "just an IT project," or less important than operational IT projects. In fact, just the opposite is true. If you do not undertake this project and complete it successfully, you'll be far behind the curve in the coming months and years as your organization begins to demand more innovative and transformational projects.

It is important to be able to articulate the scope of the project and its importance to the organization. Help operational leaders understand that this process will enhance the service you provide to the organization by sharing your expected outcomes. Communicating that this work is foundational to any future innovation or digital transformation will help garner the support you need to protect the work of this project. As an IT leader, you'll need to continuously demonstrate your commitment to completing this work through prioritizing the project and protecting the time needed to accomplish these tasks. If you treat the project as "less than," so will your team.

In the assessment chapters, we reviewed the many dimensions of each category. For example, in IT Governance, we looked at the elements shown in Table 28.1, which is a copy of the table from Chapter 17.

Each of these dimensions had associated capability statements, and you assessed your current state from CMMI Level 0 (C0) "doesn't exist" to CMMI Level 5 (C5) "optimized." You may select a dimension and decide you want

**Table 28.1  IT Governance CMMI Ratings Matrix**

| Dimension | Rating | Definition |
|---|---|---|
| **Framework** | 3 | Uses a framework. |
| **Alignment** | 3 | Aligns with organizational priorities. |
| **Requirements** | 2 | Reviews initiatives against requirements. |
| **Priorities** | 1 | Ranks initiatives to reflect organizational priorities. |
| **Use SMEs** | 1 | Appropriately involves subject matter experts. |
| **Lessons Learned** | 0 | Results are reviewed, lessons learned incorporated. |

to move it from C2 to C3, to improve your requirements gathering process, for example. In another case, you may want to go from C0 to C2 or even C3 in one leap, such as implementing a very structured Lessons Learned process.

You should avoid trying to move all your capabilities in one go. Using the prior example, you might want to improve your alignment and requirements gathering and leave the rest for a subsequent phase or project.

## Sequencing Your Renovation Work

In the next section, we will discuss creating a prioritized worklist, which will drive your project planning. Before we do that, though, we should discuss how you'll sequence the work, regardless of priorities.

Sequencing the renovation work is more than just creating a solid project plan. It's about understanding how each of the improvements you're undertaking affects the other dimensions, the organization, and the IT team. You could inadvertently prioritize two improvement projects that end up conflicting with each other because they use the same resources, they impact the same technologies, or they must be done in a specific order to accomplish the objectives.

If you approach this the way many would, you will be creating numerous smaller project plans that roll up into a master project plan. Some might call these work streams or other similar terms. The result should be a master plan that accounts for the elements listed here. These may not be elements commonly discussed in a run-of-the-mill IT project plan, which is why they're called out separately.

When you start impacting every area of IT through this renovation work, you need to ensure you are not creating bigger problems. Here are a few tips to consider when sequencing the renovation project plan (top-level and all sub-plans).

1. Avoid trying to improve two or more dimensions at the same time that require the same IT team's efforts.
2. Avoid improving two or more dimensions at the same time that impact the same clinical or operational area.
3. Avoid improving a dimension too aggressively. Moving up one capability level might be fine, two might be a stretch, but three is likely too much. Achieve one level of improvement, solidify it, reassess, and determine which next steps will improve the capability further.
4. Understand at a detailed level what and who the improvement work will impact. This requires staff who are most familiar with the work to weigh in as well as leaders to keep an eye on the bigger picture. If you work at cross-purposes, confidence in the project will evaporate, and progress will stall or halt.
5. Set the right pace for change. Some things can move quickly, and some things need to move more slowly. Setting the right pace for each change will keep momentum and focus. Your outcomes are suboptimal if you rush large, complex tasks or if you belabor small, simple tasks. Flex your timing appropriately to optimize project cadence. Ensuring you work to solidify the changes before taking on the next step so you don't slide back into old habits.

As you know, things go wrong with any project, but the more thought you give to these potential challenges as you are developing your plan, the fewer issues you're likely to encounter.

## Create Your Prioritized List

Your task is to take all your capability charts, review them, and create a list of prioritized improvements you're going to make.

You can approach this in one of several ways. For example, you might make a list of top priorities, selecting one item from each category. You might select several items from one category and none from another. Finally, you might select the top item from each category and then also identify your second and third priorities for each category, so that you are developing a roadmap beyond just your biggest opportunities for improvement. Much will depend on the overall work and the approach you've selected.

These will form the basis of your renovation plan, so it's important to finalize this step before proceeding. Table 28.2 shows an example of what this might look like.

**Table 28.2   Sample Prioritized List**

| Priority | Domain | Sub-Domain |
|---|---|---|
| 1 | Value creation | Cloud solutions |
| 2 | Cybersecurity | Patch management |
| 3 | Business intelligence | Dashboards |
| 4 | IT technology | Inventory/asset management |
| 5 | IT finance | Ops budget |
| 6 | IT service management | Knowledge management |
| 7 | IT technology | Enterprise Apps/her |
| 8 | IT technology | Automation |
| 9 | IT architecture | Technology roadmaps |
| 10 | IT governance | Framework |

# High-Level Objectives and Strategy

You've assessed your current state, you've identified your biggest opportunities, and determined your highest priorities. Based on these findings, you can now create your high-level objectives and your related strategy statements. If you recall from Chapter 4, when we discussed the building blocks of strategy, you can start by defining your outcomes or objectives for your renovation project, then develop strategies for attaining these outcomes.

For example, your high-level objectives might be something like these:

1. Improve IT strategy capabilities to drive better business alignment.
2. Improve IT governance capabilities to reduce rogue project work.
3. Develop IT staffing competencies to facilitate hiring the right skills at the right time.
4. Develop IT financial data related to technology business management to identify where the largest IT cost and benefits are in the organization.

Clearly, these are just four of what's likely to be a long list of things you want to improve. You might choose to create your full list of objectives as you see them today, but keep in mind that things will change frequently as you begin to implement your plan. Some of the items may be impacted by the first items you select to work on. Other items may become more or less important as organizational changes occur. Ideally, you should create your full list but only plan to work on a few items at a time. This will prevent you from losing focus or from initiating more change than your team can handle at any given time.

This approach also acknowledges that change is constant in HIT, and there will continue to be new projects and new demands coming in every day and every week that your teams will have to manage. Taking your renovation project, creating the whole plan, and breaking it into smaller subprojects will be the most likely path to success.

## Project Plan

From this point, you can now build your renovation project plan. This should follow standard project management processes. We'll discuss numerous aspects through the project management framework to point out opportunities and potential pitfalls. As with any large project, you should assign a project manager (PM) to oversee the project tasks and timelines. This frees up IT leaders to focus on achieving the results rather than managing the project. Having an assigned PM also signals to the IT team and the organization that this is an important project that requires the same attention and rigor as any other project.

Let's assume you decided to use the list of four items provided in the previous section. Your first item is improving IT strategy for better business alignment. That item should be turned into a small project plan. Let's review some of the key elements.

**Project charter** – What is the desired outcome of this project?
**Project owners** – Who in IT is going to drive this project? In the case of strategy, it's likely the CIO or CTO along with the IT Directors.
**Project resources** – Who needs to do the work? Again, this is likely the CIO, CTO, CISO, and/or Directors.
**Project scope** – What are you going to tackle and what are you purposely excluding from your efforts?
**Project timeline** – What's the overall duration for this project? What are the key milestones?

**Project budget** – Are you going to do this internally? If so, there may be no discrete cost for this project unless you want to track FTE allocation and associated payroll costs (that will depend on how granular you want to get). Are you going to hire an outside consultant to assist you in this effort? If so, you will have consulting and travel expenses, for example.

**Project Work Breakdown Structure (WBS)** – You can develop your list of tasks and subtasks, dependencies, constraints, and other WBS related elements to create your project WBS and Gantt chart.

## *Milestones*

It is important to identify key milestones for each sub-project and for your overall renovation plan. These are what will keep you on track when the fires and chaos of the day-to-day work threaten to push you off track. Milestones should be reasonable – meaning neither too aggressive nor too lax. If you push too hard, your project may implode. If you don't push hard enough, the project work will never be prioritized.

As you look at your project plan and milestones, consider applying some basic Agile methodologies if you're not already using Agile. One of the easiest ways to begin is to break work units down into two-week segments so that the teams can produce meaningful results every two weeks. This makes the tasks and deliverables smaller and reduces the likelihood they'll get too far off track. It also assists with accountability because you and the team will be looking at results, deliverables, and productivity every week to make sure things stay on track. You might also consider running daily or weekly huddles focused on just this renovation work so that you can quickly remove roadblocks and discuss upcoming work.

Publishing these milestones and tracking them like any other project will keep them visible and keep the work prioritized. You may also choose to report this out to your executive team or to your CEO (or your manager, whatever their title) in order to hold yourself and your team accountable to make progress. This also helps keep the effort visible and may be beneficial if the 'emergency of the week' threatens to derail your project. While there are no guarantees, having a plan and keeping that plan visible is often an effective safeguard for keeping momentum. Figure 28.12 shows an example of what your milestones might look like, using the list of four priorities discussed earlier.

| Priority | Domain | Sub-Domain | Owner | Est. Duration | Est. Cost | Dependencies/Requirements | Week or Month | | | | |
|---|---|---|---|---|---|---|---|---|---|---|---|
| | | | | | | | 1 | 2 | 3 | ... | n |
| 1 | Value Creation | Cloud Solutions | Rich | 2 months | N/A | Org. leadership participation | | ◆ | | | |
| 2 | Cybersecurity | | Scott | 6 months | TBD | IT architecture decisions | | | ◆ | ◆ | |
| 3 | Business Intelligence | Dashboards | Bryan | 8 months | N/A | Other BI demand | | | | ◆ | ◆ |
| 4 | IT Technology | Inventory/Asset Mgmt | Crystal | 12 months | TBD | Obsolesence/roadmaps | | | | ◆ | |
| 5 | IT Finance | Ops Budget | Asha | 6 months | N/A | None | | ◆ | | | |
| 6 | IT Service Management | Knowledge Mgmt | Daniel | 12 months | N/A | Team participation in article creation | | ◆ | | | |
| 7 | IT Technology | Enterprise Apps/EHR | Andrea | 5 months | TBD | Identify under-utilized functionality | | | ◆ | ◆ | |
| 8 | IT Technology | Enterprise Apps/EHR | Lydia | 2 months | TBD | Identify automation opportunities | | | | ◆ | |
| 9 | IT Architecture | Technology Roadmaps | Chris | 3 months | N/A | IT architecture decisions | | | ◆ | | ◆ |
| 10 | IT Governance | | Asha | 4 months | N/A | Improve PMO function to include OCM | ◆ | | | | |

**Figure 28.12    High-level milestones chart.**

As with any project, you will also need to determine how you're going to manage delays, which will inevitably pop up. This is especially true for internal IT improvement work. Planning for delays and having a few go-to strategies for managing these delays will help you keep things moving. For example, you might choose to have some backup tasks that can be used to fill in when another task gets delayed. You might have a list of tasks that do not have dependencies that could be pulled in or pushed out in the project timeline. Be sure to have some backup plans at your fingertips so you don't spend cycles figuring out how you can move things around when delays do occur.

## *Assumptions and Risks*

Also, as with other projects, you'll document assumptions and risks. Make note here of all the assumptions you are starting out with so that as things change, you can refer to these assumptions and see if anything material is changing. For example, you might assume that the organization will not be acquiring any new facilities in the year or that it will not be opening any new service lines. You might assume that the staff vacancies you have today can (or cannot) be filled by third-party contractors. You might assume your IT budget will remain flat or be reduced. All these assumptions play into the likelihood of success of your project. More importantly, you can review your assumptions and change accordingly. For example, suppose you assume that your staff vacancies can be addressed with third-party vendors because that's how you've been operating for the past two or three years. Suppose your budget gets cut due to financial pressures on the overall organization and you're told to cut your contractor costs by 75%. The assumptions around your available capacity for renovation and change will be impacted. Having your assumptions clearly articulated will help you determine the impact and the optimal mitigation steps.

## *Plan for Interruptions and Emergencies*

Every healthcare organization has emergency, time-sensitive IT needs from time to time; some companies seem to thrive in this just-in-time environment, while others try to minimize these unexpected requests. Regardless of which type of healthcare organization you work in, you can expect to face interruptions to your renovation plan along the way. Legitimate emergencies might arise, such as a change to a regulatory requirement or the sudden closure of a site for reasons outside the organization's control. Other emergencies, such as lack of planning or lack of process, also crop up, and IT must continue to be a good business partner and respond as best it is able. Therefore, the question is not *if*, but *when*, your renovation project gets interrupted – what will you do? How will you handle this predictable, but unexpected, bump in the road?

The short answer is to build slack into your project plan to give yourself enough buffer to address these emergencies, but that's a bit imprecise at a project level. As you develop sub-projects underneath your master renovation project plan, look at the work and the teams required. Evaluate the likelihood and impact of a serious disruption to that body of work. For example, you might estimate that there is a bigger risk of disruption to large infrastructure architecture or restructuring work than there is to re-aligning job descriptions. Therefore, build buffers into your sub-projects most likely to be impacted and not into those, like job descriptions, that can carry on even in the face of an emergent IT request or project.

Judiciously using slack time and buffers can be helpful as well since you control this project and you generally don't have external stakeholders expecting specific deliverables from this project. Allowing for a more fluid renovation schedule may help you adjust as needed to those unexpected needs of the organization.

You might also want to keep a list of alternative activities that can be performed when an emergency arises, so that Task 3 might pause but Task 14 can accelerate, for example. Be creative and be persistent in your renovation work so that when you get to the punch list stage, you really only have minor items to complete.

A word of caution here. Try to avoid allowing the organization to get used to IT dropping everything for "emergencies." This can inadvertently foster a culture of raising the flag and calling everything an emergency. One potential countermeasure is to call an emergency meeting of the IT Steering

Committee group to discuss the "emergency" along with the impact on work-in-progress. This reduces the likelihood of false emergencies pushing their way onto the schedule and raises visibility and awareness to the disruption caused by emergency IT projects/requests.

Of course, some emergency IT requests can be handled without causing any project delays. For those requests that will impact your project, you should ensure the organization is fully aware of the request and the likely impact not only on the very critical renovation work, but on all projects currently in flight.

Remember, your renovation work is a strategic project for the organization if you ever want to be able to contemplate digitally transforming your organization. Ensure this project is seen as a critical project for the future of the company and that the work is prioritized as high as almost any other work of the organization.

## *Maintaining Focus and Priority*

You may run into challenges maintaining your renovation project's momentum. It can be hard to keep this remedial type of work as a high priority when everyone is champing at the bit to move into digital transformation. It can feel repetitive to explain that you must get foundational elements fixed before anything can be transformed. It's often not a very exciting message for IT or operational stakeholders to hear. The best way to counter this is by providing clear, consistent messaging. If you have interim achievements, announce them, and make them visible. Perhaps most important, have an end date for your renovation project. Just like remodeling a building, you need to know when work will be finished, when the clean-up crew can come in, and when you'll get your certificate of occupancy. The same holds true here. You need to commit to an end date. That end date doesn't have to be the end of your improvements. In fact, your improvements from that point forward should be continuous to maintain your progress. However, at some point, you are going to have to actively engage in digitally transformative projects, and your renovation work must be substantially complete.

## *Dependencies and Constraints*

Like any good project plan, you'll make note of your dependencies and constraints based on what you know today. Your assumptions will drive many of these line items. Identifying these elements will help you see how, where, and when you will need to flex your renovation plan. If you are dependent on finance to assist with the IT finance element and they are in the midst of budget planning, that will certainly impact your timeline.

### *Organizational Change Management*

We will discuss organizational change management (OCM) in detail in Chapter 29, so you may want to reference the OCM material as you're building your project plan. Briefly, your renovation plan will create organizational change – both inside the IT department and likely outside the IT department as well. In order to foster project success, you will need to put a lot of focused effort into OCM. People resist change for various reasons, and assessing the kind of change you are injecting and the likely points of resistance will enable you to create mitigation plans to overcome that resistance to change.

## Agile Renovation Project Management

It is possible you have not yet undertaken any efforts toward leveraging an Agile approach to development work (projects, build, etc. all would come under this "development" header). Healthcare is resistant to change, and HIT is usually almost as resistant. One really low risk opportunity to give Agile a try is in this renovation project plan. How might you do that?

Begin by defining tasks as you normally would. Then, identify what the units of work or units of deliverables are and the timeframes are associated with them. For example, you might decide you need to write new job descriptions for everyone in the department after you've assessed the future-state skills you need. Just thinking about that for a moment, you might think "well, this will take about six months." Rather than waiting for everything to magically pop out the other end of the project chute, identify interim deliverables that make sense. For example, you might decide that you need to take ten steps to get this work done, as follows:

1. Assess of skills needed for future state IT needs.
2. Identify which skills are needed in which roles.

3. Perform a gap analysis on each job description.
4. Rework the job description template to reflect future needs.
5. Rewrite the job description for each role and at each level (systems engineer I, II, III, lead, etc.).
6. Submit to HR for review, approval, market compensation review, and grading (salary level).
7. Create job description cross-walk to map current roles to new roles.
8. Develop career progression mapping based on new job descriptions.
9. Create matrix of staff to show current role to new role, current comp/grade to new comp/grade.
10. Create skills gap analysis for any staff who may be negatively impacted.

You can see that these are well-suited to shorter, interim deliverables. Using Agile methods, you can continuously deliver results and make steady progress. Also, you can more quickly adjust to changes, re-evaluate backlog, and re-adjust expectations and timelines (often to be shorter) based on work completed. Perhaps most important, you see and track progress, so it's harder for projects to drift off track. A six-month project is much more likely to drift if the deliverables are months apart vs. a project plan where tasks are due every two weeks.

## Documenting Your Renovation Plan

With all the building blocks accounted for, all the assessments completed, and all the top-level views of capabilities prepared, you are ready to create your plan. You have all the data you need to begin. Don't let perfection be the enemy of good enough. You have enough information to get started. Your plan will evolve as you progress, it should. It's a living document that should help drive your renovation across all IT dimensions.

Before you begin implementing your renovation plan, there is one more critical element needed. As mentioned, we discuss OCM in the next chapter. We placed it after your renovation planning so you would have a stronger sense of what is likely to change when you review the change management material. We will discuss OCM in the context of facilitating the success of your renovation project now and your digital transformation projects later.

## Summary

Your renovation plan is very similar to any other large, complex IT project, with one notable exception. It is intended to improve your IT function from end-to-end. It will be hard to carve out time and protect this project from encroachment by other, highly urgent tasks or projects, but it is important you do so. If you fail to launch or complete this project, you will be hampering your IT function for years to come. By creating a solid plan that allows you to make incremental progress, you can continue the work and still flex to meet the needs of the organization. When you successfully complete this project, you will have created a very solid foundation from which to launch your digital transformation.

*Chapter 29*

# Manage Change

Clearing space for change is the next step in planning your renovation project. Clearing space is important because we cannot embrace the new if we're surrounded by or cemented in the old. This is true for physical projects as much as for logical projects. When we are surrounded by old technology, old policies, old procedures, and old workflows, we have too many opportunities to return to those outdated ways rather than embracing the new. In this chapter, we will examine four commonly used change management methods, in case you are not familiar or are looking for some new ideas, tips, or techniques to incorporate. We will also review actions that are likely to cause change to be successful, to actually *stick*.

Most organizations struggle to make permanent change in the direction they seek. Instead, behaviors and habits follow paths that are hard to trace, but it seems "bad" habits are more easily entrenched than "good." This is the nature of humans and the nature of change. So, it makes sense to account for human behavior in our change management processes. If we can get our staff, our peers, and our organization to embrace a compelling vision for the future, we can begin connecting the *why* with the *how* and the *when* to fully engage the organization in a successful change process.

With respect to change, we can choose to focus our energy on fighting to keep the old systems and processes in place, or we can focus on building the new. To fight to hold on to the old is always futile since change happens whether we accept it or not. Embracing change gives us a seat at the table, which is the best way to ensure we have

DOI: 10.4324/9781003377023-33

influence over what that change ultimately looks like. As an HIT leader, you cannot control what's happening in the healthcare or technology space. You *can* influence how HIT is implemented and leveraged in your organization and the way your IT department functions within those boundaries. That means planning effectively to manage the inevitable change. The discussion in this chapter is focused on organizational change management, but every aspect discussed here is relevant to your IT renovation project plan as well.

## Change Management and Project Management

Managing organizational change is not an IT responsibility, but increasingly, the success of any project involving IT hinges on effective organizational change management (OCM). With respect to your IT project management and project management office (PMO), you should consider adding OCM tasks to your project templates. For example, when a project is requested and the initial discovery or project intake process kicks off, the responsible leader (project owner or sponsor) should be asked about their change management plans. How will this solution impact patients, providers, staff, or others? How will workflows change? How will the jobs of impacted employees change? What are the plans for managing those changes outside of the IT technology changes? You can probably immediately think back on a few failed projects and see how change management would have changed the outcome.

Additionally, you need to understand how to assess how well the change has been adopted in the organization. How will you ensure you do not drift off course? Implementing change is one thing, maintaining that change consistently going forward is another. What countermeasures will you put in place to ensure change doesn't unravel over time? These are elements to consider as you plan your change management efforts.

When change management actions are turned into project tasks, they are more likely to be accomplished. While IT can't force the organization to do a good job on OCM, having tasks, deliverables, owners, and timelines makes these responsibilities visible. If you have a project Gantt chart showing OCM tasks far off track, it can help spark conversation and accountability for course correction. Figure 29.1 shows a sample of what this might look like as a few line items on a basic Gantt chart for an IT project.

| | Jan | Feb | Mar | Apr | May | Jun | Jul | Aug |
|---|---|---|---|---|---|---|---|---|
| **Organizational Change Management** | | | | | | | | |
| Impact analysis - organizational change | ✓ | ! | | | | | | |
| Change management plan | | ! | X | | | | | |
| Change management training | | | | X | | | | |
| Change management documentation | | | | | | | | |
| Change management effectiveness assessment | | | | | | | | |

**Figure 29.1   Example of organizational change management tasks in project plan.**

In this example, the project is underway and reporting April results. The OCM function started off well, fell behind schedule, and for two months has been completely off track. Having these yellow (!) and red (X) visuals in the project plan can help bring this focus to OCM efforts. This will also help facilitate conversations with organizational leaders about the importance of OCM and how the lack of effective OCM can negatively impact project outcomes.

## *People, Process, and Technology*

Change impacts people, process, and technology, though not necessarily in that order and not necessarily at the same cadence. Figure 29.2 represents a conceptual view of the relative cadence of change in technology compared to the cycles of change in humans and in organizations. In essence,

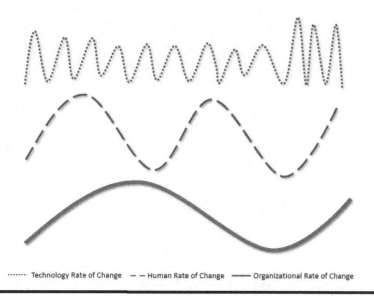

········ Technology Rate of Change   – – Human Rate of Change   ━━━ Organizational Rate of Change

**Figure 29.2   Pulses of change – Technology, people, and organizations.**

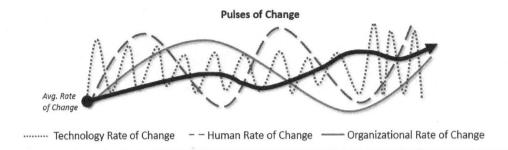

**Pulses of Change**

........ Technology Rate of Change　　－－Human Rate of Change　　——Organizational Rate of Change

**Figure 29.3　Pulses of change composite view.**

technology typically changes very rapidly, humans change more slowly, and organizations are usually the slowest to change. It makes sense. Individuals can absorb change at different speeds, organizations are amalgams of all the individuals, so that the rate of change slows further. When viewed from this perspective, it's very clear why positive, permanent change is difficult to achieve. These forces, due to their different rates of change, end up conflicting with each other at regular intervals. Figure 29.3 depicts the conceptual composite view of these three change cycles and the resulting overall pulse of change.

Clearly, these cycles look chaotic, and most leaders involved in change management will confirm this is generally what change feels like. It also means the overall rate of change is likely to be slower than desired and suffer multiple setbacks as each change cycle ebbs and flows. Though we cannot scientifically plot these rates of change and change adoption, we know that these areas (technology, human, organizational) each have their own rhythm, which in turn creates the overall rhythm of change in an organization. Understanding this can make managing change a bit easier.

In HIT, it's not uncommon to implement a technology, develop a new process around that technology, then expect people to change to accommodate the new system. Of course, we've all seen how well that works. Statistically speaking, most change initiatives fail, and many fail for exactly this reason. We can also see from Figure 29.3 that we must simultaneously manage all aspects of change in order to move forward. Let's look at how this impacts people, process, and technology.

## People

According to author Siu Loon Hoe, "Although the digital transformation plan may look perfect on paper, embedding the change in an organization would require significantly more effort. It is not just about the technology itself but the need to understand how people respond to change as well. Thus, organizations must be proactive in tackling the challenges which come with the introduction of change. The most common mistake is a lack of emphasis on the human side of change." [29.1]

Change can be hard. It can destabilize an environment. It can threaten people's sense of equilibrium, expertise, and belonging. It can lead to confusion, uncertainty, and even fear. And it is not always beneficial to all involved. Take the scenario where you have decided to automate repetitive functions, in IT and throughout the organization. Some jobs may become unnecessary. Those individuals who are impacted are not going to be enthusiastic supporters of the change unless there is a path forward for them. Of those, some will embrace new opportunities and some will stubbornly cling to their current role while the tide rolls over them. We've discussed skills assessment and competency gap analysis earlier. As you look at re-engineering your staff and your department, the people factor should be the first priority, not the last.

Remember, your organization has rewarded and promoted people on doing things the way they are currently done. Raises, bonuses, incentives, and promotions were all based on current state. That alone is a powerful incentive to keep doing things the way they are done. If your success is based on current state, moving to an unknown future state is not only professionally, but financially, risky. When we understand how much people and the overall organization have invested in current state, even when that current state is a rickety, run-down structure, we understand what is at stake in managing change well.

Additionally, each organization operates differently. Some are still very much command-and-control types of organizations where change is dictated and the overarching attitude is "deal with it or leave." These organizations are likely struggling on many fronts because good people do tend to leave those types of organizations, especially in strong job markets. Other organizations have evolved to be more collaborative, and the prevailing attitude is, "change is happening, let's find the best path forward together." With the challenges all organizations are facing with staffing in the coming decades with fewer workers available in the workforce, a more collaborative approach will be necessary to succeed.

While change can be threatening to individuals in the organization whose jobs and roles may be impacted, a well-managed change process can mitigate many of those challenges. Leading change by focusing on the desired future state and the role each individual in the department will play can reduce the resistance to change. Providing training and support in the new environment is key to sustaining desired changes.

## Process

We've talked about process throughout this book, so you should be familiar with your internal IT processes at this point. Even if you are new to your organization, you should be aware of processes that exist – whether formal or informal, written, or unwritten. Things happen in IT departments every day due to some sort of inherent process. New users are provisioned, new laptops are imaged, servers are decommissioned, software applications are modified. How does all of this happen in your environment? Is it chaotic? Automated? Or something in between? In the assessment chapters in Section Three, we reviewed the Capability Maturity Model (CMM) to understand where your department is in terms of various capabilities. More mature capabilities have better defined processes: they are written, new staff are trained, and experienced staff have ingrained these processes in their work behaviors. Ultimately, these processes become "the way we've always done things."

In some cases, we can argue that a new process that makes a job easier is likely to be adopted. We can also see that processes that appear to make a job harder, more complex, or more rigorous are less likely to be adopted. Some change is neutral in that respect. It makes some aspects easier and some harder. For example, the process of imaging a new laptop by hand means the IT techs have to take many actions. They have to install the operating system, configure various Administrative settings (e.g. to secure the device), install the required applications, install the requisite printers or external devices, and perhaps configure security applications or remote access settings. Each laptop has to be done this way by hand. Human error and variability will practically guarantee that every laptop is configured slightly differently or there is an error in one element or another.

Now, let's say an automation system is implemented. The team collaborates on the required settings, and immediately they see that some are setting X and others are setting Y due to an unclear (or inaccurate) set of instructions. As the automation software is configured, these process flaws are found and corrected through the automation software. Once that software is fully configured, tested, and validated, an IT tech can now provision a new laptop by connecting the device to the network and clicking a button to start the configuration.

How will the IT staff respond to this automation, which is both a new technology and a new process? Your answer likely is "it depends." It depends on the person, what their job is, how comfortable they are with change, how comfortable they were with the routine of building a new laptop, and how comfortable they are learning new skills. It's a perfect microcosm of how IT (and people in general) respond to just about any change. While we're talking about the process that is changing, we're also talking about how people *respond* to that change.

Some will embrace the change and adopt the new process almost overnight. They are excited to learn a new system, and they're happy that some of the tedious, manual work will be automated. They're thrilled to free up time to focus on some other part of their job they might enjoy more or that they feel is more important.

Some will be neutral and follow the leaders. They'll watch over shoulders, be coaxed into trying it on their own. They may need more time to learn, but they will eventually catch on, especially if your early adopters are also good at sharing knowledge and spreading their enthusiasm.

Then there are those folks every IT department (and organization) has who are set in their ways. For whatever reasons, they hold on tight to how things are done. They typically appear rigid, sometimes self-righteous ("this is the only right way to do things"), hostile ("you're going to mess things up terribly"), or fearful. These are the people who can undermine forward progress and they are the ones you need to spend more time with. That doesn't mean coddling them and allowing them to remain stuck. It means having open, clear, and honest conversations about the change, why the change is happening, and their role in the change.

## Technology

Change in technology is constant. In IT departments, the technology changes are driven either by the vendor (new features, bug fixes, updates, upgrades, new platforms), the organization (expanded needs of same system, new systems for existing operations, new systems for new initiatives), or the IT department itself (new features, capabilities, or systems to better run IT operations). So, every day in IT, something changes. IT teams have become accustomed to the constant technological changes and most have adapted well.

That said, there have been massive technological changes over the past five years, and these will continue to occur. Migration to cloud-based systems, XaaS, virtualization, segmentation, machine learning, artificial intelligence, and big data are the current trends changing the IT landscape. What the trends will be in three or five or ten years is hard to predict. But we do know that the change will continue and perhaps accelerate as healthcare seeks newer, more efficient, more effective ways to provide quality healthcare to entire populations.

The challenge rapidly changing technology poses to an organization and to an IT department is clear. Too much change too quickly injects massive risk to the organization. The potential to make mistakes rises, so cybersecurity, downtime, data integrity, and data loss risks are all reasonable concerns. Often, the pressures from the organization to do more (and always faster) pushes IT to its limits. Other times, regulatory updates cause changes that must be adopted and addressed quickly. There may be patient safety issues or quality concerns that drive rapid change. Sometimes, the project may have been waiting in the wings for months or years and suddenly (and unexpectedly) gets the green light to proceed.

There are many different reasons technology changes in healthcare IT, but the one we haven't yet talked about is the this: the intentional re-alignment of deployed technology in the organization. That is healthcare IT renovation. The change we will be injecting into the IT department and the organization is intentional in order to clear away the unused technology, reduce the amount of clutter and complexity, and to re-engineer our technology and process environments in ways that create a strong foundation for the future. Any digital transformation effort must be built upon this rock-solid footing of competent, efficient, and modernized IT.

## Leadership and Change

As you recall from Chapter 14, managers are expected to maintain consistent work processes, to avoid or reduce risk, to ensure work is carried out in a standardized and predictable manner. Leaders are needed to drive innovation and change. Management thought leader John Kotter said, "Management's mandate is to minimize risk and to keep the current system operating. Change, by definition, requires creating a new system, which in turn always demands leadership." [29.2]

Managers might also be leaders, but leaders don't have to be managers. In fact, many strong leaders in organizations are found in all sorts of roles. Leaders are those who step up, who embrace positive change, and help drive the organization forward. They can be particularly effective when they are in staff positions and work as influencers to drive changes in attitudes and behaviors among their peers. Since a manager's job is defined by minimizing risk and keeping current systems operating, you will need more leaders than managers to effectively drive change.

Finally, change is opportunity. It's like kayaking on a fast-moving river. The only way you have any control is to go faster than the current. Change in business is the same. If you are moving slower than the current of business and technology, change will feel chaotic and out of your control. You can embrace change as an opportunity – to clean up/out, grow, evolve, and innovate. You can gain control over your environment to a large extent and make your team and your organization better through conscious and deliberate change management.

## Change Management Overview

There are many different approaches to change management, but they all have several similar attributes.

1. **Change begins with a vision of the future state.** If we don't paint the picture of the newer, better future state, we can't enlist change agents in the process. Change without a vision is just destruction. You can go into a building and start tearing out fixtures and walls (change) but without a vision of what the finished product looks like, you're just swinging a hammer and destroying whatever it hits.
2. **Change is introduced, supported, and promoted by leaders through effective communication.** Many people resist change, even change that is seemingly good. In general, it's a defense against uncertainty and fear of the unknown. Develop a clear, concise, and compelling future state message that you use in every possible way. Making effective use of emails, newsletters, team meetings, project meetings to continue to reinforce the message is one of the success factors Kotter and others describe. Thus, the consistency and clarity of message is very important and often underestimated.

3. **Change is a process, not an end point.** Every renovation project has ups and downs, starts and stops. Change is never a straight line. Renowned management consultant and author, Peter Drucker, talked about the time dimension of management. Management "must keep the enterprise performing in the present – or else there will be no enterprise capable of performing in the future. And it has to make the enterprise capable of performance, growth, and change in the future." [29.3] Successful renovation, then, comes from both keeping the operations running and changing operations at the same time. A well-worn phrase in IT circles is "building the plane while we're flying it." This holds true with our renovation analogy – continuing to occupy the space while we are renovating it. Uncomfortable, disruptive, and sometimes downright unpleasant, but very necessary.

4. **Create useful roadblocks and obstacles.** As managers and leaders, our job is to remove roadblocks and obstacles for our teams. When it comes to change management, finding ways to *create* roadblocks and obstacles to prevent sliding back to the past is crucial. These are also known as *countermeasures*, which in this case really means taking measures that prevent falling back on old habits. You can think of many examples, but things like removing access to a legacy software system to ensure users to adopt the new one that has been idling on the sidelines for a year or two is a good example. Of course, you don't just pull the plug, but you can put in place controls or blocks to stop some of the natural tendency toward maintaining the status quo.

5. **Alignment, acceptance, and accountability are present in every model.** Regardless of which change management model you research, you will see that alignment to the change, acceptance of the change, and accountability around new behaviors to implement and maintain the change are all present. Whatever model (or combination of models) you choose, keep these three aspects top of mind always.

6. **Acknowledge that change means loss for many.** It is important to identify who is losing what in the change. It's easy to gloss over and say, "it will be better in the future," but people who have done a job in a particular way for years or decades will feel a sense of loss. Specifically acknowledging the loss and allowing for grieving (and possible overreaction), will allow people to process the change.

Marking the specific ending and celebrating the new beginning can help people move past the loss stage. To some, this may sound a bit like coddling, but allowing people to express their fears helps you understand their specific concerns and aids you in developing a successful path forward.

7. **Acknowledge and address learning anxiety.** People who have to unlearn old ways and learn new ways often experience some level of anxiety around this. They generally exhibit unhelpful behaviors including denial, finger-pointing, delaying, or manipulating/maneuvering. These behaviors often point to the need for a strong training initiative to reduce the anxiety and remove roadblocks to acceptance.

8. **Small changes, big wins.** The human mind is an amazing thing – and it can alternately be our ally or our enemy. One tenet of human change is that small changes are more likely to stick than big, all-in changes. Nutritionists advising on weight loss will say "walk five minutes per day, every day" or "drink one less soda every day." These are incredibly small changes, and they don't trigger fear responses, which kick in if you say "do aerobics for 30 minutes every day" or "stop drinking soda altogether."

   Jeff Kavanaugh and Rafee Tarafdor termed this *microchange management*. "Microchange management is based on human motivation and behavioral theory....The sum of many microchanges brings about the larger change, creating a cumulative effect that delivers nonlinear improvements with greater likelihood of overall success." [29.4]

   We often have to sneak up on change, whether in our personal lives or at work. When we can make small changes that build toward bigger changes, we are less likely to trigger the fear response. So, make small, incremental changes to build confidence in the new vision to achieve the big wins.

9. **Be agile.** Many change management methods feel slow and heavy. Sometimes something lighter and nimbler might be more useful. Again, you must gauge the right approach for your organization, but Sarah Jensen Clayton, in her article "An Agile Approach to Change Management" suggests using the "test and learn" approach. She posits that projects requiring change management rarely look the same at the end as they did in the beginning, so testing one element, learning from

it, and modifying your approach, as needed, may be more effective than setting a project plan that details out the changes over the next few years. [29.5].

To be clear, many IT teams struggle with Agile methods. We tend to gravitate toward the waterfall style, which has been ingrained into many of us for years. To complicate matters, our healthcare budget cycles and our staffing don't always support the move to Agile methods. That said, finding ways to move quickly, to remove roadblocks (and bureaucracy), and deliver smaller, more frequent units of value more often will serve you well, whether you formally adopt agile methods or not.

We've reviewed the basic components of change management. Now we'll look in more detail at four of the most commonly used methods of OCM. If you are not already using a change management model, you can consider adopting one of these four. Having a defined model will help keep you focused and organized as you navigate any organizational change, including your upcoming IT renovation project.

## Four Popular Change Management Methods

There are many different systems that describe change management and the required steps. We'll discuss four of the most popular and time-tested methods to see how they compare. There is no single 'right' method, or rather, the right method is the one that best fits how you, your team, and your organization operate. For example, choosing a method that's very detailed in an organization that prefers to run fast and loose is unlikely to succeed. You can also use elements from different models, if you are clear that you're doing so and document your method.

Finally, remember that whatever model or method you choose, you must clearly, consistently follow your plan, communicate both the vision and the change, and take small steps to ensure the change has a chance to take root. It is time-consuming and sometimes tedious, but you can fail fast or succeed slowly.

Kotter, Lewin, McKinsey, and ADKAR are four of the most often cited change management systems. We'll discuss each briefly and provide additional resources at the end of the chapter if you want to dive into any of these more deeply.

## *Kotter's Model*

Dr. John P. Kotter, Professor Emeritus at Harvard Business School and management thought leader, defined eight stages of change in his book <u>Leading Change</u>. [29.6, 29.7] These eight steps are:

1. Create a sense of urgency.
2. Build a guiding coalition.
3. Form a strategic vision.
4. Enlist a volunteer army.
5. Enable action by removing barriers.
6. Generate short-term wins.
7. Sustain acceleration.
8. Institute change.

We'll discuss each of these briefly, but if you're intrigued by this method, you can explore more of Kotter's work. He's continued to research how successful change happens and written numerous books on the subject. See both References and Resources at the end of this chapter for more on Kotter.

1. **Create a sense of urgency.** If the current state feels too comfortable, people won't be compelled to change. Being able to articulate in a clear, persuasive manner that the building is unsafe, the roof is about to collapse, the electrical system is likely to spark a massive fire, the foundation is crumbling, and the building is about to fall off the cliff into the ocean – these are things that create a sense of urgency to renovate. If the message is the paint is peeling and the windows are broken, everyone will shrug and go about their business.
2. **Build a guiding coalition.** Change is about people. Creating a coalition so that you enlist the right people at the right levels of the organization is vital to successfully initiating and sustaining change.
3. **Form a strategic vision.** Create a compelling vision of how the future will be different from the past to foster buy-in for change. Change initiatives should link to this vision so there is a consistent and clear change narrative.

4. **Enlist a volunteer army.** In order to make large-scale and lasting change, you need to have many people throughout the organization on board. Some successful change initiatives have used terms like transformation, journey, or movement to describe the magnitude of the change required and to reflect the large number of people who must actively support the change.

5. **Enable action by removing barriers.** Removing obstacles is the job of all managers, but when initiating change, this becomes a top priority. Enthusiasm and forward progress can come to a halt if there are obstacles and roadblocks preventing your volunteer army from succeeding. Remove bureaucracy so people can move quickly, knock down silos, or build bridges between them to foster innovation and collaboration.

6. **Generate short term wins.** Small, short-term wins are the fuel of success. Identifying and engineering short-term wins will begin to solidify the vision of the future in terms of real, tangible change. It will also help keep staff positive and engaged as change continues to unfold.

7. **Sustain acceleration.** There is a commonly used phrase about difficult situations: the only way out is through. In this case, change happens through continuous action and a methodical approach – through difficulties, emergencies, drama, or politics. Continued focus on the step-by-step approach will help accelerate change.

8. **Institute change.** You could also say "institutionalize the change." In other words, ensure that the small wins lead to bigger wins and that the change becomes built into the way the organization operates. Ensure there are processes in place to reinforce the new behaviors and work habits you have created through this change process.

Kotter's method is a well-used model for many reasons, not the least of which is that it is clear, concise and incorporates all the necessary steps to really drive sustainable change.

## Lewin's Model

Kurt Lewin wrote about change management in the 1940's and his method continues to be popular today. It's a short three-step process that includes *unfreezing, changing,* and *refreezing*. Lewin posited that there are three major forces present in organizations and humans: driving forces, restraining forces, and equilibrium. When we think about the environment we work in, we can see these three forces at play on a daily basis. [29.8]

**Driving forces** are those that cause change to occur to push the organization in the desired direction. They shift the equilibrium toward action and change.

**Restraining forces** are those that counter the desired change. They hinder progress because they push against the desired change. They shift the equilibrium toward actively resisting change.

**Equilibrium**, of course, is where driving forces equal restraining forces and no change occurs. Change can only happen by increasing driving forces or decreasing restraining forces.

With this as the backdrop, Lewin's model uses these three steps: unfreezing, change, refreezing.

1. **Unfreezing.** Unfreezing is the process of getting people to let go of the past or the current process that needs to change. Both individual resistance and the strong drive to maintain group conformity create resistance to change. The process of unfreezing happens by either increasing driving forces *away* from the undesired state, removing restraining forces preventing movement *toward* the desired state, or a combination of the two.
2. **Change.** The change stage is when thoughts, behaviors, processes, patterns, and systems move either strongly in the direction of the new state or achieve the desired new state.
3. **Refreezing.** Refreezing, in some sense, is driving toward equilibrium in the new state. Ideally, you want to achieve a state where the new behavior, the new process, the new attitude is locked in, becomes standard operating procedure. The sooner you can get this new state to become "the way we've always done it," the less maintenance the change will require. All change requires repetition and support to sustain it, but at some point, it becomes a new habit.

This model is powerful in its relative simplicity. It is easy to remember three major forces and three actions. It has been referenced in numerous nursing journals as an easy-to-remember method for assisting patients with making lifestyle changes to improve health, so it may fit will with your HIT culture of change as well.

## McKinsey 7-S Model

The McKinsey 7S Model was developed in the 1970's and describes "hard" and "soft" aspects of change. Strategy, structure, and system are all considered hard elements. Shared values, skills, style, and staff are the soft elements. [29.9] Though some critics argue this model may be too complex or too rigid for some environments, it effectively accounts for the various elements of change management.

1. **Strategy.** Strategy in an organization should drive initiatives, projects, and change. Developing, modifying, and understanding both the organizational and IT strategies is the first step in identifying what change is needed.
2. **Structure.** Structure describes the current organization, its hierarchy, its physical locations, its business units, etc. Understanding the current structure, along with what works and what doesn't, is a foundation of knowing (or assessing) what changes are needed. Identifying structural issues or required structural changes can help drive clarity about needed changes in the 'softer' areas including skills, style, and staff.
3. **System.** The systems that are in place are the very things that keep the status quo in place. Identifying which systems are in play in your desired change as well as which systems are working (or broken) is fundamental to understanding what needs to change.
4. **Shared Values.** Shared values are the first of the four "soft" elements of change described in the McKinsey model. It describes the culture and collective behaviors of the organization. Often, it describes the organization's mission, values, and core beliefs as well. The question is whether these support or hinder your change initiative. Though counter-intuitive, a very soft, relationship-oriented (vs. process-oriented) culture can make it more difficult to instill change because many of the influencing factors are emotional rather than behavioral-based. This type of culture is common in many healthcare organizations. Understanding the shared values and culture of the organization helps you develop effective strategies to initiate change.
5. **Skill.** When changing from one system to another, the skills of the organization's employees have become either an accelerating or constraining factor. For example, if the change is to go to the

cloud, how many of your IT staff have any cloud technology skills, training, or experience? If you happen to have hired a few staff with those skills in the past few years, you may be ready to go. If you have folks who have supported on-premise, physical servers with individual applications installed, you have a skills gap that will impact your success. How will those staff without the requisite skills approach this change? Assessing skills is covered from various angles throughout this book. It is a key element of any change management initiative.

6. **Style.** Style is about the management and leadership style of the organization. Is it command-and-control? Collaborative? Or something in between? Style indicates how an organization is managed, how decisions are made and communicated, and how leaders interact with staff. In healthcare, there is often a combination of styles. In an emergency situation - the emergency room, an operating room, or in an Intensive Care Unit - a command-and-control stye of leadership is both necessary and helpful. However, that method often isn't particularly effective outside of emergency or critical situations. Some leaders can struggle to flex from one mode to another. Assessing not only the organization's leadership style, but your own as well, will help you navigate change in a way that is aligned with how your organization tends to operate. Strong leadership skills are needed to make any change effectively, so this may be an area of focus as you assess your needed changes. There is no point in trying to create systemic change if you have poor leadership or lack the requisite leadership skills (yourself or your direct reports) to drive positive change through the team, department, and organization. You can't change your organization's culture single-handedly, but you *can* model positive leadership skills with your executive-level peers as well as within your IT function.

7. **Staff.** There are numerous references in this book to managing staff, including assessing current skills, addressing upcoming changes, training, upskilling, and communication. Ultimately, each person either contributes to the positive change, actively resists it, or sits on the sidelines awaiting an outcome. By addressing change effectively as a leader (via whatever model you choose), you'll first have to engage staff to get them to look at the upside of change and to envision the positive future they can help create.

## ADKAR Model

The ADKAR Model of change management was created by Jeffrey Hiatt, the founder of Prosci [29.10]. This model identifies five elements of change management with special emphasis on limiting resistance to change. The ADKAR acronym stands for:

1. Awareness
2. Desire
3. Knowledge
4. Ability
5. Reinforcement

1. **Awareness.** Change needs to begin with an awareness of the need for change. Awareness is not announcing that change is coming; it's communicating the *why* behind the need for change. When people are aware of the reasoning behind the need for change, they are less likely to resist it.
2. **Desire.** The next step is fostering the desire to change. People won't accept change simply because they understand the reasoning. As a change agent, you will need to work to move people from resisting to accepting (or even wanting) change. Since most resistance is anchored in some sort of fear – fear of losing their expertise, their seniority, their role, or their autonomy, for example - addressing the fear at its root helps remove barriers and foster a desire for change. Desire also can be fostered through incentives, through a sense of belonging, or through a willingness to trust and follow a leader.
3. **Knowledge.** The third element is related specifically to knowledge needed during and after the change. Knowledge of how to operate during the change and how to operate after the change are the two key aspects of knowledge in this model. One of the common failure points of organizations when introducing change is the tendency to send staff to training at some point along the way and leaving it at that. This rarely, if ever, results in change that sticks. Instead, providing training and coaching both during the transition and afterward will help ensure staff have the tools and skills they need to maintain the change going forward.
4. **Ability.** Knowing something and being able to *do* something are not the same. In this model, ability is defined as the demonstration of

the knowledge from the prior step. Staff being able to demonstrate proficiency in their tasks within the new model is key to sustained change. We've all been involved in projects where staff were trained and were unable to demonstrate any meaningful proficiency after training. This is where change fails to become sustainable and where many organizations struggle. Providing access to subject matter experts and coaches, as well as monitoring proficiency and providing additional assistance, as needed, is key to developing ability that supports change.

5. **Reinforcement.** Reinforcement of change behaviors can take many forms, including celebrations, awards, recognition, and incentives. It can also take the form of dashboards and metrics that monitor progress and help inhibit reverting to prior behaviors. Many change management processes in organizations look at change as "one-and-done," and once the project is completed, the management of change often ceases. In order to sustain change, reinforcing the new state is important, as is taking corrective action if the new state is not maintained.

As you can see, the four models, Kotter, Lewin, McKinsey, and ADKAR, all share common elements. Kotter and McKinsey are more detailed, Lewin's three-step method is easy to remember but less rigorous in terms of leading organizational change. The ADKAR model really focuses on the aspects related to reducing resistance and fostering maintenance of change.

We've also discussed effective methods of managing change, such as breaking it down into very small steps so they can be better assimilated by the organization. We know that change happens at different rates in different environments (technology, human, organizational), so we need to plan for the inevitable fits-and-starts rhythm of managing change.

As an HIT leader, you will need to determine which method best matches the personality and profile of your organization and your IT department. The key is to thoughtfully select a model, deeply ingrain that model in your own mind and that of the organization, and then follow it faithfully through the ups and downs of the change process. Whatever method or process you choose, it must provide a compelling vision and be clear, concise, constant, and well-communicated.

## Summary

In this chapter, we have discussed the importance of embracing a change management methodology in conjunction with your renovation project. The key is that you must include key elements of managing change, such as having a vision, communication, and assessment, to successfully navigate change. Each model has its pros and cons, there is no one perfect way. And, whatever method you choose, it will not be straight-line progress. There will be days or weeks when things move forward at a smooth pace and days or weeks when progress is stalled or even reversed. Maintaining your vision, continuing to communicate, and politely and professionally prohibiting the change to be derailed will be your best chance for success.

## References

[29.1] Hoe, Siu Loon, Digital Transformation: Strategy, Execution, and Technology, Boca Raton, FL, CRC Press, 2023, p. 41.
[29.2] Kotter, John P., "Leading change: Why transformation efforts fail," May-June, 1995, https://hbr.org/1995/05/leading-change-why-transformation-efforts-fail-2, accessed August 11, 2022.
[29.3] Drucker, Peter F., Management: Tasks, Responsibilities, Practices, Harper Business, New York, 1993. P. 44.
[29.4] Kavanaugh, Jeff, Rafee Tarafdar, "Break down change management into small steps," May 03, 2021, https://hbr.org/2021/05/break-down-change-management-into-small-steps, accessed August 11, 2022.
[29.5] Clayton, Sarah Jensen, "An agile approach to change management," January 11, 2021, https://hbr.org/2021/01/an-agile-approach-to-change-management, accessed August 11, 2022.
[29.6] Kotter, John P., "Eight steps to change," no date, https://www.kotterinc.com/methodology/8-steps/, accessed August 11, 2022.
[29.7] Kotter, John P., Leading Change, Harvard Business Review Press, Boston, MA, 2012.
[29.8] Petiprin, Alice, "Lewin change theory," no date, https://nursing-theory.org/theories-and-models/Lewin-Change-Theory.php, accessed February 11, 2023.
[29.9] Bryan, Lowell, "Enduring ideas: The 7s framework," March 1, 2008, https://www.mckinsey.com/business-functions/strategy-and-corporate-finance/our-insights/enduring-ideas-the-7-s-framework, accessed August 14, 2022.
[29.10] Prosci ADKAR Model, no date, https://www.prosci.com/resources/articles/why-the-adkar-model-works, accessed April 5, 2023.

# Resources

Barrow, Jennifer M., Pavan Annamaraju, Tammy J. Toney-Butler, "Change management," October 9, 2021, https://www.ncbi.nlm.nih.gov/books/NBK459380/, accessed August 14, 2022,

Basford, Tessa, Bill Schaninger, "The four building blocks of change," April 11, 2016, https://www.mckinsey.com/business-functions/people-and-organizational-performance/our-insights/the-four-building-blocks–of-change, accessed August 14, 2022.

Buckingham, Marcus, "Designing work that people love," May-June 2022, https://hbr.org/2022/05/designing-work-that-people-love, accessed online December 5, 2022.

Glaser, John, "How to ensure your health care innovation doesn't flop," December 27, 2019, https://hbr.org/2019/12/how-to-ensure-your-health-care-innovation-doesnt-flop, accessed September 5, 2022.

Igoe, Katherine J., "Change management: Why it's so important, and so challenging, in health care environments," September 20, 2021, https://www.hsph.harvard.edu/ecpe/change-management-why-its-so-important-and-so-challenging-in-health-care-environments/, Harvard T. H. Chan School of Public Health, accessed August 14, 2022,

Neeley, Tsedal and Paul Leonardi, "Developing a digital mindset," May-June 2022, https://hbr.org/2022/05/developing-a-digital-mindset, accessed February 10, 2023.

Shaw, James, et al, "Beyond 'implementation': digital health innovation and service design," August 13, 2018, https://www.nature.com/articles/s41746-018-0059-8, accessed October 2, 2022.

# Chapter 30

## Design Your Digital Future

As you near the end of your renovation work, you should begin focusing forward on designing your digital future. At this juncture, you have fully assessed your IT capabilities and implemented measures to improve and mature these competencies. Along the way, you have also uncovered information that might have been hidden or unknown prior to your project. Your renovation is not one-and-done but an iterative process of discovery, planning, and action. Yes, you should set an end point and define an end date for this project. You should consider operationalizing this work. Periodically repeating these assessments, even in small segments, such as reviewing IT staffing and leadership or reviewing strategy and governance, will help you maintain currency and avoid creating the very same situation you've just remediated. After all this hard work, maintaining it is easier than doing this full renovation again five years from now when the mess has re-surfaced. Like any other maintenance activity, you can do it in small, frequent actions, and it remains manageable. If you ignore it and try to catch up at some point, the job is significantly larger and more complex. This book was designed so you can grab a few topics at a time, review the building blocks, and perform the assessments. These are readymade for you to review and re-examine these capabilities more easily. Hopefully, that encourages you to maintain the beautiful renovation work you've performed.

Now you are ready to begin looking forward and designing your digital future. Whether you are still facing tight (or shrinking) budgets, or you have entered a period of funding, you should be ready with your plan. In this chapter, we will look at how you can tie your recent renovation work to your digital future.

DOI: 10.4324/9781003377023-34

# Preparing for Digital Transformation

The first step after you have substantially completed your renovation work is to identify your digital transformation strategy. Of course, this is not an IT project by any means. It must be organization-led, and IT-enabled. If you are dreaming up big digital projects inside the confines of IT, you're already off track. Instead, you should be facilitating conversations with your organizational counterparts to envision the new, future digital state. Once ideas for digital transformation have been discussed and a few solid ideas have been vetted, you are ready to develop your digital strategy, or at least your digital transformation project plans. These should be well-developed and detail the people, processes, and technologies needed. Since it can be easy for organizations to get a bit carried away with new technology initiatives, remember your project management basics. Well-crafted project plans with charter and scope documents will help clearly articulate the intended outcomes and guide you to developing the necessary elements to undertake your transformation project.

We discussed digital transformation at the outset of this book. Now, with your updated knowledge of your organization and perhaps a new perspective on your IT function, it's helpful to look again at a key aspect of what's happening in the larger environment. Author Siu Loon Hoe, in his book *Digital Transformation: Strategy, Execution, and Technology*, describes the challenge aptly.

> "A key challenge faced by organizations that operate traditional business models is the increasing competition from non-traditional players. These new entrants are not the conventional market players which the organization is familiar with or expects to see. These organizations face contenders coming from totally different industries and sectors. The pervasiveness of digital technology has enabled new competitors that have the advantage of direct access to consumers and their buying patterns to penetrate traditional areas and compete directly with the incumbents. They develop products and services that span traditional industry boundaries and pose a big challenge to incumbents. They can do so because of their deep customer and supplier knowledge." [30.1]

While the author is not referring specifically to healthcare, you certainly can see the relevance of these comments. We see the influence of market disruptors across healthcare, as discussed in Chapter 2. How these market drivers pan out in the long term has yet to be determined, but you can look around your environment today and see where competition is eroding your traditional market segments from consumer-friendly walk-in healthcare clinics on just about every corner to at-home monitoring, labs, and even infusion. These changes are impacting your organization in one way or another. We need to look at the current conditions and work with our operational counterparts to chart a new course. Part of that new course may be delivering care better, faster, or at a lower cost, which is important but not necessarily transformative. Part of that new course might be looking at uniquely new and innovative ways to provide high-quality, low-cost care for your patient populations. That is where digital transformation efforts will become important to your company's long-term plans.

## Clearing Out the Old

This work should have been part of your renovation activity, but before you start any digital transformation efforts, be sure you have deselected, decommissioned, removed, and deactivated (licensing, contracts, etc.) all unused or unneeded hardware and software. If you have not completed these tasks, you'll find yourself getting bogged down in clean-up work amid your digital transformation efforts.

As Hoe states, "Digital transformation is a journey, and a strong foundation is needed to bring the organization to a higher level of performance. Many organizations rush into digital transformation initiatives without first addressing the fundamental business issues and IT problems. Prior to embarking on a full-scale digital transformation exercise, it is important to first close the existing business gaps and resolve any underlying process inefficiencies. Then, the organization can focus on the basic building blocks, such as IT capabilities, and build upon them in a systematic manner." [30.2]

This is precisely the work you have undertaken in this renovation project, so you should be well-positioned for these next steps.

Additionally, this is the right time to ensure your governance processes have been assessed and revised, as needed. If you lack strong governance going into a digital transformation project, you will probably end up with failed and/or partially implemented projects. The governance process should help ensure that the digital projects requested are well-vetted, aligned with organizational strategy, and aligned with IT standards and architecture.

Finally, your IT and organizational processes should have been reviewed, improved, and automated, where feasible. However, if you are getting ready to embark on a digital journey, you may need to assess some of your processes in light of that. In other words, these processes may need to change again to accommodate new ways of running your business. Using the methods discussed in prior chapters, you can assess the relevant processes to ensure you are ready to move forward. If not, this is a great time to review and revise.

Part of your process review and improvement likely involved incorporating elements of Agile into your workflows. If not, you might want to evaluate whether this might be a good time to do so before launching into digital transformation. Going forward, delivering IT value in clear increments will be crucial for conveying and realizing IT value. The cycle time for seeing results from projects has shortened and it is often helpful to demonstrate progress through delivering smaller, usable units of work. Agile is one way to do that.

You also need to ensure you have the right staff with the right skills in place, both for today's work as well as for your potential digital transformation efforts. Your assessments should have identified skills and staffing gaps in your current state. Addressing those may bring you current, but they may fall short of what you will need to launch into a transformation project. Based on your identified digital projects, you can determine which technologies will be involved. That also means you should review your staffing again to determine if you have the right people in the right roles with the right technical skillsets for these activities. Since they are likely new (compared to your renovation work), you may be upskilling for a second or third time. Operationalizing your staff skills assessments can help you remain current and plan for the future as well.

## Starting Points

There are many places you can start in digitally transforming your organization. There are also many great books available to guide you on your digital transformation in your healthcare organization, and we have included a few at the end of this chapter in the Resources section.

According to Hoe, "A common missing piece in a strategy is a clear set of choices that define what the organization is going to do and what it is not going to do. The set of predetermined choices is crucial because it limits the options available and keeps the organization focused on the key result areas. It helps to channel all the efforts into activities that are critical to the success and survival of the organization. Only with bounded options would the organization be able to execute the strategy without any distractions and make tasks manageable." [30.3]

Helping the organization make these strategic decisions is the value of a strong IT leadership team. Technology is the enabler of any transformation effort, but the organization must decide what it wants to do and what it can reasonably achieve. From there, you can work with your counterparts to determine which technologies might deliver these results and which ones definitely will not. It will always be tempting for some to follow the 'shiny new objects' that pop up on the horizon, but if you have developed a sound IT strategy, architecture, and governance process, you'll be able to ask key questions to help keep the business and IT aligned toward solutions that will deliver results.

There is no single right answer for how, when, or where to focus your digital transformation efforts. Hopefully, through this renovation project, you've gained valuable insights about the nature of your organization and IT function. This will help y select the best path forward from among a myriad of choices.

# Summary

Digital transformation, at its core, is not about technology; it's about change involving people and processes. Technology is an enabler of these changes. When viewed from this perspective, you can avoid falling into the trap of leading change conversations with technology. The way to prepare your organization for digital transformation is to address the people and process aspects as clearly as you would the technology. As you have initiated change in your IT department, you have learned a lot about your own approach to change as well as the organization's response to change. Leverage this knowledge to craft a plan for digital projects that incorporate these key learnings and set your organization up for a successful future of innovation and transformation.

# References

[30.1]   Hoe, Siu Loon, Digital Transformation: Strategy, Execution, and Technology, Boca Raton, FL, CRC Press, 2023. Page 9.

[30.2]   Hoe, Page 18.

[30.3]   Hoe. Page 15.

# Resources

Beranger, Jerome, Roland Rizoulieres, Editors, The Digital Revolution in Health: Innovating and Acting for Sustaining Transformations in the Health System, 1st Edition, ISTE Ltd., London, UK and John Wiley & Sons, Hoboken, NJ, US, 2021.

Comella-Dorda, Santiago, Mishal Desai, Arun Gundurao, Krish Krishnakanthan, and Selim Sulos, "Building a cloud-ready operating model for agility and resiliency," March 2021, https://www.mckinsey.com/capabilities/mckinsey-digital/our-insights/building-a-cloud-ready-operating-model-for-agility-and-resiliency, accessed March 4, 2023.

Forrest, Will, Mark Gu, James Kaplan, Michael Liebow, Raghav Sharma, Kate Smaje, and Steve Van Kuiken, "Cloud's trillion dollar prize is up for grabs," February 2021, https://www.mckinsey.com/capabilities/mckinsey-digital/our-insights/clouds-trillion-dollar-prize-is-up-for-grabs, accessed March 4, 2023.

Hoe, Siu Loon, Digital Transformation: Strategy, Execution, and Technology, Boca Raton, FL, CRC Press, 2023.

Lytras, Miltiadis D., Abdulrahman Housawi, and Basim Alsaywid, Editors, Digital Transformation in Healthcare in Post-COVID-19 Times (Next Generation Technology Driven Personalized Medicine and Smart Healthcare), 1st Edition, Cambridge, MA, Academic Press, 2023.

Ordonez de Pablos, Patricia, and Xi Zhang, Editors, Accelerating Strategic Changes for Digital Transformation in the Healthcare Industry (Information Technologies in Healthcare Industry), 1st Edition, Cambridge, MA, Academic Press, 2023.

# Chapter 31

## Completion – Certificate of Occupancy

Congratulations! You have completed your renovation project. The amount of time and effort you've put into reviewing, revising, and rebuilding your IT function will pay dividends for years to come, so take a moment to enjoy a sense of accomplishment. No matter if you were able to finish a small renovation or a complete rebuild, know that the changes you have implemented have improved your capabilities and moved you closer to your goals. Like completing a physical renovation project, you are now ready to occupy your new space and begin enjoying all the upgrades and enhancements you've worked so hard to put into place.

Let's go back to where we started for a moment. We know the healthcare landscape is evolving very rapidly as consumer behaviors shift, and all organizations need to lead with digital initiatives. HIT is also changing rapidly. We know healthcare leaders are expecting (or demanding) digital transformation, though the phrase is used in vastly different ways across the industry. We know that HIT needs to be a strategic driver in the transformation conversation, but that people and processes are more critical than technology in these initiatives.

Having a highly functional IT department is crucial for healthcare organizations for several key reasons, including improving patient care and clinical outcomes; improving efficiencies and reducing the cost of care; leveraging the vast amount of data to improve operations and clinical care; and ensuring on-going compliance with an ever-changing regulatory environment. Without a competent and agile IT function, no healthcare

DOI: 10.4324/9781003377023-35

organization can thrive. With a highly skilled IT function, healthcare organizations can move quickly, improve care, improve operations, and find innovative new ways to address the multitude of challenges facing healthcare delivery today.

The next step is for you to decide if it is time to begin focusing on digital transformation in your organization. No matter what that ends up looking like or where that ends up taking you, you will know your digital house is in order and you are ready to help transform your healthcare organization.

The renovation work may be complete, but we know that maintaining this new state will take time and effort to prevent it falling back into old patterns. Hopefully, through this process, you've built in countermeasures to prevent old ways from creeping back into your organization. It's not easy, but with diligence and time, the new ways will become the accepted ways, and the tendency to fall back into bad habits will erode.

In the meantime, you'll need to set your organizational sights on what's new, what's next, and what's required to remain competitive in tomorrow's world while continuing to find ways to improve the quality of patient care, the patient experience, and the provider/staff experience. It's no small order, but it's exactly why you work in HIT.

## Summary

HIT is changing at an ever-increasing pace. The work you have done to assess and improve your IT capabilities will serve your patients, your organization, and your team well in the years ahead. You've accomplished a tremendous amount through this process and have established a very solid foundation for the future – both in terms of managing daily operations with the constraints you've always faced and in terms of the strategic alignment with the organization. The expectation is that your IT function will be able to successfully begin digital transformation efforts by building on these very strong foundations.

You've achieved amazing things during the course of this renovation project and you'll no doubt continue to drive HIT with passion and innovation to create the tomorrow we all envision today. You are making a very positive impact on your organization, your patients and, ultimately, your community. Keep up the great work.

# Index

**Note:** - Page numbers in "*Italics*" for figures and in **"Bold"** for tables.

Printed in the United States
by Baker & Taylor Publisher Services